Southbound

Jason Beem

pandamoon
publishing

www.pandamoonpublishing.com

Jacket design and illustrations © Pandamoon Publishing.

Pandamoon Publishing and the portrayal of a panda and a moon are registered trademarks of Pandamoon Publishing.

Library of Congress Cataloging-in-Publication Data is on file at the Library of Congress, Washington, DC.

ISBN-10: 099121319X
ISBN-13: 978-0-9912131-9-1

For Lori Kay

Southbound

1

MONDAY

"C'mon you damn five horse!" a man screams near the back of the room. He's standing just a couple of feet from the television, gazing up at the screen as his horse battles with another down the homestretch at Fair Grounds Race Course in New Orleans. Even though the race is being run 2,500 miles from Portland Meadows, the action and betting are just as real here on television as they are in the Big Easy.

"C'mon Garcia, whip that fucker!" the man yells as he smacks his rolled up program against his left hand. The two horses are nearing the finish line. They've battled nose and nose the entire length of the stretch. Both riders pushing and steering and whipping and screaming, imploring their runners to make that final necessary surge to put their nose down first at the wire.

"They come to the wire and it's Betty's Spots

who wins it by a head."

"Fuck yeah, I told you that five was gonna win," the man says, as he rushes over to show me his ticket, feeling the need to show not just me, but anyone within an earshot.

"Nice hit Alvin, but remember, winners never brag," I retort with a smile. I mean what I just said, but I give Alvin a pat on the shoulder anyways, just to let him know I'm happy that he got a score. I've met a thousand guys like Alvin. They're at every track. Alvin's probably fifty-five, maybe sixty. He's fat, and walks with something like a limp, but it's more like he's just pulling his right leg with him every time it's in the air as opposed to that leg actually taking a certifiable step. His scar-laced black skin and wrinkled face tell a story of a man who's had a tough life filled with heartbreak. His glasses are taped together, but not with good quality duct tape, or something like that. Rather, for him, throwing a new round of scotch tape on them each day seems to do the trick.

"How much did you get Alvin?" I ask after he gets his cash from the teller.

"She got bet down to 6/1, but I'll take it," Alvin says as he puts his newly collected money into his Velcro wallet. "I needed that. I was just about out of here."

In horse racing, the odds aren't set until the race starts and the betting closes. All the money bet goes into a big pool, and however many people have winning tickets split up that pool. After the track takes its twenty percent of course. Alvin's horse was 8/1 when he bet it. But lots of late money drove the price down to 6/1. See in pari-mutuel gambling, the players are competing against each other. Alvin and I are buddies, but we're also competitors.

Everyday thousands of men like Alvin, and even a few women, come out to these forgotten cathedrals. The grandstands are massive in scope and built to seat tens of thousands of people, but most days, only a couple of hundred will trickle through the old metal turnstiles that lead into the track.

It's not a racing day at Portland Meadows, but there's racing to bet on seven days a week. I work as the track's announcer, and on racing days I'll be perched up in my solitary rooftop dwelling, describing the racing action as it unfolds on the one-mile dirt track below. But, today, I had to come down to fill out some paperwork. Plus, I don't really have shit left to do until my girlfriend Michelle gets off work. So to pass the time, I walk around the joint, talking to the everyday players. Some of them are looking to turn their ten dollars into twenty, while others risk money that's not even theirs; trying to dig themselves out of the financial hole they're in. The place is sparse on a Monday afternoon, with maybe twenty guys spread out at different tables, all looking at the various televisions that show tracks racing from all over the States. There's a distinct smell of hot dogs and dollar tacos in the air, as most players will skimp on quality food in order to retain their money for upcoming bets.

"Hey, man, how they treating you?" I ask another guy. I'm not sure of his name, but I see him enough at least to say hello.

"Shitty," the man says, as he looks back to his *Daily Racing Form*, seemingly uninterested in a polite exchange. I pat him on the shoulder and step outside to get some fresh air. I walk up to the railing that borders the outside of the track and lean over it. The railing has been painted a hundred times over the years, but the chips and nicks caused by the hundreds of thousands of race fans who leaned against it still show through. It's my favorite spot to watch a race. At old Longacres Race Track, my hometown track that sat between Seattle and Tacoma before it closed, my dad would hold me perched on the rail so I could watch the horses race by. When you're nine years old, everything is bigger, and better. I was hooked. My dad called me a "railbird," which is slang for the track regulars who sit down by the rail, and not up in the turf club or the grandstand seats. To me, it was a term of endearment.

With the exception of some tractors going over the racing surface on the backstretch, the air is still and quiet here today. Eight hundred or so horses live just on the other side of that backstretch fence, as well as countless workers, whose lives are essentially spent back there amongst the horses, and hay, and shit. Horseshit might be the most pleasant smelling form of shit. In fact, it may be the only pleasant smelling form of shit. It doesn't smell good per se, but it certainly isn't an offensive odor. It smells like a pile of dead grass, because really that's what it is, with some barley and oats mixed in. Walking through any of the barns on the backstretch, the strong ammonia smell of the horse urine in the stalls is what has a way of blowing your nasal passages open. It stings your nostrils to breathe it in. But horseshit, it ain't that bad.

I love horse racing. I love being here at the track. Horse racing gave me somewhere to go when I needed somewhere to go. The track accepts everyone: it's one of the few places where down-and-out degenerates mingle with aristocratic bigwigs; where people with Master's degrees happily talk with people who can't spell Master's degree.

I was hooked the minute I saw Captain Condo. I was probably eight or nine years old. I always loved going to the track with my dad, but usually I just played on the kids' toy set, rather than watch the races. But this massive gray machine — "The Condo" — he was different. He would fall way back in his races. Each time, I thought he was too far back, and that he was going to lose. But, then, he'd start his big kick and catapult past his rivals, as if he'd just been toying with them. He was a gray streak when he flew past us.

Horse racing gave me almost everything I have. It put food in my mouth, and afforded me opportunities that nothing or no one else has. However, it's also taken away just as much. Horse racing will always break your heart at some point. But I don't know if that's such a bad thing. I mean, at least racing made me feel something. I'm someone who doesn't feel much; but racing made me feel. I've never rooted for anything in my life as hard as I've rooted for horses to get up and win races. Sometimes, I didn't even have any money invested; and sometimes I had all my money invested. Horse racing made me feel.

I've seen animals injured and put down right out on this dirt track in front of me. If I jumped this rail right now, I could walk fifteen feet to where I saw a rider get catapulted over her mount into the rail and break her back. I've seen jockeys and horses get seriously injured. But, for some reason, I'm always worried more about the horse. Seeing a horse running to the finish line, despite a catastrophic injury, is one of the most painful things I've ever watched. Horse racing made me feel.

I head back inside, and as I make my way toward the front exit, I spot a familiar friend with a young lady sitting next to him in front of the televisions.

"Dan. What brings you out here on a Monday?" I ask as I sit down in the empty seat next to the gal.

"Oh, hey! Ryan, this is my daughter Olivia," Dan says as he puts his hand on her shoulder. "She's a freshman at the University of Colorado in Boulder. She's in town on spring break, and we had a couple of hours to kill until dinner."

Olivia sits forward in her chair; her long, straight hair pulled back into a ponytail. She's wearing one of those fraternity event t-shirts that all freshman sorority girls wear.

"Nice to meet you Olivia," I say, extending a hand.

"Nice to meet you too," she says. "This is my first time betting on a horse race. We've got five dollars to win on the six horse, Supercilious, at Golden Gate Fields."

"How is it that with all the horses your old man has owned over the years, you've never made it out to the races?" I ask her.

"Well, she grew up with her mother in Omaha," Dan quickly interjects.

"Oh. Now I feel like an asshole," I say with a small laugh, hoping I didn't offend Dan or Olivia too much.

"Racing! The field breaks as one, as they leave the gate. But now it's Hot Lips who bursts right out to the front. Wheel For The Judge sets up in the second spot, while Supercilious is content to sit back in third."

Olivia is holding her ticket between her thumb and index finger, and it's clear from the slight smear of the ink on that five-dollar play that her fingers have started to perspire. The body reacts to gambling similarly for most people. Whether it's two dollars or two thousand, it's a palpable rush.

We sit here: our eyes fixated on the television screens above us. As the field turns to the top of the homestretch, Supercilious makes his move.

"Supercilious is coming alongside Hot Lips, who's gasping for air at the eighth pole. Supercilious now goes to the lead!"

I have no money vested in the outcome of this race. In fact, I haven't made a bet in more than a year and a half. But all that abstinence seems far away, as my heart rate intensifies along with the drama that's unfolding on the monitor.

"C'mon six!" Olivia yells out as they come to the wire. Dan joins her in rooting their horse home, even though he, as a seasoned race watcher, knows the race is already in the bag. I give a cheer; but as I look away from the screen towards the exuberant father and daughter, I feel a slight twinge of dizziness. I immediately put my finger to my pulse, checking to make sure that my heart is still doing its job. Thump. Thump. Thump. Check. Within seconds, though, my vision begins to blur, and everything and everyone around me seems to shrink. Suddenly, all I can think of is how to get the fuck out of this building. I jump up from my seat, bracing myself on the back of the chair, and immediately scan for the exit.

"Hey, Dan, I gotta run." My breath has become shallow. "Nice to meet you Olivia."

I can't get out of there fast enough. Smart doctor people have told me a panic attack is the result of the body's fight or flight response coming into play, but I've always thought it was more that I had to fight to flight. It was a struggle to leave. It was a struggle to keep my balance, to keep my breath under control, and to keep my extremities all working in their normal harmonious fashion. But I'm so well practiced at running from my anxiety, and the situations that bring it about, that I've gotten much better at getting away. I run from my anxiety daily. I've skipped out on dates, left work early, walked out of class, and even turned down sex because I couldn't calm down, and I felt the only way I was going to feel better was to leave wherever I was at.

When I get to the door, I hit the latch and pop it open. The chilly air outside creates an instant avenue to peace as it strikes the back of my throat. Now nobody is here to look at me — to judge me — to see me in this weakened, fragile state.

As I reach the car, I feel a great sense of relief wash over my body. I've reached my safe zone. In my car, I'm safe from the world and safe from other people. I look in my rearview mirror, as seeing my own reflection seems to be grounding. The mirror shows me that I'm ok, and this panic is just a lie I've told myself about how I'm in danger. The mirror also shows my hair thinning just a little bit in front. I have a couple grays on the side, but nothing to be concerned about. I've always thought I had a high hairline, but according to my last driver's license picture, it's gotten higher. Trying to breathe my way back to calm, I wonder how much Olivia made on her first bet.

Most people don't remember the first time they made a bet. With the exceptions of the big wins and narrow defeats, even the everyday gamblers can't recall all of the moments in which they've put their money, hard-earned or not, on the nose of a running animal or the turn of a card.

I don't remember my first bet either. I was just six days of age (if that actually counts as an "age"), when my dad laid me down on the floor and dealt out a hand of cards. According to my mom (who told me this story at least fifty times), I was lying there on my back in my baby outfit, confused and looking up at the ceiling, while my dad, a warehouse worker, baseball scout, and devoted degenerate gambler, gave himself two cards, and then me a pair as well.

Dad flipped over three cards in the middle, followed up with a burn card, and then delivered fourth street. By the time the fifth and final upcard was put on the floor, my shitty 2-9 offsuit was bested when dad flopped a pair of kings. Thanks dad.

2

TUESDAY NIGHTS

This door always seems to weigh a thousand pounds. Even though there are eight people sitting inside the room of this large church basement, with most of them talking, the mood still seems quiet. I stand looking through the little six-inch by six-inch window in the door. I think I'm the only person tall enough here to actually see through it. I don't want to go in, and I'd say probably twenty percent of the meetings I go to, I get to the door and then bolt.

These meetings happen everywhere around the city. In fact, they happen everywhere around the state, around the country, and around the world. The Trinity Methodist Church rests just off the Interstate Five, some ten minutes south of downtown Portland, Oregon. It looks like a larger version of the 1970's split-level homes that also reside throughout the neighborhood, just with a large cross and steeple on top.

Standing in front of the door, I straighten my shirt, calmly brush my hair back, and finally step inside.

I sign my name, my phone number, and my abstinence date on the sign-in sheet.

"December 5th, 2008," I think, as I pen those five numbers for what seems like the two-thousandth time down below the other folks who have already signed in.

"I'm Bonnie, and I'm a compulsive gambler," says the first woman to share. In her early sixties, Bonnie is dressed still bundled up from the cold, as she's taken a forty-five minute bus ride to get to the meeting. We used to see her all the time, but she's just started coming back after going "back out." She begins to weave a tale of how last week she went to the ATM three separate times until she had finally reached her three hundred dollar a day limit. She was up a hundred and fifty dollars during her first hour of play, however she "couldn't walk away." She tells of how she proceeded to keep chasing once she got down, continuing to pump Andrew Jackson after Andrew Jackson into that machine until finally she was done for the night. After losing all that she had, she called her friend Glen, and begged him to come give her a hundred bucks. It was one in the morning by this time, and she had to work at nine, but she didn't care. She just needed to get her money back. Glen was someone who she saw casually, and would fuck on occasions when they went out gambling, had too much to drink, or when she just wanted some companionship.

"My gambling had made me so lonely," Bonnie says as she stares deeply into the floor, as if some answers in life are hopefully beneath it. "I just feel so overwhelmed with work and with my kids and with not having any money. But each time I do have money, I take it to those goddamned machines. I just don't get it."

I never played the lottery machines when I gambled. The bright lights and spinning wheels of the video poker machines that litter almost every restaurant, bar, and strip club around the state can be found against the back wall in each establishment, always hidden from the view of the under twenty-one crowd. They are essentially slot machines, almost exactly what you see in Vegas, just no handle to crank. You can't find a place to eat or drink in town without a lineup of desperate souls seated with a drink in their left hand, while their right hand touches the screen, hoping that the next spin will come up with three cherries, sevens, or whatever the hell they need to win.

Many people at the meetings have always felt disrespected, like our addiction wasn't as valid as an alcoholic's, or a drug addicts. People at least understood being addicted to scotch, or pills, or heroin. But addicted to gambling?

Sitting here and listening as people pour their hearts out, I always laugh a little because consistently our stories all seem to ring the same. It started out as fun, and next thing we all knew, we were in too deep. It's nearly impossible for me to sit without my leg shaking, or my fingers tapping, or something, to release the tension coursing through my body. Speaking in public has never been my favorite endeavor; even though it's my job. Go figure.

"I'm Ryan, and I'm a compulsive gambler."

"Hi Ryan," the group says in unison.

"I've had a pretty tough week," I say as I start my share. I usually don't come into these things with a planned script, but I knew tonight I needed to get some mom stuff out there.

"It's been a month and a half now since mom died, and although I felt numb to it for the first few weeks, I have to admit it's been hitting me hard the last few days: the fact that she's gone, that cancer has now claimed both of my parents, and that there wasn't any money left in her bank account when she died. The gambler in me always expected I'd be inheriting some fortune of money. I always felt that somewhere along the line, if she ever did pass away, I'd be grief stricken because of my love for her; but I'd have money and gambling to help ease the pain. I haven't made a bet in a year and a half, and I've saved up a fair amount of money in that time.

"But, now, I just feel alone, and that my safety net is gone. She was my safety net. She was the one who supported me when things were bad. Now she's gone, and as it turns out, her money was all gone too. Between the cancer treatments, the economy doing what it did to her business, and whatever other reasons, she died essentially broke—worse than broke. We're going to have to sell her house just to pay off the mortgage and the lines of credit she had out. It's stress on top of stress. And now the sadness is creeping in.

"You know that twentieth question in the gambler's anonymous book—the one that asks, 'have you ever contemplated suicide?' Sometimes that's all I can think about. I don't think I could ever act on it, but now it seems like a viable escape option. I mean—I get how people get to that point. You know? I mean—my mom's gone, and the thing I keep freaking out about is fucking money. I feel bad that I'm even thinking about money at a time like this, but I'm pissed off she lost all of hers. I'm not even pissed at the economy. I'm pissed at her. I resent her for it, like it was somehow her duty to keep that money, and protect me—shelter me forever. I'm thirty-two fucking years old, and she's supposed to still take care of me?"

The other folks in the meeting sit quietly,

their chairs arranged in a small circle in the center of the room, as I talk of my anger. At first glance, I think I come across as a jovial person: someone who appears to be in a generally good mood no matter what the situation. Some of us just have those faces that even when we are pissed off, we still somehow look approachable.

"All I've thought about this week is gambling," I say. "At work, I've started reading the *Daily Racing Form* again, handicapping our races, and the races from other tracks. I've spent most of the time between our races looking at the *Form*, and making imaginary bets in my head. Sometimes I even keep track of how I'm faring.

"I mean—I haven't really come close to actually going to a machine, getting a voucher, and making a bet, but I've certainly been getting back into the routine. I know if I start betting again that shit will all go downhill, so that's kept me from doing it. I know I'll go into mass anxiety again and I know for damn sure I'll blow through the savings I've accrued these past couple of years. Every time I started up gambling again, it ended like that. It wasn't even because I was a lousy bettor or anything," I say.

As is typical of most problem gamblers, I can't admit that the odds are stacked against me, and that I can't overcome them. It takes a big ego to think you can beat a game where you're at a twenty-percent disadvantage to the house right off the bat. But, for some reason, I thought I would be the lucky one who did.

"I just couldn't stop. Once I started, it was all or nothing. And, if I did lose, I took it personally. I would get pissed, and take out that anger and frustration on the horse races. I'd double, triple, and even quadruple my bets: just keep chasing until I was up, and I could catch my breath and leave. Or until I was busted, and I finally had to drag my ass out of the track.

"I can't tell you how many times I sat at that ATM, staring at it, completely unaware of anything else in the world. I'd slip my card in, and it's like the whole room just vanished. It was just the ATM and me. I stood there praying that after I'd hit all the numbers, and answered all the questions, that I wouldn't be able to get the money. That pause between hitting the "Yes" button and waiting to hear the machine spit the cash out was always the longest five seconds of my day. The entire time I'd be standing there thinking, "Please God, let me be overdrawn, and don't let anymore come out," because at least that way I'd have no choice but to go home.

"Sure enough, though, the green light would start to flash, and the money would come shuffling out bill by bill. My heart sunk, because I knew this would lead to an even more futile feeling down the road. But a little piece of me soared, because I knew for at least the next ten minutes to four hours, depending on my luck, I was in the game. It's strange because it always seemed that ninety-nine percent of me didn't want to gamble, but the one percent that did won out every time." I take a break from sharing and sip from my water bottle. I hate going anywhere without my water bottle.

"By this point, I had all but given up handicapping and studying the races," I say setting my beverage down. "I might handicap the first few, but after a while, I would just start punting: picking numbers, odds, jockeys, and trainers. The damn horse could be half a cripple and I wouldn't know. And, work has made things even tougher. I mean—every day I have to stare my addiction right in the face and not partake in it. I have to watch, describe, and talk about these races, and never once do I get in on the action. I read out the prices, spot horses I think will win, watch them win, and then all I can do is sit and think 'I could have had that.'

"Anyway, that's how my week has been," I say, looking down at my lap. I always look down during these things, to avoid eye contact, and potential judgment or empathy from any of these people. I've noticed most people in these meetings look down. I think a number of us just don't know how to accept love in any form, even if it's just eye contact, and a welcoming ear.

"Thank you, Ryan," the group says in unison.

As the clock nears eight-thirty, I start to feel the nervousness and anticipation of the meeting coming to a close. These gatherings are a necessary part of my recovery, I'm told, but they are not something I enjoy. However, hearing these peoples' stories, and remembering how bad things had gotten for me, does offer some temporary relief.

However, a side effect comes with being at these meetings. Attending them is an admission of losing. It's an admission that I can't beat the game, and that I never stood a chance of beating the game. It's an admission that I'm just like the rest of these assholes. I lost. This feeling invades me like some kind of poison. The idea that I can't be good at the one thing I've always wanted to be good at—gambling—fucking makes me sick.

The minute the meeting ends, after everyone takes hands and says the exit prayer, I usually bolt straight for the door. While the others sit around and kibitz about their day, their dogs, and their problems, I just quietly button up my jacket and head for the exit.

But before I can leave, I'm stopped by the only other under forty-year-old person at the meeting; a young Croatian kid named Brad, who has never seen a poker game he didn't like. Brad always shows up to the meetings impeccably dressed, and tonight he dons a tight-fitting navy blue sweater, and a collared shirt underneath. His hair is shaven short and clean, and manicured in perfect lines. Like many gamblers, he wants to give off the illusion that he's a success, and that even though he's tens of thousands of dollars in the hole, he's still a winner.

"How's your recovery going?" Brad asks me.

"Oh fine, you?"

"I had twenty five days, until last Thursday when I ended up going to La Center," Brad says while sipping his coffee from a white Styrofoam cup. "It seems that each time I get a couple of weeks of abstinence, I think I've got it beat, and I head right back up to that card room."

"I used to go there too. Tough games up there, right?" I'm trying to feign interest. But, even though I'm itching to get the hell out of the building, my desire to be liked, and appear interested, often supersedes my agoraphobia.

"I always seem to get up early," Brad states. "But, inevitably, I just can't leave, and the next thing I know I'm stuck two or three thousand. My dad says he's going to kick me out if I don't quit, but he's said that before, so I'm not too worried."

"Have you thought about eighty-sixing yourself?" I ask, as barring myself is something I've done at a few of the card rooms in the area just to keep myself out.

"Naw. I just need to be able to not go," Brad says. "I need to be able to look myself in the mirror and say, 'I'm not going to gamble ever again.'"

I nod in agreement, knowing that Brad will probably be headed back up to the La Center Casinos sometime within the hour: if not, then sometime within the next few days or weeks. He has no shot at abstaining, because he really doesn't want to quit: at least not at this point. They say in recovery: "It's always the threes that get you." Three days, three weeks, three months, and three years are the most dangerous times during someone's recovery. Three days because, when you're busted, it usually takes a few days to get money from relatives or friends who believe your lies about not having money to make the power bill, or that your car died and you need cash for a new battery. Telling them you have to repay a gambling debt can also work. You say you owe the money to a big fucking Yugoslavian who's going to break your pinkies if you don't pay him. People who don't hang around racetracks and casinos actually believe that these loan shark and collector types exist. So, preying on their belief of Hollywood fictional characters can usually get you a couple hundred bucks.

The three-week relapse is usually after someone has started a recovery program. Usually their spouse has threatened to leave them, so for the first few weeks they are inspired, and they think, "I'm finally going to quit. This is the time I'm going to get it done." But that itch that they were using gambling to scratch is still there. So, since they don't know any healthier ways to deal with it, they go back out.

Three months in, people usually just relapse because they're fucking bored. By this time, they've gotten the adrenaline from the addiction out of their system. But, then, they start having to pay off bills they've neglected for years, as well as debts they've accrued from whatever loan places they've hit up, if they aren't fortunate enough to have a good job.

Plus, after three months of Gambler's Anonymous meetings, going bowling with your pals on Saturdays, taking walks with your wife, or whatever other god-awful distractions you replaced gambling with, you really just want to go place a bet.

Three years is always the interesting relapse, and usually the most dangerous. Often, in recovery, people say "I have another relapse in me, just not another recovery." These are people who have worked their programs, kept their noses clean, and have managed to somehow, someway, find a different distraction. They have been able to avoid doing the one thing that they knew best in the world. Then, all of a sudden, sometimes deliberately, sometimes by accident, they make a bet: a single, solitary bet. That's all it takes, then it's on. It's more than on. The cortisol and adrenaline shoot through their veins like plunging rapids as their minds race, their thoughts focus in, and worst of all, they begin to dream.

Gamblers are the biggest dreamers there are. We sit and think about all the wonderful and glorious things we will do with the money once we finally break through and get that big win. The biggest philanthropists in the world aren't Carnegie or someone like that. Rather a gambler, in his or her mind, has that title. Gamblers know that once we hit that big score we are going to pay off all our bills — first thing. We're going to put money aside for the kid's college fund. We're going to help our cousins, and nephews, and the neighbor down the street with cancer. Everything will be fixed, once we hit that score. But that big score usually doesn't come, and when it does, the money just goes right back into the games. I know this feeling. Of all the big hits in my career, I never gave a nickel to anyone, and I rarely paid an overdue bill.

Driving home this Tuesday night, winding

through the suburban back roads you have to take to get to that church, I think about Brad and how he's probably already on the freeway to La Center. I think about this weekend's races at the track, and how my pal Ben hasn't trained a winner in two weeks. I also think about some of my greatest successes, and how if I could just go back in time, I would have been more responsible with that money. But I know that's all bullshit.

There was the $7,500 Pick 4 at Emerald Downs back in 2005. It was a crisp Monday evening card of racing with only a smattering of people actually at the track. After beating a favorite in the first race, I selected two runners in a ten-horse field in the second race: one 15/1, and one 22/1. The 15/1 shot, a claiming nag named Henry's Laughter, got up in the final strides and things got interesting. A 9/1 horse named Holmdale Snap went slow early on and stole the third leg of the Pick 4 sequence, setting me up for the final race. I walked all the way down to the top of the stretch to watch the last race. My buddies all knew what was going on. When a big score loomed, I always wanted to be alone. And with maybe 500 people at the track that night, it wasn't hard to find a spot to be by myself. I never check the payoffs, and when the announcer Richard Sanchez, a friend and mentor of mine, started to read off what the winning bets would pay, I covered my ears, walked towards the top of the home stretch, and hummed as loud as I could, so as to not hear what my looming windfall was going to net me.

Sure enough, a nice 4/1 runner named Kaiser's Dweej took the last race, and when I walked back to my friends, they all screamed out that I had taken down the whole pool! Seventy-five hundred bucks. Of course, after the government got a hold of twenty eight percent, it went down to fifty-four hundred and change. I've always resented giving anything to the government, let alone two-thousand dollars in cash winnings. After tipping the teller, I walked out with fifty-three hundred dollars, and my buddies and I proceeded to head over to the Iron Horse Casino down the street to blow off some of the day's winnings.

3

MICHELLE

As I park my car, the streets of Portland seem weirdly quiet tonight. At least more quiet than normal on a Tuesday at nine thirty. The part of the city I live in is known as the Pearl District and has become the "it" neighborhood in the recent decade. The Pearl is just blocks north of downtown, and is loaded with high rise condominiums, chic restaurants and bars, and tons of neat little shops. During daytime hours, the centrally located Jefferson Park is littered with families picnicking, and hipsters smoking their hand-rolled cigarettes talking about how big corporations are the cause of all their ills. I rarely patronize any of businesses in The Pearl, and tend to do most of my shopping up in the north end of town near the racetrack. Growing up in the middle class suburbs around Seattle, the idea of paying more just to shop at these swanky shops has always seemed somewhat ludicrous, especially when Fred Meyer and Burlington Coat Factory are only a five-minute drive away. The only reason I live down here in the first place is Michelle.

She invited me to live with her after my recent lease was up at my little studio. While the idea of sharing a six hundred square foot apartment had been something that we both were concerned about, after two years together, it seemed the logical next step in our courtship.

After finding a parking spot, I head towards the building and pass the doorman, who stands in his black trench coat and old style derby black cap. He rarely says hello, but always gives a tip of the cap to residents and guests who enter. It's the only place in Portland with a doorman, and is a beautiful fifteen-story condo unit with a jet-black glass exterior called The Baker Building. Upon getting in the elevator and hitting the seventh floor button, the door starts to close before a long, black arm interrupts its momentum. The gentleman who scurries in is on the phone, speaking a language I've never heard. After a brisk upward journey, I nod to the guy as I exit into the seventh floor hallway. Taking a left turn off the elevator, I enter apartment seven-nineteen, and am greeted by only pitch black and silence.

Michelle is sleeping in the queen-size bed to the right, with the door to the bedroom open, and the lights out. She's in her third year of her surgical residency at the local hospital, and getting up to work at four-thirty in the morning, and then staying at the hospital until seven or eight at night, leaves her little time for anything but work or sleep.

Our apartment consists of artwork that Michelle has gathered over the years, as well as furniture that her parents gave her after she finished medical school. The only possessions I added to the place are a panoramic framed shot of Santa Anita Race Track, and a few extra forks and knives.

"Hi sweetheart, how was your meeting?" she whispers from out of the dark.

"It was fine. Nothing too exciting," I say, as I change into my pajama bottoms.

"How was your day, did you get to cut

anybody open?"

"I don't want to talk about it," she says. "Dr. Hollingsworth got pissed at me again for something totally stupid. I swear that guy hates me for no reason. I need to sleep though sweetie, are you coming to bed?"

"Naw. I'm going to go surf the net for a while," I say as I kneel down and kiss her on the side of her cheek. When she's been sleeping, her skin gets so warm. I always love to kiss the side of her cheek in moments like this, because she's like a human furnace when she's been sleeping. Michelle always sleeps surrounded by pillows on all sides. It's as though she sets up a bunker within the bed, with pillows touching her entire body. Her curly brown hair even seems to get its own pillow, as her head rests on a big red pillow with the hair draped onto a separate feather-filled pad. When she's not in bed sleeping, she's a tall and impressive woman. She wears glasses, and has a little crease in the center of her nose that's beyond adorable. Her hair is curly, and even though she gets it straightened once a month, within a few hours of the procedure the hair starts to curl again. She still makes me smile when I see her after two years.

I met her while sitting in a hotel bar just two blocks from where we now share an apartment. Michelle had just moved to town to start her residency after finishing up her time at Yale Medical School, and was staying at the hotel while she awaited her apartment at the Baker Building to be ready. I was at the hotel bar visiting my friend, also named Ryan, who was tending bar. I talked with Ryan the Bartender, who had plenty of down time, as he only had two other customers to attend to on a quiet Monday evening. With the great Dave Niehaus calling the Seattle Mariner's baseball game on the television, we both discussed our love of Seattle and the hapless Mariners, when the woman just a few stools down interjected.

"Mariners fans. Eww," the woman with the glasses and teacher's sweater said with a smile.

"Eww? How can you hate on my M's?" I asked. My attention was now directed towards her, as opposed to my comrade behind the bar.

"Because I'm an A's fan," Michelle said with

a smile, pointing at the television, as the A's were indeed besting my Mariners on this night.

We began a conversation, and within a week, we were having a first date, eating pizza at Nostrana. Within another week were sharing our first kiss at Pix Patisserie. I always tease her, wondering why an Ivy League surgeon is dating a guy from the racetrack. When I first met her family, I was shocked by how normal and well adjusted they all seemed. "Whose parents still live together, and are married in their late sixties?" I thought. "That's like so thirty years ago."

I shut the bedroom door and plop down in the recliner chair out in the living room. When I pull open my laptop, I do what I always do. I go straight to one of a series of horse racing websites. Sites where fans and gamblers get together to talk about the sport, talk about betting, or just complain about their most recent losses.

From the time I first got into racing, I always thought "why are these guys so bitter and jaded about everything?" However, after six years of working in the business, and ten years of gambling seriously on the horses, jaded would be something I'd consider an uplifting mood. Gambling on racing does something to your psyche. Getting nosed out of a photo for a couple thousand dollars because a jockey got the horse stopped, or the horse spooked from a shadow, or any of a thousand other things that can happen during a race, can literally cause a person to go mad.

As I comb the Internet, I come to a site where a guy who is only known as "Cre8ive" starts a thread where he complains about how the people who work in racing can't stand the gamblers.

Tempted to post a smart-ass reply, or an honest response, I know that it's in my best interests to just stay out of it. There isn't much sense in starting an Internet fight with someone who is faceless, and is essentially just a name on a screen. The Internet seems to have given the power of anonymity, and a soapbox, to every chucklehead with a computer. After scanning a few other racing sites, I decide to check in on my other favorite online haunt: Craigslist. Although Michelle and I have been an item for two years, I tend to find companionship via the Net more often in recent months.

"BBW looking for a fun younger guy—39— NE Portland"

Craigslist has become my anonymous way to meet and find women who are as desperate as I am. Not just for sex, but desperate for attention: desperate to be held, desperate to talk with someone, and discuss more than how his or her day went. I love Michelle, but I find that as our relationship continues, our distance has grown, due not only to her extraordinarily busy schedule, but also due to my own desire not to be open. Sometimes I'm just bored.

About six months into our relationship, she caught me out with another woman. I had told her I was just going to stay in for the night, and being the rocket scientist that I am, I took this gal to a restaurant that's two blocks from Michelle's house, and in the same building that her friend, Sarah, lived in. I told Michelle that this gal was an old friend, and that I didn't think she'd understand me wanting to just hang out with another woman. I lied. It was total bullshit. I was totally planning on sleeping with this other girl. It seemed we lost a lot of momentum in our relationship after that. Lately it's been ok, but we just exist as friends these days it seems. It's weird lying in bed with someone you know well, and still have them feel like a stranger. But she's been the strongest rock in my corner throughout my recovery and my mom dying. The fact that I love her isn't in question, even though my ancillary actions on the Internet, and in the world, may say otherwise.

"Thirty-two year old male, 6'1", dark hair, and hazel eyes," I start to reply. "I work in town as a sports announcer. Successful, and a smart guy. Shoot me a message if you want to talk more."

It's fifty-fifty whether or not this is even a real person, or just some robot that just collects e-mail addresses, but it's worth a shot. I reply to a few more responses in the Casual Encounters section, which, essentially, is where you go to get laid.

"I Need a Cock—25—Downtown." Surely, this isn't a real person. The title is way too lewd, and inside the message it says anyone from eighteen to fifty-five can reply. Meaning, everyone with an e-mail address please send me a message, as I want to collect as many addresses as I can.

"Big gal looking for a big guy—31—Tigard." Definitely a real person. If they're looking for a fat guy, then they're usually real.

I simply copy and paste my same introduction to all these people, and sure enough within fifteen minutes, the thirty-nine-year-old gal I e-mailed first replies.

"Got a Pic? Can you host?"

I upload a picture of myself with a microphone that was taken at the downtown radio studios where I do my weekly radio show. It's not only a slimming picture, but, hey, maybe she'll think I'm some kind of important person.

After informing the big gal from the Northeast that I can't host a rendezvous, since my girlfriend is sleeping on the other side of this wall, I hit the send button in hopes she'll reply. The wait for Internet responses has somehow become a little bit of a jones for me — similar to gambling. It's that uncertain possibility of something good happening — the possibility of hitting a score — it's a game of chance that will hopefully lead me into a stranger's bed within the next hour. Michelle knows I get antsy and sometimes need to get out of the house, even if it's taking a walk at eleven o'clock at night. So, even if she were to wake up and find me not there she wouldn't freak out.

But alas, she didn't respond. Maybe she thought I was ugly.

4

PM

I park my silver Chevy Trailblazer in the south-end employee parking lot, and walk in with roughly an hour before the races are set to begin at one in the afternoon. In my betting days, I would have shown up by ten in the morning to play the first few races from Philadelphia Park, Aqueduct, or even Suffolk Downs during the warmer months. As I open the door, I quickly poke my head into the main office, grab my *Daily Racing Form*, and see if my boss needs anything promoted for the day.

"Just make sure to talk about Oregon Championship Day. And tell everyone about the Barbeque Tent, and that it's open despite the bad weather," my boss Keith says.

"Do you want a bagel with schmear?" he asks, pointing at the continental style breakfast spread on his table. My boss refuses to come to work without having at least five meals worth of food in the fridge, or spread out on his table. He's a food pusher. One of those types who'd rather have you call him a bad name, than turn down his offer of some weird food from his homeland.

"No, thanks. I just stopped by New Seasons and grabbed some lunch," I respond.

Portland Meadows Horse Track sits just six miles north of the Pearl District, but they are worlds apart. The Pearl is cosmopolitan, and decorated with young and vibrant people, fancy stores, and a general buzz that exists in a place where people want to be. Portland Meadows sits in Delta Park, which, other than the actual park itself, pretty much consists of a couple motels, Elmer's Pancake House, a Burger King, and some kind of auto parts store. There's a hardware store as well, which backs up against the track at the quarter mile pole. But it's off the beaten path a bit.

The grandstand at Portland Meadows is three stories tall and has a huge neon horse flashing to look like the horse is running in place above the main entrance. Unfortunately, the neon on the legs malfunctions, so the horse looks as though it only has three good legs, which, given the talent level of the horses that compete at this track, is somewhat apropos. The building is anything but spectacular, but as a racetrack, it's serviceable and does its job admirably.

The track was built in 1946, and looks like a huge warehouse as you pull into the parking lot. The parking lot is filled with potholes, and hasn't been repainted since Bill Clinton was in office. The parking area is massive in size, and probably has room for about three thousand cars. On a typical day of racing these days, it only has to have room for about three hundred vehicles, with a quarter of those being horse trailers and vehicles used by the trainers who condition the horses. The parking lot is used more these days for various auctions, as well as serving as a huge open space for dad's to teach their kids how to drive, or for people to find an anonymous place to get a blow job, or smoke a joint, or whatever they need to do in some degree of privacy. I've actually never done any of those three things here. Seriously. I promise.

From the main office, I head down the narrow white halls and open up a door into the main gaming area of the track. Within five feet of entering the main area, I stop to talk with some of the regulars situated at Carl's Paddock Bar. These guys all sit leaned back in their chairs, copies of the *Daily Racing Form* in hand, dingy, old sweatshirts and jeans the standard attire, looking for their next winner from any of the televisions.

"Hey, what the hell is this Obama's problem?" says Marco, a seventy-something-year-old Yugoslavian transplant who's at the track seven days a week. He hasn't worked an actual job for as long as anyone knows. Marco spends his days at the track with his *Daily Racing Form* in front of him, a diet coke, and five televisions located just above him so that he can bet on multiple tracks from across the country.

"Eh, be nice to the guy, he's just trying to clean up Bush's mess," I sarcastically reply. I usually play devil's advocate when discussing politics.

Our entire relationship consists of short and spirited political interactions, with Marco generally saying something negative about the democrats, and about how smart Rush Limbaugh is.

"This morning Rush was talking about Obamacare," Marco screams so the other five players near Carl's Paddock Bar can hear him.

"Whatever, Marco. Who you got at Churchill in this next race?" I ask.

"I'm on the five," Marco replies.

I stand behind Marco and his pal Mitch, who's seated at Marco's table, as Churchill's announcer utters those three magic words.

"And they're off!"

Marco and Mitch sit together each day, and if you saw the two guys on the street, you'd never picture them hanging out together or even having any combination of similar interests. Mitch is much younger, maybe forty, is always clean cut, and is usually mild mannered. He's always polite, but when his horses aren't running well, and he's getting behind on his bets, he certainly gets testy.

"What the fuck is this jockey doing?" Marco screams at the television. Even though the races are simulcast in from thousands of miles away, horse players still tend to scream at the jockeys and horses as though they can a) hear them, and b) give a shit what these guys say.

By the time the horses at Churchill come into the home stretch, Marco, Mitch, myself, and pretty much anyone else who's ever watched a horse race knows that Marco's horse is out of steam, and has no shot. He drops back to fifth, and by the time the lead horses hit finish line, his horse isn't even on the television screen.

"Alright guys, I'm heading upstairs," I say as I collect a bottle of water from Carl the Bartender and head on my way. Carl has been serving drinks at the track for decades, and if he isn't taking a food order or pouring a cold one, he's probably at the betting machine putting his most recent two-dollar tip on a horse.

As I make my way through the main lobby back to the press box elevator, I pass by the sixty or so gamblers who are there taking in the morning simulcast races from the East Coast tracks. The tellers, the people who take the bets, are all lined up behind a counter on the left, each looking more sour to be there than the next. A huge bank of big screen televisions hangs above the player's seating area. All the guys sit in these little cubicle-type desks. Each of them studies their copies of the *Daily Racing Form*, and checking the odds on the televisions before heading over to the tellers to make their plays. It looks like a library in some ways, which it kind of is.

There's Harry, the retiree who made his fortune owning and operating small convenience stores in the area. He owns a couple of horses that race at Portland each year, and he spends a minimum of six days a week at the track, usually spent wandering aimlessly talking to whomever will engage him in conversation. He's a millionaire many times over, according to some sources, and yet he insists on wearing the same sweatshirt every day, and has been wearing the free Belmont Stakes hat the track gave him for the last year and a half.

There's Bennie, who, like Harry, is here every day. But unlike Harry, he's not financially secure. Bennie lives in low-income housing, and gets disability since he retired from the parks department, where he'd worked for twenty years before taking a buyout on his pension because he had hurt his back and couldn't work anymore. He took the money from his buyout, rumored to be about two hundred and forty grand, and went to Reno to try and make a run at becoming a professional horseplayer. He made it for about fourteen months before finally blowing his last dollar. In fact, it was Marco the Yugoslavian, his long-time compatriot from the track, who had to drive down to Reno, pick him up, and bring him back to Portland to help him get set up again. Bennie always has a bad-beat story ready to tell anyone who's willing to listen.

In gambling, bad-beat stories are never in short supply. They're tales gamblers tell of the hard-luck losses they've suffered—of the times they've been beaten by a nose at the finish line, and it cost them hundreds or thousands of dollars.

Earlier in the year, Bennie had a nice score when he hit a Place Pick 9 at Arlington Race Course in Chicago. The beauty of the racetrack nowadays is that you can sit and bet on literally every track in the country as well as many in Canada, Japan and Australia, seven days a week. Bennie's Place Pick 9 involved him picking a horse in each of the nine races at Arlington, and in order to win that bet, his horse in each race had to finish in either of the top two spots. In horse racing, a "win" bet is one that requires the horse to win the race. A "place" bet means they can finish first or second, and a "show" wager means that if the horse finishes first, second, or third, the player wins, albeit not as much money as the other two options. When Bennie took down that ninth and final race, the results went official, and he collected just over ten thousand bucks for his efforts.

I was standing next to Bennie when he took down that score, and the first thing I noticed was something I recognized from my own gambling days: the look on Bennie's face wasn't the ecstasy you'd expect to see of someone who'd just won ten grand. It was a look of relief. It was a look of utter relief. For the compulsive action gambler like Bennie, or me, ten thousand dollars assures us of what we want most, which is to stay in the game. It's a way for us to be able to continue to fund the addiction, and to chase after more and more. Your average player might bet two dollars a race, or five, or sometimes twenty. Guys like Bennie and I, our blood doesn't get pumping unless we're risking an amount of money that means something to us at the time. Betting ten dollars a race is something we do just to pass the time.

Bennie was relieved that he could pay his rent that month. But, he was more relieved that he could go after the Pick 4 at Los Alamitos later that night. He was relieved that for at least the next few weeks, he could bet as much as he'd like, and maybe run up his bankroll. He knows the money is going to go away again, but this hit allowed him the opportunity to pretend he's going to be a lifelong winner, at least for a little while. I've had those big hits before, and after spending some fun money at a strip club or casino, hitting my head on the pillow at night with a wad of cash in my wallet was one of the most content feelings I'd ever known.

When I finally get to the press box elevator, I breathe a sigh of relief to be off the gaming floor and away from the action. Watching all those players, and all those races on the televisions, does nothing but get me excited anymore. When I first quit betting the races, I would spend all my time out on the gaming floor looking down at the ground and avoiding watching the races at all cost. But in recent months, I've started watching again. If an acquaintance has a horse going in a race, I'll sit and watch with the guy rooting that horse home, as if it's my own. It's my way of getting some action without actually putting my skin in the game.

The elevator seems older than the building itself, and when I get in and push the button with the word ROOF on it, the slow upward journey begins. After all the shakes and creaks of the elevator ride are over, the door opens up to a dark tunnel that leads out to the press box.

I pass by the Steward's office first. Essentially, they're the referees of racing. They're employed by the state, and make all rulings at the track.

Continuing down the hall I pass the photo-finish office, the television camera area, then the television department, whose wooden door is cracked, weak, and looks like it wouldn't take much to break through, even with the padlock on the door.

The final door of the press box says "Announcer/Chart Caller" on it. I open it and step into the room. It's essentially two offices in one. I have to walk through Gary-the-Equibase guy's office to get to my booth. It's like an office within an office. I've been calling the races for six years at Portland Meadows, and got my start at Mohawk Downs in Dayton, Ohio. My booth is no more than four-feet wide, and probably twelve-feet long, with a small white desk, and a big 1994 Sony television to go along with the expansive windows that overlook the track and the infield. It isn't much, but it's one of my favorite places. On a clear day like this one, I, and any rooftop guests, can see the majesty of Mt. Hood to the east, as well as Mt. Adams, as well as the blown-off top of Mt. St. Helens, which resides fifty miles to the Northeast, and which lost twelve-hundred feet of its crown when it erupted on May 18, 1980. I like having Gary in the room next to me, as I spend most of the day talking with him between races about politics, women, jockeys, trainers, and much more. He's a total kick, and maybe the most stubborn guy I know. But he's got a good heart.

I start my day's announcements.

"Good afternoon ladies and gentlemen, and welcome to Portland Meadows. The main track is fast for today's nine-race card, and post time for the first race is just thirty minutes away. Here are today's changes . . ."

I still get a giddy feeling hearing my voice go out over the speakers.

After going through the motions of giving out the jockey changes—over weights, and scratches for the day's races—the real fun begins. Six runners step onto the track, as the trumpeter plays the call to post. And by trumpeter, I mean the cassette tape that I hit the play button on. As the horses start parading, I repeat their names, while I stare at the jockeys silks, or colors, as they're also known, so that I can memorize the horses' names by the silks the jockeys are wearing. Since I watch the race through my powerful binoculars, I don't have time during the race to look back and forth at my program.

"Tiz O Gold, Tiz O Gold, Tiz O Gold."

"Shamundi, Shamundi, Shamundi"

"Little Bob Johnson, Little Bob Johnson."

The horses finally get to the starting gate and begin loading up. One by one, the six runners are led by an assistant starter, who holds a short chain, and leads the twelve-hundred pound animal into a small steel contraption, with maybe six inches worth of wiggle room on each side of the horse. Once the horses are all in the gate, the head starter waits until they are all pointing their heads forward, and when everyone is ready, he hits the small button in his hand and the gates fly open. I keep my attention on the horses, as I look through my green Swarovski 10x50 binoculars. I hold them tight as the horses take their first steps out of the gate, and I start the call of the race.

"And they're off," I shout to the eighty people out on the apron, and the few hundred more watching around the country who actually pay attention to our small track.

"Little Bob Johnson heads out for the early lead, with Shamundi right there in second. Moonlit Master moves up into the third spot, with Tiz O Gold right to his outside in fourth. They've pulled some five lengths ahead of Cape Truth and Warren's a Legend, who is the trailer."

The field continues into the home stretch, and I lower my binoculars. The horses have come within view as they run inside the final eighth of a mile.

"Little Bob Johnson continues on the lead, but in the center of the track, Cape Truth is starting to make up ground. It's Little Bob Johnson, but here's Cape Truth on the outside, and Cape Truth and jockey Annie Houlihan get up for the win."

The horses run the six furlongs, or three quarters of a mile, in one minute and fourteen seconds. One minute and fourteen seconds is all an average horse race takes at Portland Meadows. Just over one minute can mean thousands of dollars to the owners who own the horses, and hundreds of dollars for the trainers and jockeys who earn ten percent of the owner's winning share. The horse and rider return to the winner's circle after the race and pose for a picture to commemorate this event. It's a thirty-seven-hundred dollar race on a Wednesday at Portland Meadows, so odds are this race won't be stamped in the memories of many people for too long.

For me, it means I've finished one of the nine races that will make up my workday. An average day like this at Portland Meadows will feature probably four- or five-hundred-thousand dollars bet on our races. Only about thirty thousand of that is actually bet here. The rest is bet from people playing at other tracks, or watching at home on their computers or televisions. Between races, there's about twenty minutes to relax, watch TV, talk with Gary-the-Equibase guy, eat, or whatever.

On this day, though, as it has been for many days in recent months, my idle time is spent reading the *Daily Racing Form*, and watching the other races from around the country. This probably isn't something I should be doing, as in some ways it's a tease, and in all ways it's a trigger, but fuck it, I'm not betting.

Santa Anita's second race of the day is just six minutes away, so I immediately flip to the page in the *Daily Racing Form* with that race's past performances. The *Daily Racing Form* lists the horses' past races and pretty much any information you could think of about the horse. It even says whether or not the horse has his testicles, or whether he's been gelded. It's that expansive. There are so many bits of minutia that a bettor can find from the *Form*.

Santa Anita is a gorgeous horse-racing track in Arcadia, California, which lies just north and east of Los Angeles proper. It sits up against the San Gabriel Mountains and is one of the most picturesque racetracks in the world. The massively tall palm trees, and monumental fountains in the infield, add a touch of modern class to the old school charm of the massive green and gold painted grandstand with its overhanging roof. Horses like Seabiscuit, Sunday Silence, Spectacular Bid, and so many of the greats of the last seventy years have raced there. Hall of Fame jockeys and trainers make it their home year-round, and they run for huge prize money. Gamblers bet anywhere from eight to twenty million dollars a day on the races there.

I've visited Santa Anita numerous times, and whenever I'm asked what my dream job is, I always answer, "I'd love to announce at Santa Anita." My dad took me there when I was twelve as an aside to a Disneyland vacation, and each time we went to Los Angeles, Santa Anita was always a side trip for us.

I even got to watch a race from the announcer's booth there with Bill Tomlinson, who is considered by many to be the top guy in the business. Tomlinson, a gentle man in his late fifties, calls races with class and precision, and rarely misses a name or anything that happens during a race.

"Portland seems like a fun place to call, yes?" Tomlinson asked me politely.

"Yeah, it's alright. It's a fun job for sure," I told him, even though all I could think of was how jealous I was that he gets to call here in paradise.

Tomlinson called the race at Santa Anita while I sat back and watched one of my idols perform his craft dutifully, never once taking my eyes off Bill to watch the actual race. The race on the track was a bottom-level maiden race, essentially the worst horses at Santa Anita. After the race concluded, Tomlinson turned around and reflected on what had just happened.

"I'm sorry you had to see that race. That was the worst race we've ever had here at Santa Anita," he said with a chuckle.

I laughed, knowing that any of the five "nags" from that race would have been favorites in nearly every race run at Portland Meadows on a given day.

I think of that encounter as I study the past performances for this upcoming race at Santa Anita. I can see by the television signal that the sun is bathing the track with its warmth and light, and that it's a glorious day in Southern California. As I analyze the race, which is now just two minutes away, I notice it appears that the number two horse, Saint Loup, looks like he could be "lone speed" in the race, meaning he could be all alone early on. Being all alone early in a race would allow him to relax, and when he's unpressured he might be able to shake loose and go all the way. If someone does push him early on, then he could be doing all the hard work early, and not have enough steam left late in the race to keep going and hold off the horses that will be closing in.

As the race kicks off, Saint Loup goes right out to the lead as I had predicted. As he gallops around the track, Saint Loup never gets pressed and cruises to an easy win at 5/2 odds. A simple two-dollar win bet on him returns seven dollars and twenty cents. My normal win bet of fifty dollars would have returned me one hundred and eighty bucks back in my gambling days. A one hundred and thirty dollar profit for one minute and two seconds of work by a dark bay horse named Saint Loup.

I think about how easy that was and how often I was able to pick winners. Picking winners was never my problem. When I lost, however, I went on tilt. Tilt is something that every poker player or serious gambler has experienced over the course of his or her career. Essentially, going on tilt means you're pissed off and you start to bet carelessly and over-aggressively. I would quit looking at the past performances altogether once I was on tilt. The game of skill would quickly turn into me simply picking names, numbers, and odds, and throwing increasing amounts of money on them hoping to get back to even. The amount of times I've blown my entire bankroll after going on tilt can't be counted on my fingers and toes. It was a near weekly, and sometimes daily, occurrence at my worst.

During the summer of 2008, after not betting for a couple of months, I was stuck at home for a week recovering from a minor surgery. I had torn my left retina at some point and one day randomly saw some black spots in my vision.

After visiting the eye doctor, and getting my eyes dilated, the doctor told me the bad news.

"You need to have surgery on this, like tomorrow," the doctor said in a serious voice. "You can choose not to have the surgery, but you'll go blind if you don't."

"Well that seems like a no brainer," I thought.

So, within eighteen hours, I went under the knife to insert a small piece of plastic behind my left eye called a scleral buckle. I was home and on the mend within four hours of being in surgery. With two weeks of ordered rest and relaxation, a simple afternoon of betting while being stuck on the couch led to maybe my biggest tilt episode of all.

It all started out well, with a thousand dollars deposited into my account, I was off and running. Within two days, I'd run my account up to thirty-three hundred and was on a roll. Then, on the fourth day, the shit went downhill fast. Down a couple of hundred bucks after a few hours, I decided to put a hundred-dollar win bet on a 3/1 runner at Saratoga, trying to get my money back. That horse ran up the track, and next thing you know, the hundred-dollar chase win bets were turning into two-hundred-dollar straight exactas, and five-hundred-dollar win bets. Three more deposit requests later, I had lost fifty-three-hundred dollars on the day, and I went from being up twenty-three hundred to down three grand. Tilt and addiction tended to give me an exacerbated case of tunnel vision. All that damage happened before I could even clear my head to realize what had happened, and how fast nearly a month's worth of pay had evaporated in a few clicks of my computer mouse on bettingtheponies.com. Sitting there, with the realization of what had just happened starting to sink in, I felt as though someone had just kicked me in the gut with a pointed boot.

That bad week led to the next few bad months, which inevitably led to trips to the emergency room for panic attacks, as well as financial and emotional bankruptcy. The adrenaline rushes from the ups and downs of betting led to wild swings of emotional and physical sensations. I thought I was dying. In the midst of a panic attack, the body locks up. Everything seems uncontrollable. Breathing rate increases, palms begin to sweat and dizziness sets in. Your limbs start to feel like jelly and the simple act of standing becomes possibly the largest task a human being can face. The sensation and desire to flee wherever you're at during that current moment becomes not only something you desire, but something you'll put ahead of essentially everything in your life. If fleeing means losing your job, or your house, or other things you've worked years to acquire, you'll give them up in a red-hot second and run away during a panic attack.

I know these feelings all too well, as I began to have panic attacks at age twenty-one after my dad died. Sometimes they would happen on a daily basis and sometimes not for months at a time—but they were always there. And they were always far more prevalent when I was gambling. I visited the emergency room twice during that fall of 2008, both times after full-on days of binge gambling. My betting literally started with the first race at Monmouth Park at nine-fifty in the morning, all the way until the late Pick 4 at Los Alamitos nearing midnight. After a vain attempt to quit following the Breeders' Cup that year at Santa Anita, I made my final bets on a couple of races at Philly Park on December fifth. Realizing that I wasn't able to quit on my own, I broke down on the elevator up to my announcer's booth. I called my Aunt with a plea for help, as I didn't want my mom to know just how bad off I was.

"I can't quit," I said to her with tears in my eyes. "Every time I try to stop, I inevitably go back. Once I get going, I just can't stop. Ninety-nine percent of my brain says not to bet, but I listen to that little fucking one percent each time. I'm so fucking sick of it—all the bullshit of it. I've missed so much shit because of it. I swear I've said, 'I wish I could have been there' more than any other phrase in my life. My life has become centered only on betting. It's cost me almost everything I've ever made, and I've fucked away almost every good relationship I've had. But I just always go back. I always go back to the gambling. This is just fucked!"

5

BUNNY GIRL

As the last race of the day gets set to start at Portland Meadows, I gaze over the infield to the backstretch where the horses are warming up. It's quiet, and the only people left on the apron, the area below where people watch the race, are a couple of hipsters in their old tattered suits, and a family with two kids running around. It's really one of the best times to be at the races, and in particular, up in the announcer's booth. For all its age and rust, Portland Meadows, like almost every track in the country, has a certain beauty to it. There is a nostalgia and majesty of the old game. Much of that comes from the animals that give their lives for the sport, and for its perpetuation. The way they move, and the way they give every ounce of themselves, it's impossible not to have a love affair with them.

The horses finally go into the gate, and as the bell rings in response to the starter's order, the final race of the day is off. All is going well until a runner named Feels Like Rain suddenly pulls up out of the race and comes to a stop, as jockey Javier Perez finally gets her to quit running. The race continues with Acts Like a King getting the win in relatively facile fashion. But it's difficult to watch the race and not focus your attention back to the quarter pole, where the apparently injured horse is coming to a stop. Perez hops out of the saddle and tries his best to hold the horse still, which he does with some success. The veterinarian who follows the horses around in a car about an eighth of a mile behind the pack catches up and quickly gets out to examine the horse. Within a few moments, I hear the vet radioing for the horse ambulance. But her instruction to take the horse back to the trainer's barn indicates that it's not a catastrophic injury, and that the horse should be fine.

It's a bad way to end the day, but the workday has ended nonetheless. With just one more day left in the racing season, my off-season work usually consists of helping out with media and marketing, hosting events, and other odd jobs. Most tracks have distinct racing seasons of three to seven months. Some race year-round, but most don't. We race in the fall and winter because the track in Seattle, Emerald Downs, runs in the spring and summer. Many tracks will operate on a circuit, so that the jockeys, trainers, and employees have somewhere to work year-round, even if it's in different cities.

The announcing is what I love, though, and the sole reason I stay in the game. Plus, where else can you get paid a few hundred bucks for just five hours of work that really isn't work at all? After a quick on-air goodnight to the bettors and guests, I sign off and head to my car to go home. Driving home through the afternoon Portland traffic has become a breeze since moving to the Pearl District, as everyone on the freeway is driving out of downtown while I'm one of the few who is driving back in.

I pull up to the apartment and am greeted by the doorman in his typical Wednesday fashion. It's getting somewhere near spring, so he's given up his winter trench coat for a simple black button-down jacket. We exchange our typical "good evening" to one another and the interaction is over in just a matter of seconds. Quickly up the elevator and into the front door, Michelle sits waiting on couch.

"You're off work early, how'd you get so lucky tonight?" I ask.

"I need you to leave," she quickly replies with a look that shoots straight through me. I know I've done something wrong, because she is not a reactionary. "I know you've been cheating on me."

I know I'm fucked, but I'm trying to look calm, as my brain is moving at three million miles per minute, trying to figure out what she found out.

"What the hell do you mean?" I say as I try to buy myself time to sort through the cavalcade of lies that are popping up in my head, trying to navigate my way towards the one that will get me through this.

"You left your computer open, and when I went on it to check my e-mail, there was an instant message from some girl — Pdxbunnygirl, or some shit like that."

"And that means I was cheating?" I protest.

"Her first message was, 'when will I get that dick again?'"

"I don't even know what the fuck you're talking about," I say.

"I kept talking to her," Michelle says, looking me straight in the eye. I can't bear the idea of giving her a look back.

"She said she saw you last month and was wondering when you could get together. I played along like I was you. She knew all about you. It was obvious she'd known you and seen you recently. God dammit!"

Silence, and some attempts at mild denial, is all I can muster for responses.

"Why would you do this to me?" she asks.

Realizing that things weren't working out, and that I'm caught in my lies, I finally find the guts to retort.

"I don't know what to tell you," I say. "I have no excuses, I just don't know what to say. I hardly ever see you."

"Why couldn't you just tell me," she pleads, as she starts to sob uncontrollably.

"What did you want me to tell you?" I say, still looking down at her feet. "We hardly ever see each other, you work a hundred fucking hours a week, and your days off are the days I work. And when we're both home we're fucking exhausted, or just not interested in each other. I'm not making excuses, but things just aren't working."

"You're going to blame me for why things aren't working out?" she says. "Why don't you blame your dick for it? Because I certainly didn't force you to go fuck some other girl."

"I don't know what to say. I'm an asshole," is the only bit of truth I can come up with.

"Please just get your things and get out," she says. "Just don't make me look at you while you sit here and lie to me. I'm going over to Sarah's house for the night. Please be gone by tomorrow."

"I'm not going to leave, let's talk about this," I beg her, sitting on the couch and motioning for her to come sit next to me. "I know I fucked up, but I don't want to lose you over this. This was just a stupid one-time thing."

"How can you look me in the face and lie to me like that!" she screams, bending over at the waist and sobbing into her hands. I reach out to put my hand on her shoulder, and she immediately recoils and takes two steps back.

"What do you want me to say?" I ask. "What do you want me to do? I'll do anything, just try and calm down, and let's talk about this."

Michelle wipes her tears and tries to compose herself. Finally ready to talk, she sits on the edge of the couch, just far enough away.

"I don't want you to say anything," she says. "I just want you to leave and I don't want to see you anymore. You don't talk to me anymore. You make me feel unwanted. And now you're cheating on me. What is there to say?"

And that was it. The fastest breakup I've ever had, the end of my longest relationship, and all I can do is sit here and feel like an asshole. I don't feel guilty for what I did, but am rather upset for getting caught. Michelle starts to walk out after grabbing a handful of her clothes. I had reduced this strong woman to tears and it was like a kick in the stomach for me, because I knew she meant everything she said. I was exactly where I hate to be—in a position of feeling vulnerable. There may not be a worse word in the English language to me than vulnerable. What a terrible thing to be. Sitting here with my head in my hands, she grabs the last of her overnight bags.

"I love you, and I'm sorry things have to end like this," she says with the door half open. "I hope you find what you're looking for."

And then, she's gone.

6

RIALTO

I sit slightly dazed in the apartment. Still blindsided by what's just happened, I try and call Michelle. It goes straight to voicemail, and just hearing how happy her voice sounds during the greeting makes me feel shitty.

"Michelle, come back. We can work this out if we just talk about it," I plead, knowing in my heart that my efforts are futile. After ten minutes pass and she doesn't return my call, or subsequent texts, I decide to leave. I round up my clothes and pack them into some garbage bags, since my suitcases are in storage. I load up my toothbrush, and bathroom supplies, and head out the door. This is Michelle's place, and ninety-nine percent of the furniture, kitchen appliances, and towels are hers. Not much sense in rummaging through all that crap just to grab the one or two things I had supplied to our short-lived shared home. After passing by the doorman for probably the final time, I quietly walk to my car, throw the bags in, and head away from the Baker Building.

I drive aimlessly around for twenty minutes, confused, annoyed, not wanting to eat, but certainly wanting to distract myself somehow, and food always seems to work. As I drive down Broadway, I spot some parking attendants out in front of the Hotel Vintage and I pull over. It's a swanky, expensive hotel, but it's close, and to be honest, the idea of soaking in the big hot tub in the room seems nice.

"Good evening sir, and welcome to the Hotel Vintage," says the parking attendant. "Will you be needing any help with your baggage tonight?"

"Naw. Just park the car please."

The Hotel Vintage is a narrow building reminiscent of any boutique hotel you'd find in Manhattan—to me at least. As I walk into the lobby, I hear Enrico Caruso playing softly over the sound system, while guests gather around a complimentary wine and cheese bar that's been set up.

After checking in, and riding the antique

elevator up to my room, I collapse on the bed. It's amazing the feeling that can come from flopping onto a hotel bed after setting your bags, or in my case garbage sacks, down. It's the kind of exhausted joy that comes after running a marathon, a night of intense love making, or after the end of an extraordinarily long day at work.

After sitting for fifteen minutes enduring a combination of hunger pangs and heartache, the desire to take a walk motivated me off the bed and into the streets of Portland. I know my way around downtown, but the only place I can think of to grab a quick bite within walking distance is the Rialto on Fourth and Alder. The Rialto is an off-track betting site. I've been there for work, and I've hosted numerous parties and handicapping contests in the cozy confines of the pool hall/bar/OTB. Upon arriving, I'm greeted by Bill, the betting teller, who recognizes me.

"Hey, how are you doing?" he asks.

"I'm fine. Just came down to grab a bite and see what was going on."

"Not much, for a Wednesday. Just Mohawk

Harness, Jacksonville Greyhound, and Woodbine," the teller says.

Most tellers, or bet takers, have the same tone no matter what the day, time, or situation. They smile only when there are no customers at the desk. They've spent literally decades of their lives hearing complaints from patrons about why they're losing, and what jockey stiffed them, and what bad luck they've had. Tellers are in the business of customer service, but they rarely think of themselves that way. They're union employees, so they essentially have the protection of the union. They cannot be ordered to smile and be happy, or to try and make the customer's experience a good one—things you'd expect of customer service representatives who wanted to be good at their jobs. It doesn't matter if you're in Oregon, Oklahoma, or Ozone Park, New York, tellers are a special brand of grouchy.

"Well, I'm going to go eat. Enjoy the rest of the night," I tell Bill, who offers me up a wet noodle of a handshake as we part.

The Rialto is a poolroom, and the kind of

dark, oak-walled place you expect if you were designing an average OTB. The food isn't half bad, though, and I plunge my emotions into each bite of my Rialto Burger. While enjoying my mountainous bacon-covered monster, I scan the room, taking in all the players watching races on the elevated television monitors.

"C'mon with that deuce!" one player yells. "C'mon whip him. Whip him. WHIP HIM— shit!" The man quickly scans his *Racing Form*, looking for the next race to punt on. His tattered shirt, and unkempt, fading hairstyle is similar to the other players still taking in the races. Even though there are seven or eight guys in the room, each is locked up in their own special brand of loneliness. Each man's eyes are either focused on a television, a program, a *Racing Form*, or a cigarette.

The favorite in horse racing wins about thirty-five to thirty-eight percent of the time at most tracks, and on a given night, most of the stiffs at the Rialto can count on winning two or three out of every ten bets they make. Of course, there are the guys who go after long shots, or after the big scores via Pick 4's, Pick 6's, or even Superfectas, where they try to pick the order of the top four finishers in each race. The odds of hitting these bets are shitty. But when you hit, you get paid. I always liked to play the Pick 4's. That was my bread and butter. Recently, I looked up my online betting account and found that over the course of three years, my return on investment on Pick 4's was high, while pretty much every other thing on the ledger was a loser. I rarely played the Pick 6's because you need to have a huge bankroll to play those kinds of bets.

While I sit at the bar, I think about all those past hits as I watch most of the players sitting here making their two-dollar win bets. Some of them are making a few bucks and most of them are losing a few. I never understood how someone could play the game for such inconsequential amounts of money. I mean, if you're going to play, then fucking play.

My leg is shaking, as it always does when I'm out and around people. The constant up and down bounce of my foot is similar to what you see of people waiting around in a doctor's office. Each race I watch on television just increases my level of tension and excitement. I feel like a horny teenager in a room with pornos on every television, only I have a chastity belt on.

After finishing my burger, and with just two minutes to post time for the next race, I glance at the program for Woodbine. It's their last race of the day and it's a cheap maiden race. A maiden is a horse that has never won, so essentially a maiden race is full of either first time starters or life-long losers. I look at the race and notice the favorite is an even money shot named Disco Dan, who's going to be breaking from the far outside in the six-furlong race.

I take my wallet out and set it on the bar counter. I part the wallet gently with two of my fingers and see a single, solitary, twenty-dollar bill. I take the twenty out of my wallet and start to caress it. I know Disco Dan is going to win. It's just one bet. Fuck it. I start to make my way to the betting window. I've thought hundreds of times in recent months about making a bet, but there was always something to stop me. Now, there's only twelve feet of tattered green carpet between Pandora's box and me, but as I approach the teller, instead of stopping and turning around, I keep striding forward. I shouldn't be doing this. I shouldn't be doing this. Okay, just this one time, but only once. I arrive at the teller's window. I'm standing as tall and straight as my legs will allow me in their present state. I feel like a quick gust of air would drop me right now.

"Give me twenty to win on the eleven at Woodbine," I call out to him.

Once I hand the teller over the money, it clicks. My life has now changed, in milliseconds, as the machine prints out a small two-by-three-inch sheet of paper that reads "Race 8, $20 Win #11."

Over a year and a half of abstinence, hundreds of Gamblers Anonymous meetings, thousands of tears and thoughts of possibly never betting again all vanishing as that little piece of paper pops out of the machine and into my hand. Hello, old friend.

I walk back to my seat as my pulse continues to race with the horses loading into the gate. The reality of the split second decision I've made is finally starting to catch up to me. That old familiar feeling—the one that came to me only when I was making my biggest, riskiest bets—was back: an instant adrenaline rush; that tingling in the tips of my fingers, and the flush sensation that rushed to my face are all back with a vengeance. The instant escape, where no one else around matters, or is of consequence. It's one of the few times I can exist in the space of others and revel in some kind of twisted peace. It's just me and that television.

And I'm fucking excited about it.

"They're off!"

The race unfolds just like so many do, with some zillion to one long shot going out way too fast, way too early, and cementing the fact that he has no shot to win. Disco Dan is positioned on the outside. He makes his way over to the two path as they go into the far turn, and starts slowly inching towards the leaders without any urging from the jockey, who's as still as a statue in the stirrups.

I keep reminding myself to breathe. I'm standing at the bar watching the race unfold, and trying to act as calm as possible. It's the only race currently going off, so everyone's gaze is set upon the race at Woodbine. I hold my ticket as tightly as possible, as my heart thumps against the wall of my chest. I can feel my pulse in my neck, my torso, and even in my fingertips. My face is warm, like I just drank my first glass of wine. I finally sit on my barstool, and look away from the screen to reassess the reality of my surroundings. This is happening; but it all seems so slow.

At the top of the stretch, when most surefire winners make their move, Disco Dan kicks into gear and blows by the early leaders. By the time he arrives at the midway point of the homestretch, he's all but home free and not looking back. He hits the wire in front by four lengths and I don't even make a motion. Not a fist pump, or a cheer, or even a nod. I feel like I've been in a fight. My exterior looks fine, but inside I'm exhausted. Beat down. Tired. Lonely.

Scared. And that was after a win.

A few minutes later the "official" sign goes up. $4.20. That's what Disco Dan pays to win for every $2 wagered. I sit, still in shock from the last two plus minutes. Such an innocuous amount of time, and it seemed like it took an eternity. I have a new abstinence date for my GA meetings now. March 18, 2010. But I know this isn't my last bet. Those feelings of thrill, terror, risk, and excitement grip me immediately. Trying to compose myself by taking the deep belly breaths I learned about in my anxiety outpatient program, I walk up and cash out my ticket with the teller. I leave the two one-dollar bills on the machine for his tip, drop fifteen bucks down for the burger, and I'm out the door. I'm up five bucks for the night, and heading back to The Vintage with plenty on my mind, the least of which is Michelle.

7

CLOSING DAY

I feel a bit apprehensive walking into the track today. After making that bet the other night, I spent my days off reading the *Racing Form* for various other tracks, but decided not to bet. My intention was to prove to myself that I could control my gambling this time around. But like I've said many times, relapse occurs in three days, three weeks, three months, and three years. Even the sickest of addicts can make it two days. But still, I'm kind of proud of myself. I sent Michelle a couple of texts. No response. I was tempted to go to her apartment, but she doesn't want to see me.

On race days, it's easier for me not to bet. First, there isn't a wagering terminal located up in the press box. Second, it's against the rules for employees of the track to bet while at work:

something I obeyed at least twenty or thirty percent of the time during my old gambling days. When I walk into the main office, I see a note in my box from my boss.

"Come back to my office when you get in," is all it says.

"Hey Keith. What's up?" I ask.

"Have a seat, will ya?"

"So, it's no secret we've lost a shit ton of money this year and the last couple years," Keith says. "We aren't going to be able to keep you and a few of the others on during the off-season."

I immediately adjust myself in the chair, holding onto the handles as I listen to my boss tell me he's taking away my income. "I apologize for the late notice, it's just our budget can't afford anything that's not completely necessary right now. The reason we waited so long is I tried everything I could think of to keep you guys on."

"Don't sweat it Keith. I get it," is all I can get out. Even with the money saved up in my bank account, all I can think about is "what am

I going to do for food and rent?"

"We might need to have you come in if we do any promotions in the off-season, but I can't make any guarantees."

"I understand," is all I say as my brain begins to race, trying to figure out what to do next. Of course, I could always get unemployment, as it's something I've never had to claim before. Plus, between work and a small inheritance I got from my dad's estate when I turned thirty, I've managed to save a fair amount of money in the last few years.

I'm trying my best to soak in this last day of work. Not because of the last pay day, but rather because when racetracks start laying people off in such big numbers, and with the rumors of Portland Meadows's financial instability, which has been rumored since before I was born, there's the possibility that this could be my last day at this track, period.

Sitting up in my perch, I start to fill out my programs and get ready for the races. The sun even peaks out from the clouds for a bit; something that hasn't been seen for what seems like months, and may literally have been months. I spend the day calling the races, reminiscing with Gary-the-Equibase guy, and searching Craigslist for possible off-season jobs. I have no clue what I'm going to do next because, even with a college degree, I don't have any real experience outside of a racetrack.

As the final race field comes onto the track for the post parade, the time when they parade in front of the stands before the race, I give out the horses' names, the names of their owners and trainers, and finally the names of each rider. I do it with a slight smile, and even though I should be scared shitless right now, I'm enjoying how great this is.

When the gates fly open, I call the race with the passion and vigor of doing it for the first time, and not as something I do nine times a day, eighty days a year. The race goes off without a hitch and a horse named Callaghan's Chief wins the last event of the season. Shortly after the final winner's circle presentation, I pack up my binoculars and head down the rickety elevator for the final time.

There are usually three types of people milling around the main gaming area after a day at the races: the winners, who are either at the teller windows collecting their winning bets from the last race or cashing out their vouchers; the losers, who are either hitting the winning players up for a twenty to try and get back in the game, or heading out into the cold Portland evening; and the horsemen, the men and women who train, groom, and own the horses that race at the track. They gather around Carl's Paddock Bar and talk of the good luck, bad luck, or no luck they've had for the day. Mostly they sit and reminisce about the good times and the good old days.

"I remember when the grandstand was filled every night," says one old lady who has been working on the backstretch for any one of twenty different trainers over the last several decades. "They've let this place die. Look at the walls, the carpets, and the paint job. The people that run this place don't care about us, they never have."

I could easily go to the bar and get lost in a

conversation with any of the horsemen at the track. But instead, it seems more important for me to move on, simply find my way to my car, and start that final drive home, with home being a hotel room.

Upon arriving back at the Hotel Vintage, I hop in the shower to rinse off the salt and sweat of a hard day's work up in the announcer's booth. Five straight hours of working for two minutes and then having a twenty-minute break before the next two minutes comes due. It's a perfect job for gamblers, who inherently want something for nothing. We want the easy way out, the quick buck. Announcing races is ideal for me, as it allows me a creative outlet, but also doesn't force me to have to do any heavy lifting or hard work. But unfortunately, for me it's over: at least until the track hopefully reopens in October.

The break that is now upon me offers up time and freedom, which on one hand is something I relish and look forward to. On the other hand, however, it can be terrifying to have that much time and open space to fill. Lying in the bed, I start to think about what to do and where to go. I can't afford to keep staying at the Hotel Vintage all summer long at two hundred dollars a night. I could go back to Seattle and try to find a job at Emerald Downs doing something around the track, as they open up in a few weeks. But the idea of doing something other than announcing, for not much money, isn't all that enticing.

I pull out a couple of my books from one of my garbage bags, including my AAA road atlas. I've had the same one for seven years, and it's tattered from dozens of road trips. It's been almost a decade since I last stepped on an airplane. It was my twenty-first birthday, and some friends and I had flown to Las Vegas for the weekend. I was already anxious about flying, and I didn't know that planes taking off to leave Vegas have to climb quite steeply to clear the mountains. Then, when the pilot backed off the thrust, it felt like the plane was dropping, even though we were still climbing, just at a slower speed. I immediately panicked and looked at the young lady sitting next to me who also looked horrified. She said, "What the fuck was that?" I didn't even answer. I just spent the next two hours white knuckling the arm rests of my seat.

I always felt that by age thirty-two, I should be settling into a marriage and eventually having kids. I'd found my career, and Michelle was certainly the perfect candidate for marriage and someone to raise a family with. She has a big heart, is a loving person, and she's beautiful to look at. But my decisions to break not only her trust, but her heart as well, alienated her and forced her hand. I shot her another text message, simply asking if she was okay. But after thirty minutes passed with no response, I resigned again to leaving her alone—at least for tonight.

As I lay in bed, with Letterman playing on the television in the background, I finally find some contentment in an idea to take a journey. The desire to run away and escape has been the driving force in my life, and finally, with no job, no family, and no girl, this is the perfect time to run. Tomorrow morning I'll wake up, hop onto Interstate Five, and drive south. I've thought about taking this trip a thousand times. What the fuck. What do I have to lose?

8

SOUTHBOUND

It's forty-eight degrees outside and raining as I sit in front of the concierge desk at the Hotel Vintage. It's Sunday morning and the town is quiet, as the hipsters aren't awake yet to grab their breakfasts at Bijou Café, or Lovejoy Bakery, or any of fifty other amazing breakfast places in the town. Plus the churchgoers usually head out to the suburbs for their services. March is often thought of as the time of year when the weather turns: when spring begins and all things suddenly change for the better. March in Portland, Oregon, however is usually on par with February, January, December, November and October, as well as April and May, for that matter. It rains here. A lot. It's not just a rumor spread to stop Californians from moving up here.

Having checked out, I realize that my plan for taking out a pile of cash for the trip will be delayed by twenty-four hours, as I forgot that banks aren't open on Sundays. So, I grabbed what I could out of the hotel ATM. Working weekends for a decade has a way of jading a person to the idea of a normal Saturday/Sunday break. With three hundred in cash, a full tank of gas, a backpack filled with books, my laptop, and some garbage bags full of clothes still unpacked from my quick exit at Michelle's, I head to the freeway.

There are two schools of thought on how to proceed on a trip like this: one is that I can go balls to the wall, stopping only for gas, food, urinating, and the occasional stretch. That kind of trip would put me into Los Angeles by Monday afternoon, Monday evening at the latest. However, since I don't have to be back to work until October, there is really no sense in rushing.

Driving through Oregon is something I'm familiar with. Having grown up in Seattle, Washington, my years of driving to Vegas and California during my early twenties have ensconced this drive into my brain. Name an exit or milepost anywhere between Seattle and L.A., and I'm sure I can tell you what's there.

Oregon stretches for three hundred and eight miles on Interstate Five from border to border, and there are two distinct parts. The first portion of the trip is from Portland to Eugene, which takes you through Salem (the state's capital and home of nothing really exciting), then through Albany (which is even less exciting but at least has some cool restaurants), and finally, you reach Eugene, the state's second largest city. All total, it's about one hundred and five miles of flat-as-a-pancake, straight-as-a-string freeway: the kind of stretch that normally excites road trippers because you can make great time. However, Oregon's sixty-five-mile-per-hour speed limit tends to hinder the fast pace that all men crave while making a road trip. In the book of man laws, "making good time" on a road trip ranks high on the list of things men brag about most. The others being: getting a stripper to go home with you, and/or how close of a parking spot you managed to find at any crowded event.

Eugene is a college town and home to the Oregon Ducks Football team, who are the pride of Oregon sports. They have become a national powerhouse thanks to all the money Nike pours into the school, and the town is actually quite a scenic area.

Eugene is where the second part of the Oregon drive really starts. After you pass through Eugene the road begins to tilt upward and starts to wind, as the next one hundred and ninety five miles are full of hills, valleys, turns, and semi-trucks that unfortunately require me to put my full attention on the road and not on the lush greenery of my surroundings.

There aren't many memorable points between Eugene and Medford. It's essentially just a hundred and fifty miles of very pretty country. It all runs together: a series of hills, valleys, and more hills. There's Jumpoff Joe Creek, where I guess a guy named Joe once took his final plunge. Shortly after passing Jumpoff Joe Creek, and making my way to Grants Pass, I find myself passing over the top of a hill that opens up to a massive expanse of a view. I'm starting to get antsy as I look down into the valley, which stands hundreds of feet below the road. My hands begin to sweat as I try to focus solely on the road, but being scared of heights, and pretty much everything else in the world, I keep thinking "What if the car steers itself over the cliff? What if I freak out and need to pull over and call an ambulance? What if I pass out momentarily and go over the ledge?" By the time the hill descends to lower ground and into Grants Pass, my worries start to slowly fade. Deep breaths. In through the nose, out through the mouth. Belly breaths.

As lunchtime nears, I pull off exit twenty-seven in Medford to grab some food and produce from Harry and David's. I get chips, salsa, and a ripe pear to go along with some bread and peanut butter for sandwiches. Road tripping, loaves of bread, and a jar of peanut butter, have always gone together in my mind. I leave Medford with my groceries in tow and drive another thirty-five minutes or so.

As you get closer to the California border, there's a massive but beautiful climb through the mountains, and eventually a gain of over four-thousand feet in elevation. When I reach the top, I see that many of the truckers and passenger cars have pulled over to enjoy the view. However, I know exactly where my next stop is going to be. I drive ten more miles into California and pull over at the first rest stop in the state. I stumbled upon this little park a few years back on one of my trips to Vegas and I've made it a point to stop here each time I'm passing through. I don't know what the name of the river is, or the park for that matter, but its beauty is nearly unmatched during this drive. The park sits down at the bottom of a hill, just before the start of another incline. It's a perfect spot to picnic.

After lunch, and back on the road, my favorite part of the entire drive begins. The one hundred miles between the rest stop and Redding, California, are some of the most beautiful on the West Coast. Passing through towns like Weed, and then alongside majestic Mt. Shasta, tends to invigorate a drive of this distance. An hour and twenty minutes later, I finally cross over Lake Shasta and into Redding, my resting place for the evening. The sun is in its waning stages, and as I glance west over the lake, I have to squint to enjoy the sun falling. Glancing east, I can see the sandy hills surrounding the lake, the tree-lined crest perfectly illuminated by the last traveling rays of sun, and the redness of those hills just bleached in sunshine, resting in absolute perfection.

Redding was supposed to be the capital of Jefferson State when the conservative residents of extreme Northern California got sick of all the liberals in the Bay Area and Los Angeles setting all the laws. But as it sits, it's seemingly the capital of the far north of the Golden State, as there isn't a good size town within a two-hour drive in any direction. The main attraction to me, and the reason I always stop here, is that Redding is home to the northernmost In-N-Out Burger restaurant. After checking into my motel and relaxing for a few minutes, I shower, put on some presentable clothes, and head over to the In-N-Out Burger. As with every In-N-Out, the lines are huge and the wait is somewhat long by fast food standards, but the greasy Double-Double I get with a side of fries is well worth it.

I've only got a short drive planned for day two of my trip, as I'm planning on taking in the races at the Sacramento harness track in the afternoon and then staying in Sacto for the evening. I go online, purchase a racing program for the harness track, and start to study and map out my bets for the next night. I'm going to have to buckle down and take things slow and serious if I'm going to make my money last through the off-season and avoid going broke too soon. I decide that I'm only going to make three bets the entire card in Sacramento. Now, normally I'd bet on all the races, and if I was losing, I'd double down and keep doubling down until I got even, or until I went home busted and disgusted. But this time has to be different. I have to keep the betting under control. I know how things turn out when I'm not disciplined, so if there is to be some kind of change, it needs to start right away and stay that way.

Morning in Redding is calm. There's a slight

hum of traffic out on the I-5, but it's an otherwise sleepy town. Interstate Five takes on a very straight and gentle rolling quality in the two hours between Redding and Sacramento. The hazy, dusty, and yellow scenery gets quite arid and sparse, and at most points it's hard to believe you're in the most populous state in the country.

Pulling into the Cal Expo Harness Track in Sacramento isn't exactly like pulling into Santa Anita. It's more like pulling into Portland Meadows back home, but with fewer people. The grandstand looks like a high school grandstand with a horse track in front of it instead of a football field and running track. Harness racing differs from the thoroughbred racing I've always focused on, and love, as there are no jockeys, but rather drivers sitting in a little buggy called a sulky. I've never really paid much attention to the harness runners, with the exception of watching my boss's horses that race back east. But horses are horses. I've picked a few gems out on the card and I'll be making separate twenty dollar win bets on all three. The first race of the day will be one of my bets, and as I make my way to the windows I'm greeted by a smiling teller, which tells me he must be either new or just starting his shift.

"Twenty to win on the three," I call out as I hand over a crinkled Andrew Jackson.

"Here you go, sir. Good luck," the teller says as I walk away.

The horses come trotting by, and as they start their one-mile journey, my horse blasts right out to the lead. I bet on the big favorite in the race: a 4/5 shot named Woodford's Champagne who has won two races in a row. Normally I wouldn't bet on a horse with such low odds, but I wanted to stick to my plan of betting what I set out to bet and not changing or getting emotional. Sure enough, as the field comes into the home stretch, Woodford's Champagne starts to pull away easily and draws away to win by what seems like a country mile. I cash my ticket, and take my thirty-eight bucks with me to find lunch and a comfortable seat in the grandstand to relax. My next bet isn't until the fifth race, so I kill the hour texting my buddy in Los Angeles.

"Hey Jon, you drunk ass, I'm coming to L.A. Be there tomorrow night," I write.

"Awesome, where u stayin?"

"Not sure yet, gonna hit up Santa Anita and probably just stay near the track. Gonna stay for a while, so gotta find an actual place to crash, but it's gotta be cheap."'

"Cool, let me know when you get down here. You can crash here for a night or two."

"Maybe. I'll call you on the weekend," I reply to end the conversation.

The fifth race draws nearer and the horse I had planned to wager on is actually a juicy 6/1 odds, higher than the 4/1 morning line that the track handicapper had predicted. I put my twenty dollars to win on the horse, and within five seconds of the race starting, my ticket essentially becomes confetti as the horse breaks off stride and gets pulled all the way to the back of the field. He eventually passes one other horse and finishes sixth out of the seven horses in the race.

"What a stupid sport this is, harness racing,"

I mutter disgustedly, but somewhat jokingly.

My last wager comes just one race later with a 3/1 second choice who is trying to beat a favorite that's beaten him three weeks in a row and is 4/5 odds. Last time out, the favorite, El Rondo, got an easy trip on the lead, so I'm hoping that this time someone pushes him and tires him out enough that he'll run out of steam, and my horse can catch him. But alas, nobody pushes El Rondo as I'd hoped and he romps to his fourth straight win, with my horse, Catchdavidsmiling, running second again.

Three bets and down twenty-two dollars for the afternoon. In the grand scheme of things, I could lose twenty-two bucks every day for the next five months and be fine. But this was just a warm up. This was the minor leagues. This was betting a track and horses I don't follow, and where there isn't any money to be made. Los Angeles is where the big scores and big bets lie for me, and it's just five hours down the interstate.

9

CITY OF ANGELS

There isn't much in the way of scenery on Interstate Five between Sacramento and Los Angeles. It's essentially three hundred and fifty miles of barren land once you pass through Stockton. I blitz through the dusty fields that make up central California. Other than a stop for lunch and gas in Kettlemen City, I just want to get this driving over with. Once Bakersfield is in the rearview mirror, you start to climb and spend the next ninety minutes or so driving through mountains. It's where Southern California begins. The difference between Bakersfield and Los Angeles is only about 100 miles, but the two cities couldn't be more polar opposites.

After driving through the hills, I pass through Santa Clarita and the other mountain suburbs that start to appear as you near Los Angeles. Once I hit the Two Ten Freeway I start to drive east to Arcadia, a comfy little suburb in the Northeast. The closer I get, I don't know whether it's the anticipation of almost being to my destination or the fact that I'm just tense and nauseas from the non-stop driving, but I can't sit still in the car. I switch driving hands every thirty seconds, keep adjusting myself into different positions, but nothing seems to relax me.

Santa Anita doesn't race this day, but it's the first stop on my itinerary. I finally exit the freeway onto Colorado Street. Within a mile of getting onto Colorado Street, in the distance to my right, I can see the grand cathedral. Santa Anita Race Track has been sitting on this plot of land for well over seventy years, and it's as beautiful today as it ever was. The parking lot isn't completely empty, as there's simulcast betting going on today with a moderate crowd of regulars betting the races via the television sets throughout the facility. I notice as I pull into Santa Anita's expansive parking lot that there's a Motel 6 conveniently located right across the street. Seems like the perfect place to hole up for the weekend of racing before trying to find a more permanent residence.

Walking into the Santa Anita grandstand is like walking back in time. At least it's how someone my age envisions olden days being like at the track. The paddock area is gorgeous and manicured so perfectly it's almost a wonder that the flowers and bushes are real. As you walk into the grandstand, the old tile floors, old-fashioned food stands, and the nineteen fifties odds-board all just sweep you back to a time when all the men wore suits to the track and the women wore dresses. When everyone had a hat, and people only bet to win, place, or show.

Much of that ambiance is still here. But then, I bump into one of the thirty guys here who thinks it's acceptable to rock sweat pants in public. Since it's a dark day with no racing, I quickly dart out to the rail. It's quiet and there's nobody around as I soak in the beauty of what stands before me. The palm trees that rise up hundreds of feet in the air, their beauty amplified with the San Gabriel Mountains providing a dull brown background for the green of the trees to bounce off of.

My decision to make this my home for the next five or six months is something that should terrify me as I know what betting has done to me before, and what it could do to me again. But I'm oddly comfortable with the decision and excited to face the challenge that I've laid out before myself. I place my hands on the railing and lean into it, as I do at every track I've ever been to. The rail is what separates the horses from the spectators. It's the closest possible place for a fan to get to the action. It's a reminder of my younger days, sitting on my dad's shoulders "on the rail."

I'm so tired, though, that as much fun as sitting around and soaking in the place is, I really just want to get settled in. I stop by the customer service desk on the way out and buy a *Daily Racing Form* for the races tomorrow. I hop back in the car and drive over to the Motel 6. I head to the front counter to get my temporary residence set up.

"I need to get a room," I tell the front counter employee.

"Yes, sir. For how many nights?" the young gal responds.

"I'm going to check out Sunday afternoon, so four nights," I say.

"That'll be sixty nine dollars a night plus tax, do you have a credit card?"

My credit card is something I've kept for emergencies ever since I quit gambling. Back in my early twenties I ran up about twenty-five thousand in credit card debt at one point, as I reasoned that instead of quitting or playing within my means, I would just bet more and more until I got out of the financial trouble. Unfortunately, I ran out of credit before those winning bets could start coming in. Luckily for me however, there was always mom to bail me out, as when the debt collectors came knocking at the door, she was glad to help with an open checkbook. When I finally did quit gambling for good, I paid off all of my credit cards except for one Visa that I've kept in my back pocket for safekeeping, just in case I ever needed it. Today felt like a good time to pull it out, as I don't have much cash on me after the drive down.

"Do you know where there's a Wells Fargo around?" I ask the gal at the hotel counter as I initial the motel's no smoking policy.

"Just go to the other side of the racetrack and there's a massive mall," she says. "There's one right on the outside of the big parking lot of the mall. I'm almost positive it's a Wells Fargo."

After unpacking my bags, and getting settled into the room, and with an hour left until banking hours are over, it's time to get the bankroll. The bankroll for gamblers is the universal term for money that's strictly to be used for gambling. This money doesn't go towards food, hotels, or toothpaste—just bets. A bankroll is something I've never used, because when I was betting, *all* my money was my bankroll. Money that was supposed to be for rent, books, school, or food was still gambling money, even if it wasn't labeled as such at the time. But if I'm going to be able to do this and have a chance to not have things slip into oblivion, I have to do it differently.

"Welcome to Wells Fargo sir, how can I help

you?" says Candy, a nice fifty-something woman who looks pleased that her workday is coming to an end.

"I need to check my account balance, and then I also need to make a very large withdrawal," I say quietly, trying to not act as badass as I feel right now.

"Ok do you have your account number?"

I hand her my account card and she quickly pulls it up on the screen, and since there are other people around, scribbles my balance on a small blank deposit slip and slides it across the counter.

$31,748.

I knew it was right around there because I saw my balance last week when I checked my account, but it still jarred me a bit seeing it sitting all alone on that little ripped paper slip. It's about the most money I've ever saved up with the exception of when I got an insurance payment of about the same amount after my dad died. It's certainly enough for a single guy with no attachments to live comfortably for the six months I'm going to be unemployed. But I could easily blow it in a few weeks if I'm not careful.

"I'd like to take out twenty thousand in cash please," I say.

"Okay. I'll have to get the manager to help with this transaction, would you mind having a seat?"

"No problem," I say as I go to the waiting area and pick up one of those awful bank magazines with a picture of a happy family on the cover.

"Mr. McGuire," the bank manager says as she extends a hand. "I can help you with your withdrawal if you'd like to come back to my office."

I head back with her and we fill out some paperwork to facilitate getting my money.

"We just don't like to hand out large sums like that out at the desk," she says.

"I completely understand, and I appreciate it."

She walks to the back area of the bank where I presume there's a massive safe with hundreds of thousands of dollars, and francs, and deutsche marks, and whatever else a bank has in the back. This is after all Wells Fargo, the pinnacle of high finance.

The manager walks back in, takes the one-hundred-dollar bills out of their little bands, and begins counting them in lines of ten. She counts them out quickly, but I can see every bill just long enough to realize what each one means. Each passing hundred is a few days' food or shelter. Within about two minutes there are two hundred Benjamin Franklins staring back at me. All those six-inch dull green bills come as a tangible reinforcement of how real this all is. We so rarely see what our cash looks like. It always looks like a number on our ATM receipt. But now, two thirds of what I've been able to save up over the last few years is lying right in front of me. It's one of the most beautiful things I've seen in my life.

"Can you please put it all in a large envelope?" I ask.

After getting back to the Motel 6, I promptly lay my *Daily Racing Form* on the bed, flop down on my belly, cue up my laptop, and turn off the television. The life of a serious handicapper is one of hard work and loneliness. A day at the races for most people is a relaxing way to spend a Saturday or Sunday out in the sunshine, betting a few bucks, having a couple of beers, and just enjoying a great day. It's Americana at its best.

On a typical Santa Anita Saturday, you're usually going to see around twenty to thirty thousand people taking in the races. But on a Thursday afternoon, like the day that awaits me tomorrow, there is likely going to be just a smattering of horsemen and gamblers taking in the card that gets underway at 1 p.m.

I open up my *Daily Racing Form* and the juices start to flow as I read through the names of all the runners in the first race of the day. Opening up a new *Daily Racing Form* is something that every bettor knows as one of the most optimistic times in a gambler's life. It's essentially fifty pages of new possibilities. Each race brings with it the opportunity for a huge score and something memorable to happen, be it good or bad. And while most gamblers will tell you about the wins they've had, and say they only play to win, I've always felt that there's something romantic in the bad beats of loss as well. Sometimes those tough luck losses not only teach us the lessons we need to learn about betting, but life in general. They also give us a good story. Bad beat stories are never in short supply on the racetrack and if you hang around long enough, you're bound to hear a new one after every race. I think, sometimes, that it isn't the gambling I was addicted to, but rather the losing. It sounds strange I know, but I'm serious.

"Fucking five horse."

"Goddamned Hernandez stiffed that runner!"

"The stewards took my horse down and it was a total fix."

Those are just some of the wonderful phrases you're likely to hear after each race that's run. Bettors always believe something was up, and that it was someone else who cost us a win. It's never our fault. It's never that we maybe just picked the wrong horse. Or maybe it was just bad luck. It's always someone else's fault.

I spend the entire Wednesday early evening

pouring over the *Daily Racing Form*. Analyzing each horse's past races, speed figures, trip notes, and about forty other factors that are available in the *Form*, I start to circle those horses that I think have live shots at winning throughout the day. A gambler's copy of the *Daily Racing Form* generally looks like a three-year-old got a hold of a red pen and doodled all over the fifty some pages of past performances. Key information is underlined, good horses circled, bad ones get an X through them, and notes are written in the margin.

After a few hours of staring at the *Form*, I start getting itchy to get out of this room. My eyes are starting to play tricks on me, as they've been strained from reading the last few hours. I switch my computer browser from my trusty horse racing replay website over to my even more trusty Craigslist. Switching the page to the Los Angeles site, I click on the Casual Encounters tab and then click on "Women for Men." Literally hundreds of these ads get posted each day in each big city around the country. Many are not real, and most are listed for just sex. However, many people are just looking for someone to fill a few hours with and distract them from whatever is going on in their lives. It seems like there are many more hours to fill in a day when you're not working forty hours a week. And when you're as dysfunctional as I've been in life, you don't exactly have friends and family beating down your door to hang out.

My anxiety has always seemed to peak in the evening hours: my arsenic hours, as my mom used to say. It's this time of night that I usually seek remedy in some kind of distraction, to keep my mind and body busy until the bliss of tiredness seeps in and slows everything down.

"28-year-old, just wanting to cuddle," says one ad that sticks out to me. I copy and paste the response I made to previous ads, send it off with a picture, and the waiting game begins. As I'm replying to more ads on Craigslist, my e-mail button clicks to notify me of an impending new message.

"Re: 28-year-old, just wanting to cuddle," I see in the subject line.

"Hey, how's it going? I liked your picture

and you sound like a nice guy. I'm just out of a relationship so I'm not looking for anything serious. In fact, I really just want someone to hold me, and to talk to for a while. I can host or can travel to you. I'm in Monrovia. What part of town are you in? Here's my number if you want to talk, or we can text."

Within maybe seven or eight seconds, I'm punching in her number and sending off a message.

"Hey, this is Ryan. You just e-mailed me. I'm in Arcadia but would prefer to come to your place if you want. I just moved here, so still getting situated."

Knowing full well that no woman in her right mind would come to a strangers Motel 6 room at nine o'clock on a Wednesday night, I figure if I'm going to keep this one on the line, I better head her way.

"I'm at 2106 NE 66th St., about five minutes from the 210. Want to be here in an hour? Promise me you're not a crazy person," she replies.

"I promise I'm not a crazy person. See you in

an hour." I still have not figured out how to assure someone over the Internet that I'm not a psycho-killer without sounding like a psycho-killer.

I jump in the shower with a newfound pep in my step and get ready for my evening out. I haven't even seen a picture of this young woman, but I really don't care. Similar to her, I'm fine with just having some company to keep me occupied. For years, the gambling was my muse during idle times, of which there was always plenty. And even though gambling is now back in my life, it will be important to have some viable distractions.

Pulling up next to a run down two-level apartment complex in Monrovia, I text this mystery girl to let her know of my arrival and ask another question I figure is important at this time.

"Hey, I'm here. Okay to come up? Also, what's your name LOL?"

"Yup. I'm Krystal."

I feel nervous walking up the stairs to unit twenty-one zero six, and I tap extra lightly on the door. A part of me always wants to say, "Fuck it," and run away before these little outings, but I always stay. The risk of something good, or bad, happening is always part of the titillation. Within a few seconds, the door opens slowly and I notice most of the lights are turned off. A very sullen looking Krystal greets me. She says hello and I quickly flash a big smile to try and lighten up the mood. She politely grins back. She's a big girl, both in height and in proportion. Her hair is a dirty brown color and is tied back in a simple pony tail, while her face, although pretty, looks to have aged prematurely at just twenty-eight years of age. She's wearing cotton shorts and a tank top, and aside from her lack of a warm smile upon greeting, I couldn't help but notice her massive chest. I've always fancied myself a boob man and even though I'm not particularly attracted to her, I'm finding it difficult not to get aroused.

"Come on in," she says as she walks to the couch. "Do you want a water or soda, or something to drink?"

"Water would be good. So you said you just had a break up, what happened?"

"My ex broke up with me out of nowhere on Sunday. But it was only a three-month thing so no big deal."

She brings me the water and sits down on the couch, which sits two people comfortably. However, with both of us being of above average girth, it puts us right into a cuddling position. I quickly put my arm around her, hoping not only to ease her apprehension at the situation, but also to try and facilitate the kind of physical contact that I'm desiring. I know she posted in her ad and in her reply to me that she wasn't looking for any sexual encounter this evening, however, I'm confident based on my past triumphs in similar situations that she may eventually think otherwise. At least I hope so.

"So, what kind of work do you do?" she asks.

"I'm a professional gambler," I say with a quick response. I love the way that sounds, even though if gambling were my only occupation, I'd have a career salary of about minus twenty grand a year. Not exactly the kind of performance that most people would consider a worthwhile job.

"I play the horse races for a living," I add. "I'm from Oregon, but am going to spend the spring and summer down here playing at Santa Anita, Hollywood Park, and Del Mar. I'm planning on going back up to Portland in October. I really do like it up there, but I just had to get out of there for a few months. The weather can get you down in that place."

"That's cool, I've lived here my whole life," she says.

I find that Krystal has the intelligence and wit of many of the girls I've met on Craigslist over the years. It's not that she's dumb or uninteresting, she just seems to have a desire to keep things simple and pretty on the surface, and speaks without sounding interested in me, or interested in anything really.

The conversation continues, and eventually she finds herself easing into my cradle. I kiss her lightly on the head a couple of times and even on the cheek, but I'm not getting any kind of feedback that she wants to go further. My mindset when it comes to women has generally always been to divide and conquer: get them bedded and then leave as soon as possible. With the exception of Michelle, and one or two other serious girlfriends over the years, my anxiety and just general discomfort, have prevented me from wanting any kind of intimacy with women except for purely sexual contact. Even with Michelle, within a few weeks I was out banging whomever I could find on the side.

"Do you want to go to my room?" Krystal asks out of nowhere.

"Yeah, sure," I reply, trying to act cool about it even though my brain and pants are both moving quickly at the idea.

We arrive to find a room littered with clothes on the floor and a small mattress in the corner with a sheet and a comforter. She lies right down with her clothes still on, so I follow suit and other than removing my shoes, I hit the bed in my full regalia. I go in to kiss her and she politely accepts and immediately meets my tongue in between our mouths. Now I'm in, and covertly start to caress her large breasts that I haven't been able to get my eyes off of since I arrived. She lays on her back and while she lets me do whatever I want, she essentially just lays there and accepts the attention, showing no real sign of wanting to touch me back. Maybe she's just selfish? She turns her head away from me, opening up her neck to be kissed upon. I begin to gently kiss her neck as I slide her tank top and bra strap off of the side of her shoulder. Her breast quickly slides over the side once exposed. Gravity even hits at twenty-eight.

As I start to make out with her flush nipple, I finally decide to make the big move. If she goes for this one then I'm in. So, I slide my hand down towards her pants, and as I go to massage her nether regions, she grabs my hand.

"I'm on my period," she bluntly says.

Fuck.

A bit befuddled, and more than a little frustrated, I go for plan B, which involves getting back to her breasts.

"I told you I just want to cuddle," she says.

"Oh, okay, sorry. I thought once we were kissing, and since you invited me back here, that maybe you wanted to play."

"I thought this was play. I just can't right now," she says looking away.

She rolls over into the spooning position, which is possibly the least egalitarian form of cuddling. While she enjoys the warmth of someone behind her, holding and cradling her, I'm left with a face full of greasy hair, my left arm starting to go numb under her head, and an awkward boner. Now resigned to a few more minutes of this torture and then a drive home to masturbate as my future, I stay with her for another fifteen minutes or so. Doesn't seem much point to put in effort once I know there is a limit on how far things will advance. I'm not going to ever see her again. So, I try to make the best of it, and at times, I squeeze and hold her as tight as I would Michelle if she were here. Michelle. Michelle is great.

"I should get going," I say.

"Ok, thanks for coming over."

Within a few seconds, I'm out the door, back in my car, and on my way back to the Motel 6. While I feel mildly irritated that things didn't end up with a hookup, the mission of distraction, and having someone to spend some time with, leaves me feeling at least temporarily satisfied. For as much as I avoid people, and get anxious around them, I do get lonely. Having someone to play with and fill in some of those empty hours scratches at least part of that itch.

10

MAHONEY AND MARIA

I'm a morning person. Always have been and probably always will be. Up with the sun at seven in the morning, I have six hours until the first race of the day. What the hell to do? After spending three and half hours scouring the *Daily Racing Form* last night, I certainly don't think staring at the races again would do me any good. So, breakfast at Clockers' Corner it is. Although it's kind of a Santa Anita touristy thing to do, Clockers' Corner is a perfect place to spend a morning before the races. Hundreds of horses gallop around all morning long, some just jogging and stretching their legs, some putting in full-fledged workouts, all with the backdrop of the San Gabriel Mountains looming over the race track. Each horse that jogs by huffs and puffs, as their breath steams and evaporates a few feet after it's expelled from their nostrils.

The hostess takes me to my seat and I happen to be seated next to trainer John Mahoney who is eating breakfast with a few of his clients. Mahoney is a middle-aged trainer who started out training Quarter Horses in Arizona and New Mexico before switching to thoroughbreds about ten years ago. His career blossomed quickly. He's had great success. I've seen him on the horse racing television stations numerous times. He's a burly man, probably six-feet tall, and close to three-hundred pounds. His reddish hair and goatee are trimmed short to go with the rest of his clean-cut look.

"I'm really excited about this horse, John," says one of his owners; an elderly gentleman that's dressed immaculately and probably has a ton of dough.

"Yes sir, Mr. Barnes, I am too," Mahoney says between bites of his eggs benedict. "He's been training so good in the mornings, I'd be shocked if he didn't win today."

Well, that was an interesting nugget. Trying to act cool, I casually flip through the pages of my copy of the *Form* to the race and horse that

Mahoney and his owner are talking about. Mahoney has two horses in, and since only one of them is a boy, and he said "he," it must be Delirious Laughter in the second race. Delirious Laughter is a first time starter, so today will be his first time running in a race. Mahoney isn't normally someone who wins with many first time starters, and he's famously humble when it comes to his horse's chances. So, the fact that he seems to have a massive amount of confidence in this horse seems to be a good sign.

I had intended on playing the early Pick 5, which calls for a bettor to pick the winner of the first five races on the card. I initially loved another horse in the second race and wasn't going to even use Delirious Laughter, but I think it's more than coincidence, possibly some sort of "Gambling God" divine intervention, that I overheard Mahoney touting his runner. I have to use this horse now. So, my seventy-two-dollar ticket I had anticipated playing has quickly become a one-hundred-and-forty-four-dollar play with the addition of Delirious Laughter onto my ticket. I brought four hundred bucks with me for the day, which I figure is a safe amount to keep me in action all day, but also not too much to get me in trouble too early on in this journey.

Overstuffed with eggs and English muffins, and after a trip back to the Motel 6 for a post-breakfast nap, I arrive back at Santa Anita properly attired with some nice slacks, a button down shirt, and the Portland-hipster touch of a good fedora hat. I head straight to the paddock to watch the horses for the first race start their warm up. I'm playing four horses in this race that has eight runners. I've got two favorites and two long shots on my ticket. This is my spread race. I'm hoping one of my long shots will come in.

As I make my way towards the saddling area where the horses are preparing, I hear a familiar voice speaking over the public address system.

"Good afternoon ladies and gentlemen, and welcome to Santa Anita. Here's a look at the horses for today's first race."

It's Maria Martinez. She works as Santa

Anita's paddock host. Her job is to preview each race at Santa Anita and tell the bettors, both on track and out in simulcast land, what's going on with the horses, who looks good in the paddock, and who she's planning on betting. I've watched her picks and she tends to do pretty well. She's lovely, and not in a typical Southern California way. She's tall and thick, with hips and curves that are by no means out of place on her figure. Her tan complexion stands out against her white dress and hat. Her face shows a bit more age than her birth certificate would allude too, but she's a beacon of light in a place that's often filled with the darker aspects of human behavior. Her long dark hair flows as she tosses it back while giving out her selections for the race. Every degenerate at the track has had some kind of fantasy about taking Maria home. Or, at least having her pay some sort of attention to them. The fact that she's not a supermodel makes them all think they have a chance as well. There's something hotter about a girl who's pretty, but not too pretty. She's getable, I think. I wish. Ok, probably not.

Maria was raised around horse racing. Her dad was a long time gambler and even worked as a groom for a few years, taking care of horses for big name trainers like Clark Branson and Billy Hawkins back in the 70's and 80's. Maria's parents bought her riding lessons for her fifteenth birthday and she instantly fell in love with the animals. Her riding horse was a retired racehorse named Grandstand Gabe who had competed on the track for four years before being retired after he no longer was winning. His new career as a jumper brought him a new lease on life, and found Maria her passion.

Her parents took her to Santa Anita often, but she spent more time out in the kids play area than watching the races. After meeting Grandstand Gabe, though, she started following her dad to the track all the time, practically every weekend during high school. She attended the University of Arizona, the only school in the country with a racetrack program, and even interned at Del Mar in San Diego during the summers. After college, she was hired fulltime by Del Mar, and within three years of working in the publicity office, she took over as the paddock host. Santa Anita snatched her up after that summer, and for the last three years, she's been the queen of Southern California racing.

"Hey Ryan — Ryan McGuire," a jubilant voice calls out from behind me.

"Kenny? Holy shit," I say.

Kenny is Kenneth Mitchell, a long time writer and former handicapper at Emerald Downs in Seattle. He has been doing the picks for the *Los Angeles Times* for the last couple of years. He's only thirty years old, and already he's regarded as one of the top handicappers at any newspaper in the country. He got the job at the *Times* when the previous handicapper, Jerry Ranter, retired after being there for just short of 300 years. Kenny is dressed sharper than I ever remember seeing him in Seattle. He's sporting khaki pants and a nice Tommy Bahama style shirt, and he looks great. I guess I was used to seeing him back in his ratty-t-shirt-and-mesh-shorts days in Seattle. But his skinny ass even looks to be filling out from that fancy press box food.

"What brings you down to Santa Anita?"

Kenny inquires.

"Got laid off after the Portland season, and didn't have shit else to do," I say. "Planning on just staying down here for a few months, playing the races and maybe collecting some unemployment, gotta get some of that free money," I joke.

We continue our conversation, and before I even know it, I hear Maria's voice again, only this time it's not over speakers.

"Kenny, I didn't think they let you out of the press box," Maria says as she approaches us.

"Only on Thursdays," Kenny jokes. "Maria this is Ryan McGuire, he's the announcer up at Portland Meadows."

I shake hands with Maria as she smiles and asks me "Got anything you like today?"

"Delirious Laughter in the second," I quickly say with a sneaky smile.

"Yeah, good luck with that. I gotta run. I'll see you guys later. Nice to meet you," she says as she starts to leave. I don't take my eyes off of her as she struts away. I feel like an eighth grader whose dream girl just somehow acknowledged him.

Realizing there's now only seven minutes until the first race, Kenny and I make our way up to the windows to make our wagers. After calling out my ticket to the teller (they're still as crabby at Santa Anita as at every other track), we head out to the apron to watch the race.

"A one-hundred-and-forty-four-dollar ticket, huh? Didn't know you were such a big player," Kenny says as he pokes me in the side.

"Just getting started my man," I say. "I really do like Delirious Laughter in the second, and I think this first race is wide open."

The horses get to the gate for the opener. I have the two favorites, plus a horse at 8/1 odds, and a 12/1 long shot that I took strictly because that horse raced at Portland, and I have a soft spot for the local guys.

Horse racing is pari-mutuel game, which means I'm competing against all the other players, not only here, but also across the country. So, in my Pick 5 play, if there's $200,000 in the pool, and two people hit it, they each get $100,000. If 200 of us hit it, we all get

$1,000. The payout will always be the total pool divided by the number of winning tickets, and more long shots, equals less people having winning tickets.

"And awayyyyy they go."

The horses break from the backstretch and Kenny and I watch the race with little emotion or speech. Between the two of us, we've probably watched fifty-thousand races. We know that there's little reason to start screaming or even rooting during the first few furlongs, unless your horse gets pulled up and you need to scream an expletive so all the people around you know you were on that runner.

"The opening quarter mile in twenty-three and two-fifths seconds, and it's What a Trippi on the lead."

What a Trippi is my 8/1 pick. He's getting away with an easy lead, and is unopposed through the early stages of the race. I'm feeling quite pleased with how the race is unfolding, but with a loose-on-the-lead long shot like this, I can't really get too excited until they get to the homestretch with that same unobstructed advantage.

"They turn for home and it's still What a Trippi on the lead by two, but Mountain Man is starting to roll."

Now my blood is starting to pump. Not only with the excitement that What a Trippi is just two-hundred yards from pulling off a nice upset to start my first bet in Southern California, but because Mountain Man isn't on my ticket, and that stupid son of a bitch is starting to dig into the lead with each and every stride.

"C'mon, What a Trippi," I scream, finally letting out a verbal holler at my runner. The jockey can't hear me. I know this. I hate when other people do this. But, I get why they do it.

"What a Trippi by a neck, Mountain Man with one final surge — What a Trippi holds on!"

My heart feels like it's trying to crack my ribs, as I give a small fist bump and a large exhale relief. Almost half of my bankroll for the day was at stake in this first wager, and to get knocked out in the first leg would be more than a little upsetting.

"Nice start Ry. I gotta get upstairs to the

press box, want to come up?" Kenny asks.

"Yeah, sure," I say, as we weave our way to the press box elevator through the herds of people who are either cashing their winning tickets, or getting in line to punt their next wager.

The Santa Anita press box is a mecca for anyone who has worked in racing media. Many of the great journalists in the sport's history have spent their days up there, watching the races and penning their works of textual art. However on a Thursday in March, it's not exactly packed. Kenny sits in the last seat on the main row, as he's the newest guy to the press box. The names and faces in there make up a *Who's Who* of racing folks. Danny Dellatore from the *Daily Racing Form*, whose analysis I was reading just the night before, sips his drink and greets Kenny.

"Danny this is Ryan McGuire, he calls the races up at Portland," Kenny says. "He's gonna hang up here for a few races."

"Nice to meet you kid," Danny says, getting back to writing his analysis for Saturdays races, as his deadline is just a couple hours away. He looks like a racing writer from the 1980's: his unlit cigarette dangles from his mouth as his fingers pop his keyboard. His hair is gone on top and struggling for survival around the sides, and his mustache looks like a bristled broom hanging over his top lip.

After exchanging pleasantries with a couple of other writers and media guys, Kenny and I sit down, and I focus my eyes directly on the odds of Delirious Laughter. The three-year-old's odds are nineteen to one, up from his morning line of fifteen to one. This tells me, Kenny, and everyone else out there, that most people aren't that hot on him. My other pick, Catchmeifucan is the current favorite and figures to be tough to beat, as he has raced twice and finished second both times, just missing by a neck in each of those starts. He's even money, which means if you bet two dollars to win on him, you'll get back four bucks. Catchmeifucan is everyone in the press box's pick, and even Maria on the television is finishing up her analysis talking about how it will take something special to beat him.

The horses fly out of the gate, and just what I wanted to see, Delirious Laughter breaks like a horse that's done it a million times, and bursts right out to the lead. Within a few jumps, though, Catchmeifucan comes right up to the front along with Delirious Laughter, and they battle it out in the early going.

"As they go into the turn it's Catchmeifucan and Delirious Laughter, and those two are head and head, going right at one another."

They turn into the stretch, and my two selections continue nose and nose. But when they straighten away, Delirious Laughter seems to find another gear, and in a matter of maybe thirty yards, he kicks away and starts to open up. Delirious Laughter is visibly tired after the early battle, but Catchmeifucan is completely out of gas, as a late runner named Malamar passes him. Delirious Laughter finds the finish line first, with at least a length and a half between him and Malamar at the wire.

I try to remain cool, as I don't want to alienate the rest of the press box within twenty minutes of having met them by bragging and screaming for my long shot, especially since they were all on the horse my runner had drilled into the ground with a speed duel.

"Nice pick, man. I should have listened to you," Kenny says as he rips up the ticket that he had on Catchmeifucan. "I should have at least put a few bucks on that horse to show. What did you like about him?"

"Just had a hunch. I like Mahoney horses in their first start," I say, knowing that had I not gotten up for some morning eggs at Clocker's Corner, I would have been dead in the water with everyone else.

My Pick 5 ticket continues its march onward as the second choice named Pickthreeguru takes home the third race with relative ease. And favorite Dubai Race Night wins the fourth, over my other pick in that race Braddick's Hat. I know I'm sitting on a good score. I have three runners out of the seven that are going to be running in the fifth and final race of the Pick 5 sequence.

As usual, I don't wait around to hear the

"will pay" announcements. Instead, I head toward the top of the stretch, which is away from the grandstand and down by Clocker's Corner. Unlike most tracks, there are actually people down at the end of the stretch at Santa Anita, however, there is still plenty of space for me to be all by my lonesome. These are moments for a gambler to celebrate. Even though the win isn't in the bag, this is the nervous energy we spend our time chasing. Anytime I play a bet like this I want to win. But part of me loves the fact that I get to be pleasantly tortured for the next twenty minutes with anticipation. As I'm walking down to Clockers' Corner, I hear that familiar voice again in my ear.

"Hey, nice pick Portland," says Maria, who I didn't see coming as I had my face buried in the program.

"Thanks! Just a hunch I suppose," I say with a chuckle, trying to appear not only calm, but also cool, badass, and ultimately do-able. "I'm live in the Pick 5 to the three, four and seven, root them home for me!"

"I really like the seven, and it's paying . . ."

"NO! DON'T TELL ME!" I shout. Maria snaps her head back in reaction.

"Okay. Sorry?" she says, confused.

"Naw, it's okay, I just think it's bad luck to know what a bet's gonna pay," I tell her, trying to re-establish her belief that I'm a sane person. Surely, she should understand a gamblers superstitious nature, but she's looking at me like I just killed a puppy or something.

"Oh, okay. Well good luck!"

"Thanks Maria," I say. "If I hit it I'll buy you a drink after the races," I say, knowing that she probably gets propositioned daily and knows how to turn a guy down by now and still keep him liking her.

"I'm gonna go to the Firecracker Restaurant after the races and I'll take you up on that. If you hit the bet that is," she says with a smile that's hard to read as genuine or sarcastic.

"It's a deal," I say, completely in shock. At some point, I learned that with girls, confidence means more than most other things. Maybe that's right.

Maria heads to the paddock to do her report,

and I go find a seat in the grandstand near the top of the homestretch. Santa Anita is one of the few racing tracks where the grandstand goes all the way to the top of the stretch. It's massive in scope. However, the girth of the building is only really needed on big days like Santa Anita Derby Day or when the Breeders' Cup is in town, like it is later this fall.

"And awayyyy they go," the announcer says as the gates fly open in the race that will decide my Pick 5 play. My three runners are all close up with Brandywine, the #3, going out for the early lead. Maria's pick, the #7, Ron The Sneak, is third early on and racing out on the outside.

"They come by the quarter pole and it's Brandywine in front, and Ron the Sneak is starting to roll."

The seven runners fly by me, and judging by how the #3 and the #7 are pulling away from the rest of the field, I start to realize that this bet is pretty much a cinch.

"Ron the Sneak up alongside and right on by, and Ron the Sneak to win it going away by two."

Bingo.

I know this ticket is going to pay in the thousands. Ron the Sneak was 4/1 and the third choice in this race, so I'm banking on probably three-thousand or four-thousand bucks with the two long shots early on. I instantly start to walk back towards the winner's circle with a smile on my face. I walk upright and proud. I've bested my competition, many of which are stirring around me, throwing their losing tickets to the ground.

"Results have been posted as official," the announcer says to my delight. *"The Pick 5 has returned five thousand, eight hundred and seventy nine dollars."*

Fifty-eight hundred. Fifty-eight-hundred fucking dollars. My first day at the track and I've already jumped my bankroll up to enough where I could lose four hundred a day for the next two or three weeks and still be up. But right now, I just know I'm heading to the IRS window to collect my bounty. The teller counts me out $4,585.60 after the government gets their twenty eight percent. Fuckers.

"Thank you very much," I say as I collect my

winnings and leave the eighty five dollars and sixty cents behind for the teller, who seems about as excited as if I'd given him a buck. There are still three races left on the card, but my day is essentially done. I might throw a twenty or two on some horses in the last few races, but the heavy lifting is over. I head up to the press box for the last few races to talk with Kenny about the big score. I enter the room to Kenny and Danny clapping their hands for me.

"Aw, thank you, thank you," I say as I jokingly bow. "Can I treat to a round of drinks or buy lunch guys?"

"We get free food and drinks up here Ry" Kenny says with a sly, shit-eating grin.

"Fine, if you don't want my money," I reply sarcastically. I smile and think of how great it is to have hit such a nice score so early on in my trip. But as we watch the sixth race field warm up in the paddock, I watch the television and instead of being transfixed on the odds or the horses, I'm only enjoying the fact that within two hours I'll be heading to the Firecracker. After all, I owe Maria a drink. Hopefully she didn't think I was joking.

11

CARNE ASADA

The Firecracker restaurant isn't exactly the kind of place I was expecting. It's a hole-in-the-wall Mexican restaurant in a strip mall a few miles from the track. It's a long rectangular space with the counter and kitchen located in the back, and some flimsy tables and chairs in the front. The place is somewhat crowded, though, as a mixture of Mexican grooms from the racetrack and suburban white families nosh on their tamales. Maria is nowhere to be seen, so I go up, order a bottle of water, and sit down at a corner table. The man behind the counter barks out orders to the cooks in the back. He appears to be the owner, and seems to know everyone else that's sitting around the restaurant. Since nobody is up at the counter ordering, he goes and talks to a few of the racetrack grooms, in Spanish, so the only words I comprehend are "caballo" and "bien." They all share a laugh, while two of the guys in the group look right at me. So, of course, like every non-Spanish speaker, I'm completely positive they must be talking derogatorily about me.

The door opens and I turn my head quickly to see Maria stroll in. She immediately sees me and comes over.

"Hey Portland. How are you?" she asks.

"Today was a good day," I understatedly reply.

"Are we having dinner or are you just buying my first margarita?" she asks.

"How about both?"

We go up to the counter, and the owner comes over and gives her a hug before heading behind the counter. It's clear now that this is one of her regular haunts after the races, or just in general.

"I'll have the chicken enchilada plate and a blended margarita," she calls out to the man.

"Y tu?" says the owner as he looks at me.

"I'll have the carne asada, please."

I hand the guy a twenty and we take the little red number fourteen sign to the corner table.

"So did you come down to Santa Anita for the week?" she asks.

"You know, I got laid off after the season ended, so I'm down here as long as my bankroll can last," I say as I laugh, trying to make it seem like I'm not as sick of a gambler as I really am.

"That sounds like a real fool-proof plan," she says. "But at least you're off to a good start."

"Yeah that was amazing," I say. "One of the best hits I've ever had. I haven't been betting much the last few years, just wanted to focus on announcing and spending more time doing non-racing related things. I found that for a few years, when I first got into it, handicapping, betting, and announcing were all I was doing." As much as I want to be honest and open with Maria, telling her right away that I was a full-blown addict doesn't seem like a good way to win her over.

"Yeah I get that," Maria says as she sips her newly set down margarita. "I dedicate about three hours a night to studying the next day's races. When I first got to Del Mar, I got a lot of crap for being another ditzy, pretty, racing host. And I so badly didn't want to be known as that. I spent so many hours at Del Mar watching workouts, interviewing trainers, jockeys, handicappers, just dedicating my whole life to it. When my parents died, I found it a great distraction."

"Your parents are gone?" I quickly retort. I'm usually a passive listener, but she got my attention with that one.

"Yes. My dad, a total health nut guy, he woke up one morning and wasn't feeling good. He went to work at the track that morning, still wasn't feeling well, and something like an hour into the morning workouts, he fell down. He died before they even got him to the hospital. He had a heart attack. He was only fifty-one years old. My mom had ovarian cancer that was already far along when she was diagnosed about six months after dad died. She only made it another nine months before she passed away."

"Was this recent?"

"Dad five years ago. Mom three and a half," Maria says.

"Jesus. My parents are both gone as well. Both from cancer: dad in 2001, and mom just this past Christmas."

"Were your parents involved in racing?" Maria asks.

"My mom probably saw twenty horse races in her life, and that was just because she'd come to watch me announce once in a while," I say. "My dad was a gambler. He took me to the track all the time when I was a kid. I didn't go much during high school and college, cause I was playing sports, chasing girls, and hanging with my friends. I started going more once dad got sick. We went to the track one weekend, and he died on the following Tuesday. After he died I just kept on going to the races."

"Wow, I'm sorry," she says.

"It's okay," I say, shrugging, and taking a sip of my ice water. "I took some time off after he died. I needed to get away. I found that going to the track was all I wanted to do. I finally went back to school after he died, but I spent most of the time at the local OTB or card room. I've always felt comfortable in those houses of ill repute. All the middle-aged single guys walking around, chasing a winner, and hoping to cash a bet. I think even when I lived in Spokane for a while, I was at those places and watching those kind of guys, thinking that somehow my dad was going to show up, even though he was getting cold in a casket three hundred miles west."

"How old are you?" she asks.

"I'm thirty two. You?"

"I'm twenty six," she replies.

"Well I think we're both far too young to be sharing stories about how both of our parents died."

"I agree!" Maria says nodding.

The Firecracker owner brings over a monster plate of enchiladas and a huge slab of carne asada to the table. He sets down some Tapatío hot sauce per my request and leaves us be.

"Can you eat all that?" I ask, staring at the row of three enchiladas.

"Twice a week I can," she says with a smile.

"You must come here often," I say. "I figured as much since you were hugging on the owner."

"Ha! He's my uncle," she says pointing towards the man behind the counter. "My dad's older brother. My cousin is in the back cooking," she says with a smile.

"That's awesome," I say. "My mom had a restaurant and card room in the Seattle area where I grew up. All through college, my friends and I would go there with our dates and tell them we were big shot gamblers. We said that was why we got free food, and why everyone kissed our butts."

"And that worked?" she queries.

"Well, it worked to get the dates. None of us had any moves, though, so we certainly didn't get laid," I say as we both laugh.

We sit at dinner for another thirty minutes, talking about our families, our jobs, and the food before Maria cuts the evening short. She has to do her analysis for the next day's races, which coincidentally is what I have planned for my night as well. We part ways with a hug and both get ready to head back to our respective homes — hers an apartment somewhere, and mine, the always-classy Motel 6 on Colorado Avenue.

"Can I get your number in case I need to give you anymore 15/1 first-time winners?" I ask with a smile before she gets in her car.

"Sure, give me your phone," she says as she grabs my phone and types her number into it.

"See you soon," she says.

"See you tomorrow at one o'clock."

12

MONDATTA

Back at the Motel 6 and still beaming from my big score at the track, and in my opinion, my score at the Firecracker Restaurant with Maria, I start to look over the card for the next day's races. I also look at Saturday's races, which include the Santa Anita Handicap.

The Santa Anita Handicap is one of the biggest races of the year at Santa Anita and is for the top older horses in Southern California. It's a "handicap" because the best horses in the race have to carry more weight, to try to even out the chances of the lesser horses. The weight is supposed to handicap the best horses.

It's a huge day for the horsemen and bettors alike. There's a Pick 6 bet, which requires players to pick the winners of the final six races, and the pool is going to be at least a million bucks. I know I'm going after the Pick 6 on Saturday, and normally I wouldn't play too large of a ticket because of the difficulty of actually hitting the wager. But with my fresh bankroll boost from my first day, I figure it might be a fine time to take a bigger stab at the life-changing payday.

I'm going to allocate four hundred to five-hundred bucks towards the Pick 6 as well as my normal Pick 4 plays. There will probably be thirty thousand people at Santa Anita on Saturday, so it's important to have your bets and tickets lined up before hand, because the lines at the betting windows are always staggering on these big days.

Dawn cracks at Santa Anita on Saturday, and same as I did yesterday, and the first day I arrived, I head down to Clockers' Corner for breakfast. As with most gamblers, I believe that if something worked the first time, you must continually do it over and over again, because surely you won't win if you don't. I order orange juice, while I'm waiting, I recognize the man sitting next to me who's ordering a cup of coffee.

"John Mahoney. Hey, I'm Ryan. I had a nice

hit with Delirious Laughter the other day, thanks a lot," I say.

"Yeah, he sure ran lights out," says Mahoney. "Hopefully we have the same luck with Mondatta this afternoon."

"Oh man, she's a cool horse. I'm pulling for you," I say as I turn my chair towards the trainer. "You know I actually announce the races at Portland Meadows, and I always watch the Southern California races on the simulcast. I love watching your horses and root for you."

"Well thank ya. Maybe someday we'll send one up to Portland," Mahoney jokes.

"The worst horse in your barn might be a stakes horse up at Portland Meadows my friend," I say, not exaggerating at all.

We continue our conversation over coffee and juice, and just as my breakfast potatoes and eggs are being placed in front of me, Mahoney gets up.

"I have to head down to the barn. Nice talking with you. Come back and visit my horses sometime," Mahoney offers.

"How about this morning?" I quickly and

probably annoyingly reply.

"Finish your breakfast and just come on back. I'm in barn thirteen," Mahoney says as he walks away. "I'll put your name on the guest list at the barn gate and they'll get you a guest pass."

I eat my breakfast at the speed of a hungry Doberman, pretty much neglecting the *Racing Form* and the workouts. I can't wait to visit the famed Santa Anita barn area. During my time in Portland, I would often sneak back onto the backstretch to visit the horses and trainers and grooms. The backstretch is unlike any place you'll ever visit. It's almost unbelievable that these places exist within the massive metropolitan areas in which they call home: barns filled with horses, trainers, hay, poop, and immigrants all working and caring for these thousand-dollar, sometimes million-dollar, equine athletes. Stepping onto a backstretch is like stepping back in time. You hit the gate at Santa Anita's backstretch entrance and it's hard to believe that this place lies just some fifteen miles from downtown Los Angeles and

Hollywood.

I walk past the first few barns with trainers'
names on the sides of them that I've only seen in
bold print on the cover of the *Racing Form*. Then
I come to barn thirteen, and I notice the black
sign with the gold initials "JM" inside a
diamond. The same colors as John Mahoney's
silks, or colors, also adorn the walls of his barn
as well as the stall guards in front of the horses.
I poke my head into the office and notice an
older Mexican man sitting back in the chair
eating a donut.

"Is John here?" I ask.

"Si, he's down with Mondatta," the man says
as he points to the right.

I walk down the aisle, and one by one, I look
at each horse as I pass by. Most have their
heads poking out of the front of the stall, hoping
for a quick pet, or better yet a visitor with
carrots. One chestnut horse has his ears pinned
back and is whipping his head to and fro, clearly
signaling he isn't looking to meet new friends.

I'm getting towards the end of the shed row
when I hear some rustling from inside a stall. I

look in and see Mahoney finishing up putting some warming mud on the legs of a tall, beautiful animal named Mondatta. Mondatta is a four-year-old filly, and she's by far the best horse in Mahoney's barn. She's running in this afternoon's Santa Margarita Handicap: a Grade-1 event, which means she's running against the best horses in her age group and gender. She's 10/1 on the morning line odds, given the fact that she is making her first start against Grade-1 type horses.

Mondatta has run seven times in her life; not many for a horse of her age and breeding. Her mom was a stakes winner in New York named Mondo Mama and her dad won the Kentucky Derby before being sent off to early retirement. Mr. and Mrs. Warren purchased her at a sale in Kentucky for $120,000. That sounds like a mighty sum to pay for a horse, but Mondatta was actually purchased below the sale average for that year's event. She had some knee issues when she was a two-year-old, so she didn't get to run her first race until April of last year, her three-year-old season.

She finished second in that first start at Santa Anita and dominated a field of maidens (horses who have never won a race) in her next start at Hollywood Park. She followed that up with three straight second-place finishes before she won the Grade-3 Santa Clarita Stakes earlier this meet at Santa Anita. She followed that up with a win in the Grade-3 Reseda Stakes, which was her first start on the main track. She'd run strictly on turf early in her career, as her mom was a turf horse, and her dad (despite winning the Kentucky Derby), also had good success on the grass.

The Reseda was supposed to be run on the grass, but as luck would have it, the rains came, and washed the race off of the grass and on to the main track. Mondatta seemed to relish running on the dirt, muddy as it was, and splashed her way home to a convincing five length win. Mahoney thought enough of that effort to let her try running on the dirt again, this time against the big girls. She's scheduled to take on Sister Susie and Bubba Girl, two of the top older mares on the West Coast today. So she'll need her best game to get a win.

"Hey, Mr. Mahoney," I say after watching him for a minute.

"Hey Ryan," he says as he sticks to the work at hand. "This is the big mare, Mondatta."

"Yeah, she's getting a real test today, huh?"

"Not for nothing Ryan, but I think she's the best horse in that race," Mahoney says unwaveringly. "She just keeps improving and getting better, and I have a feeling she might be really special. Like Breeders' Cup special."

"Well, let's hope so," I say as I lift my right hand towards her massive face.

Mondatta is as kind a racehorse as you'll ever find. She nuzzles her face right up against my jacket, while I pat her face and scratch the side of her neck. She's a picture of beauty; not overly large for a four-year-old filly, but muscular, and defined like any athlete in the prime of her career. She has a tiny white spot on her head, as though someone took a vial of paint and splashed it across her face. I continue to pet her, and enjoy the soft touch of her hair.

"She sure is a sweet thing," I say.

"Yeah she's great in her stall," Mahoney says as he gets up off his knees and starts to walk out of the stall. "But when she gets onto the track, it's like some different animal takes over her body. She gets mean, nasty, and pissy all at the same time."

"I can't imagine that," I say as I continue to pet her. "She's too sweet to ever be pissy."

"Wait about seven hours and watch her in the paddock," Mahoney says. "Then we'll have this conversation again."

Mahoney introduces me to Mondatta's stall neighbor, a plucky little guy named Delirious Laughter. My face lights up. This little horse, who looks similar to half the other horses on the track, given his dark bay and brown color, was the horse who keyed my big hit Thursday.

"I gotta run home and grab a nap before the races," Mahoney says.

Taking his cue, I start to walk out of the barn and back towards the gate with Mahoney as we kibitz about Mondatta's big start later on.

"I'll catch up with you later. Thanks again for letting me come back here," I say.

"If she wins, come on down and get in the Winner's Circle picture," Mahoney says.

"For sure!"

First post time hits, and the crowds pour in for Santa Anita Handicap Day. Families barrel through the turnstiles on their way out to the infield, which is filled with blow up jungle gyms and pony rides. The real gamblers, also known as the guys who are middle-aged and alone, all find their table to set up home base for the day. I do what I always do and go to the paddock. I like to look at the horses as they warm up, but also, for me, it's a way to keep my mind occupied between races.

When I'm gambling, it's important for me to take serious and substantial breaks. My biggest losses have always come when I've gone on tilt and just started blowing off at whatever track I could put down my next wager. If you go to any track, or off-track-betting parlor across the country, you'll see guys like me when I'm at my worst. Guys who are "on tilt." We're the ones scanning the bank of televisions with no idea of which horses we are betting on. We simply look up for the track with the smallest number of minutes to post, find a number, or odds, that we like, and run to the window and bet. Usually, when I reached this point, I was "chasing," trying to get back my losses by betting bigger and bigger.

One of my worst chases came at Santa Anita just a few years earlier. I had gone down to California to visit some friends for New Year's Eve, which is opening week at Santa Anita, as the track starts the day after Christmas. I spent New Year's Day at the track after partying all evening the night before with friends.

After getting stuck a couple hundred after the first few races, I found myself getting ticked off and looking for a quick score to get back to even. I went back into the simulcast area and started putting one hundred dollar win bets on any track that was running.

After swinging and missing at races from the Fair Grounds, Turfway Park, and Golden Gate Fields, I looked into my wallet and saw three Ben Franklin's smiling at me. I looked up at the screen, and saw there was one minute until the next race at Turf Paradise, which is in Phoenix, Arizona. I looked and saw a 2/1 favorite and figured that if I hit this bet I'd be up to $900 bucks and essentially even for the day. I walked up to the teller, who looked irritated at my arrival, and quickly bet the three hundred on the horse. Its name was Disco Infernal.

Literally one stride out of the gate, Disco Infernal took a weird step, tripped, and with his nose heading to the ground, proceeded to flip his rider right over the top of him. It's one of those things that happens occasionally in racing, and it sucks when it's your horse it happens to. It was salt in an open wound for me, and I was at the ATM before Disco Infernal's competitors had even hit the wire.

I had perfected the art of the ATM withdrawal. The key is to always take the money out before midnight the day before gambling. That way, your five-hundred-dollar limit, or whatever it may be, is available again to you the next day. Plus, you hopefully still have some of that withdrawal you took out before midnight to add to the new day's withdrawal.

This was to be my last three hundred for the day, and instead of putting it on a Pick 4, or spreading it out, or making it last, I bet it on an even money runner at the Fair Grounds—simply trying to double my money. My horse took the lead turning for home, but quickly found the long home stretch too daunting, and got caught by a long shot in the final fifty yards, sealing my fate for the afternoon, and sending me back to my car totally reliant on a credit card to get me back to Seattle.

As the horses warm up in the paddock, Maria comes onto the airwaves and begins her analysis of the first race. She's wearing a business suit of sorts, teal colored and matching shoes, and, as always, she's a rose among the dandelions who inhabit the track. As the horses come onto the track for that opening race, she starts to walk towards the track. I greet her.

"Hey happy Big Cap Day," I say with a smile.

"Hey, Portland, give me another winner like the Thursday," she says as she stops.

"I like Mondatta in the Santa Margarita," I

say, showing her the big circle I placed around Mondatta's name in the program.

"What's with you and Mahoney horses? You got a crush on him?" she asks.

"He's my buddy now, and he hasn't steered me wrong so far. I'm one for one."

We walk out to the track together and watch the first race of the day. The first race features some cheaper claiming horses: horses that are all for sale for sixteen-thousand dollars. A horse named Lubak Charmer pulls off a 6/1 small upset. I've decided to play the Pick 6, which doesn't start until much later in the day, and after my meeting with Mahoney, I'm thinking a large win bet on Mondatta might be in order. With three hours until the Pick 6 starts, I head back to the Motel 6 to grab a shower and shave before coming back to the track.

The Motel 6 in Arcadia offers something that's of the utmost priority when it comes to finding a decent, cheap motel—decent water pressure. Without it, a man can feel incomplete when he gets done with his daily ablution. The feel of soap still on your skin can play havoc with a person's general wellbeing. The shower at the Motel 6, however, seems to have the ability to blast dirt off the body and blast the soap off that carries that dirt. I find myself spending upwards of twenty minutes in the shower these last few mornings, enjoying the cleansing feel of the water chipping away at my skin. Most Motel 6's have shitty shower pressure, but the one in Arcadia seems to be a fortunate exception.

Since today is Santa Anita Handicap day, it's only fitting that I upgrade my usual racetrack wear. Normally jeans and a t-shirt would suffice; maybe khaki shorts if it's warm outside. However, you're only as good as you look and feel, so I opt for a nice pair of black trousers and a collared shirt from the 2005 Preakness Stakes, the year the plucky Afleet Alex almost fell, but still won. What the Motel 6 offers in water pressure, however, it lacks in ironing equipment. So, I go old school and splash water on the pants, and try to hand pleat and smooth them out. After ten minutes of stroking my pants, and remembering I'm going to the track and not a friggin' job interview, I belt up and make my way to the races.

It's only about a half-mile walk to the track, but I drive, as I always feel better knowing that my car is close by. Sometimes in fits of gambling rage I've found that it's best to have an escape, as running out to the car and taking some breaths, or listening to Howard Stern, or just leaving, can sometimes save me a ton of money. Plus, with my penchant for the occasional panic attack, knowing that I have an escape close by always helps to ease the worry. My car has always been an escape for me. I somehow created it as a safe space, so it's where I run to.

The March sun in Los Angeles has a certain kind of perfection to it. It sits kind of low in the afternoon as daylight savings hasn't hit yet, but it offers up a golden temperature of seventy-one degrees, and is bright enough to illuminate the natural beauty of the San Gabriel Mountains to the north of the race track.

Five races into the day, and with the Pick 6 about to start, I've managed to only make a couple of five-dollar win-and-place bets, just to have some action, and to keep my mind fed for the couple of races before the sequence starts. Down just twenty dollars for the afternoon, my Pick-6 play has come out to four-hundred-and-thirty-two dollars. And I've included Mondatta, as well as Sister Susie, in the Santa Margarita Stakes, which is the first race of the sequence. Mondatta opens up at odds of 11/1, so it's clear that there isn't a lot of early action or word of mouth buzz on her.

As I head down to the paddock, I don a quick smile towards Maria, who's just about set to start her talk, and I notice out of the corner of my eye, a horse wearing a green number-five blanket and saddle, rearing up and pitching a fit. Just as Mahoney had said, there was a different side to Mondatta. She rears up on her back legs, kicks her front legs up, and lets out a huge whale of a noise, so pretty much everyone within an earshot of the track can hear her. Her dark brown hair is beaming in the afternoon spring sunshine, as she finally calms down enough to allow her jockey, Jose Camillo, to hop onboard.

Camillo is a young Peruvian rider who came to the United States just three years ago. He immigrated, and then went to Northern California to ride at Golden Gate Fields. After having a strong first year up North, he decided to try the big leagues of Southern California. In just two years here, he's established himself as a top-ten rider in the standings; not an elite guy yet, but still doing well and making a few hundred thousand a year.

Camillo gets onboard Mondatta. She immediately seems to calm down and puts her game face on. She bows her head down to her chest, as she and her rivals parade in front of the grandstand before the race starts. The dapples on her hindquarters stand out in the sunshine and shows all who see her just how proud she's feeling right now.

As the field heads towards the starting gate, Mondatta's odds finally seem to be settling down at 9/1. My two-hundred dollars to win, and my Pick 6, rest on Mondatta getting home in front, although Sister Susie would keep the Pick 6 alive, as I included her as well. Mondatta goes into the starting gate just as smooth as ever, and when the last horse loads, a long shot named

Bella Fortuna, the field is sent on their way.

"And awayyyy they go! Bella Fortuna and Sister Susie go right to the front, with Bubba Girl sitting just behind them in third. Rampart Girl and Triathlon are together fourth and fifth, and then it's three lengths back to Hurricane Jane, and Mondatta is the distant trailer."

I notice the first quarter-mile of twenty-three-and-one-fifth seconds goes on the board, and I'm encouraged by the fact that they are going fast early to set it up for Mondatta, however discouraged by the fact that Sister Susie is one of the two duelers up front.

"They head to the final turn and Sister Susie has put away Bella Fortuna, but Bubba Girl is now breathing down her neck, and from the back, Mondatta is starting to roll along with Hurricane Jane."

The horses arrive at the top of the stretch, and while there was a buzz in the crowd throughout the race, an intense roar begins as they hit the home straightaway. People who were sitting now stand. Fans that were quiet now start to yell. The next fifteen seconds or so will change lives, at least for a while.

"Bubba Girl takes over the lead as they pass the furlong pole. Mondatta and Hurricane Jane continue to rally on the outside."

I start to whip my leg with my curled up *Racing Form* as they come into the final one-hundred yards of the race. Mondatta is bumping a little bit with Hurricane Jane. They're nose and nose, and still a length behind Bubba Girl, who is a tough customer.

"They come to the wire and it's gonna be close and it's gonnnnnaa beeeeeee...Bubba Girl to win it by a neck. Mondatta and Hurricane Jane in a photo for second."

"FUCK ME," I scream out, even though there's a young family of four within an arm's length of me. The dad sends a bit of an evil eye towards me, but the kids are too lost in the thrill of the homestretch battle to have noticed.

My two-hundred dollar win bet is essentially confetti as I take the ticket out of my wallet, look at it, gently tear it up into pieces, and toss it onto the ground. The racetrack is one of the few places left on Earth where littering is actually encouraged. It's a tradition that dates back almost as long as racing itself. Even though tracks like Santa Anita have recycling bins and garbage cans a plenty, in the moments following a devastating loss like the one I just suffered, taking those tickets and throwing them on the ground is probably the most constructive way to take out the anger and frustration. It's better to take it out on the paper than yell at a teller or another patron.

I walk down to the area near the winner's circle where the losing horses all unsaddle, and I can hear Camillo telling Mahoney what happened during the race.

"I think she ran good," Camillo says as he catches his breath. "She got bumped a little bit by that other horse, but she never gave up."

Camillo's words are no consolation for me at this point, however, as I watch Mondatta try and catch her breath as she's led back to the barn, I still feel a sense of fondness for her. She was nine to one, it was her first time taking on the big girls, and she finished third beaten just a neck by a horse who is one of the top older mares on the West Coast. What a game little runner she is. I know she'll be back.

I realize I have just two Ben Franklin's left in my wallet and over an hour and a half until the Santa Anita Handicap, a race in which I don't really have a strong opinion. I head back under the grandstand and notice that there's just five minutes until the next race at Golden Gate Fields. I look up at the tote board and see that it's just a field of six, and that two horses are 9/5 favorites. Instead of checking the *Form* real quick, or waiting and taking a walk to burn off the stress of the big loss, I go right to the window and put a hundred to win and place on the number-five horse. Five has always been my lucky number. The number five horse breaks right on top and coasts to an easy lead before going all the way and returning $5.80 for every $2 win ticket and $4.00 for every $2 place ticket, as the other favorite runs fourth. I get back four hundred and ninety dollars for my two hundred dollar investment, and just like that, I'm back down only three hundred and change. I've now recouped the loss from my Mondatta win bet.

How sweet it is.

For some reason, a win during a chase always seems to slow me down. I collect my four-hundred-and-ninety dollars and head back outside, realizing how easy it would be to try and double up my bet on the next race at Oaklawn or Fair Grounds. I keep trying to remember that this is a marathon summer and not a sprint. The last thing I need is to be going broke in a few weeks and have to crawl back to Portland to look for some shitty part-time work before the racing season starts.

As the runners for the Santa Anita Handicap make their way into the paddock, I head back there to not only scope them out, but to go and watch Maria. She's captivating, as she stands there in the middle of the famed Seabiscuit walking ring, named after the famous horse that ran here back in the late thirties and forties. As she looks at the camera, it's almost as though she's oblivious to all that's going on around her. She describes each horse in the race, which doesn't take long as there are just five of them set to go to the starting gate for the $750,000 pot. There will probably be two-million dollars bet on this race, with wagers coming in from all corners of the country, and even from Canada. With just five horses in the race, it isn't as though there is a ton of ways to play the race other than maybe a big win or exacta bet.

"Choctaw Nation looks majestic in the paddock as he warms up," Maria tells the crowd.

She's right too, the four-year-old chestnut-colored horse is truly something to behold as he strolls around with his groom leading him by a chain. He's muscular and fit, and carries himself with a confident demeanor. He's the third choice in the race right now at 4/1 odds. Rturntoserve is the heavy favorite at 6/5 with Calypso Noted also getting a lot of support at 2/1 odds. Ben E Sabadoo and Hello Lucas are the two long shots in the field, and in reality, neither one has a chance at beating the top three. They both, however, will pick up a nice check just for running fourth or fifth. Plus, in horse, racing you never know what will happen in a given race.

As the field heads out onto the track, and the

trumpeter begins to play the call to post, I go and catch up with Maria.

"So, who's the play?" I ask her directly.

"I love Choctaw Nation. He looks like a monster. And I think the trainer was just giving him an extra workout in the last race. I don't think he was fully cranked up."

"I like him a lot too. Are you going to bet on him?" I ask.

"I rarely bet the horses," she says. "I want to be as unbiased as possible. Plus my dad spent too much of his check on the races. Always made me nervous about doing the same thing."

"Yeah, I get that," I say, even though a big part of me has always thought, "what good is racing without betting?" When I was a kid, I loved the horses and the sport, and there are times when that still rings true, like when I'm calling the races. But a day at the track for me has always been more about trying to find the simplest, easiest way to make the most money (or to lose the most money, as has happened a time or two before).

"Well, I'm gonna go put some on Choctaw," I

say, as we part ways with a smile.

"Two hundred to win and place on Choctaw Nation, please," I say to the teller, as we exchange four-hundred dollars for a small paper betting slip.

A few moments later, I make my way through the sea of humanity that's currently residing on the tarmac of the racetrack. I find a spot on the rail about thirty yards from the finish line to watch the race. Next to me stands a father, who's probably about my age, and his six-year-old son: an image you don't see at the track as much as you did when my dad took me to the races. It's a scene that certainly makes you smile. I watch as the dad lifts the kid up onto his shoulders, so that he can see the race. I remember sitting on my dad's shoulders like that, a quarter-century ago, staring out at the open grass and the tall poplar trees of old Longacres in my native Seattle. The image I have is always of his hands holding me up there: my dad's hands, his fingers, his nails. I can still see them. Those hands meant safety. It's funny the things you remember about someone, even after they've long since passed away.

Longacres was one of the most beautiful tracks of its time, and like so many places in our youth, it's much larger in scope in our memory than it probably was in real life. But at seven years of age, to me, it was the greatest place in the world. Watching horses like Chum Salmon, and Captain Condo, do their magic down the homestretch at Longacres is forever stamped in my memory. Hearing the great announcer Gary Henson's staccato voice booming out of the speakers as he went through the field describing the action, made the hair on my arm stand up. His voice is etched so far into my brain, I can still hear its rumble.

After the races at Longacres, I'd go home and ride my bike around the block, whipping it with a stick, and reciting Henson's calls from the afternoon. The neighbors all thought I was weird. What kind of chubby kid wants to be a jockey? But my imagination has always been strong, and with the majesty of those races playing out in front of me in my youth, what better way to initiate a child's imagination and wonder.

The young boy on his father's shoulders gazes out to the track and sees the horses lining up behind the starting gate. He looks about as captivated as a human being can be. They say kids' attention spans aren't what they used to be. But this boy seems to buck that theory.

"Who're you rooting for?" I ask the kid.

"I want the number one horse," the kid says without hesitation.

"And away they gooooo!" The announcements begin.

"Ben E Sabadoo the long shot is going out the lead with Rturntoserve the big favorite right alongside. Calypso Noted sets up shop in the third spot with Hello Lucas in fourth, and it's a long way back to Choctaw Nation who trails."

I'm not worried yet, because Choctaw Nation always drops way back. He usually waits until the top of the home stretch to unleash his powerful, late move.

"The field turns to the top of the stretch, and Rturntoserve takes command and kicks for home. Calypso Noted is trying to pick him up in second,

and Choctaw Nation is starting to roll down the far outside."

Now Choctaw Nation starts to kick his rally into gear, and jockey Randy Figaro is using his right-handed whip to implore just a little more effort and speed out of his horse.

As the field comes past me, I can see Rturntoserve is still in front and Choctaw Nation is getting closer, but I know he's not gaining fast enough.

"They come to the wire, and it's gonna be Rturntoserve to win it by half a length. Choctaw Nation ran second, with Calypso Noted in third."

I'm upset, but since I covered my bet with a place wager, I'll essentially break even give or take a few bucks. I walk to the winner's circle to take in the pageantry, which includes Rturntoserve being draped with a blanket of white roses with the Santa Anita logo in the center. The jockey, an ageing veteran named Bernie Dalindo, has ridden Rturntoserve in all of his twenty-five career starts. Dalindo had always been a middle of the pack rider in Southern California, but Rturntoserve has been his once-in-a-lifetime runner. Rturntoserve just got nosed out in the five-million dollar Breeders' Cup Classic last year. And even though he earned a cool million for his second-place effort, that nose cost his owners two-million bucks. As well as an extra couple of hundred-thousand for Bernie, who at his age, and with probably only another couple of years left in the saddle, would have been a nice start towards retirement.

Rturntoserve and Dalindo will be back in the Classic barring any unforeseen injuries. But for now, everybody associated with Rturntoserve is enjoying this payday. The winning owner's share of the seven hundred and fifty thousand dollar purse is four hundred and fifty grand. The owner, Mr. Michael Powell of Los Angeles, made his fortune in the shipping business. Like so many of the owners at Santa Anita who buy and sell million-dollar horses all the time, the payday is nice, but really the money is inconsequential, as he's probably a millionaire a hundred times over. But for Bernie, who takes home forty-five thousand for the win, and the trainer Bobby D'Lorio, who also gets forty-five thousand, or ten percent of the winnings, it's a life changing score as they've made most people's yearly salary in just over two minutes.

I head back to the Motel 6 for a night's sleep and a couple of days off from the races. I'm planning on dinner with my friend Jon, whom I went to college with, as well as packing up and looking for a more long-term place for the spring and summer months before Del Mar starts.

But first up is Hollywood Park.

13

THE TRACK OF THE LAKES

AND FLOWERS

Hollywood Park is located in Inglewood, California, adjacent to the formerly famous Great Western Forum, where Magic Johnson and the "Showtime" Lakers played back in the eighties. Everything that Santa Anita is, Hollywood Park isn't. However, it has a charm and wonder all its own, and truth be told, I love the place. I stroll into Hollywood Park for what seems like the two-hundredth time this spring, when in reality, it's only the thirtieth day of the meet. After ending the Santa Anita season with some nice scores and my bankroll twenty-eight hundred more than when I came south in March, the Hollywood Park meeting has proven to be a sobering couple of months.

There was the disqualification on opening day when I had a live Pick 4 ticket going into the last leg, but the stewards ruled that my horse had interfered with some horse at the start, which was enough to warrant disqualifying him and costing me somewhere in the neighborhood of eight-hundred bucks. Then there was Gold Rush Day. Gold Rush Day sent me into overdrive, and gave me not only my biggest loss of the season, but my first emergency room visit on this trip. After getting behind early on, I proceeded to chase and chase and chase until I was out of cash and didn't have time to get back to the motel. I got so desperate, I went to the ATM and took out a thousand bucks — my newly adjusted ATM maximum withdrawal amount and something I promised I wouldn't do since I took my bankroll out of the bank — and bet it all to win on a big favorite in the Gold Rush Day Classic, who proceeded to get beat in the final jump.

"FUCKING COCK-SUCKING MOTHERFUCKERS!" As I walked out in disbelief, I passed by the paddock and delivered a powerful right-hand punch to one of the posters hanging on the back wall of the grandstand. The poster read, "Strike it Rich on Gold Rush Day," which really pissed me off. Upon impacting the poster, which, of course, had a solid wall behind it, I instantly felt a sharp pain jolt from my fingers to my elbow. Adrenaline can be a powerful thing, and I was so jacked up and pissed off, my now broken knuckle didn't hurt nearly as bad as it probably would have had I simply taken a fall, or got my hand sat on by a fat guy in the bleachers. A quick spin over to Inglewood Memorial Hospital, a small cast for three weeks, and I was on my way home, like it was just another long day at the office.

"Home" during the Hollywood Park meet is pretty much exactly what you'd expect from a rent-by-the-week motel in Inglewood. It's essentially a den of prostitution, gangsters, degenerates, and me. When I first arrived, I conveniently got a corner room on the ground floor, and loaded up on earplugs in case noise became an issue, which, of course, it did. For some reason, people at this motel don't believe in quiet hours, unless it's between six and ten in the morning, when most motels are actually at their busiest.

My loudest neighbor is Alice; a dark-skinned black prostitute who's probably fifty or fifty-five, and who still turns tricks for a living. She has the body of a much younger woman, but a face that looks like it's been run over by a John Deere tractor. Alice insists on playing music when her "dates" come over. You'd think that for a romantic evening with a classy courtesan like Alice, she'd be playing something soft, nice, and romantic. But, alas, DMX, or something like it, is what she plays in the background while she plies her trade. And, of course, her stereo is about three millimeters from the adjoining wall to my room. But, it's better to hear DMX, than some old granny giving blowjobs at forty bucks a pop.

Alice did, however, get me a great deal on a small handgun. I'd gone shooting at a range for the first time a few weeks back, and I enjoyed it. Plus, in Inglewood, it doesn't hurts to have protection. I've never been a "gun guy," but for some reason, being down here in this strange town, and in a bad part of said strange town, I felt it necessary as a "just in case."

Hollywood Gold Cup Day has finally arrived, and my bankroll has officially reached the red for the trip. With food, lodging, the looming medical bills from my hospital stay, and of course, a brutal run of bad bets, my twenty-thousand-dollar initial withdrawal, which I had up to over twenty-seven thousand during the Santa Anita meet, has dwindled to fourteen-thousand five hundred.

Del Mar is beckoning in just a few weeks. So I decide to tame things down and leave myself just two thousand for the remainder of the Hollywood Park season. I want to go to Del Mar with at least ten grand left in my bankroll, so my old fraternity pal Jon has agreed to hold onto my twelve thousand five hundred for the time being. I told him that I wanted to change up my luck a little bit, and that maybe by having someone new hold my money, it would wash away all the bad mojo that particular pile of cash had been housing.

Hollywood Gold Cup day brings about the

return of a couple of horses that I've had on my mind since Santa Anita ended: Mondatta and Choctaw Nation. Both lost and cost me some dough, but I've been waiting for them to come back, and hoping that they'd be ready to make me some big money in their next start. Mondatta was given a few weeks of rest after the Santa Margarita, and she's running today in the Grade 1 Matriarch Stakes, while Choctaw Nation is going in the half-million-dollar Hollywood Gold Cup against his old nemesis Rturntoserve.

Mondatta isn't going to have to face Bubba Girl, who beat her in the Santa Margarita. She sustained an injury in training a few weeks later, and because of her success and value as a broodmare, she was retired. Mondatta will have to take on Hurricane Jane and Sister Susie, as well as nine other fillies and mares, as the race drew a full field of twelve. Since I don't want to get too out of control, I stick with just small exacta and win bets throughout the early portions of the day.

Down about seventy bucks when the Matriarch arrives, I head to the paddock to size up the runners. I can see John Mahoney in the walking ring talking to the owner, and to jockey Jose Camillo, who's back to ride. Sadly, Hollywood Park doesn't employ Maria. She stays at Santa Anita and does office work while Hollywood is in season.

As Mondatta is led out into the walking ring along with her competitors, Mahoney helps Camillo up onto his steed, grabbing the jock's ankle, and giving him a leg up to help him onto the big gal's massive back.

"Stay back and make a late move at the quarter pole," Mahoney instructs. "And try not to get her blocked, because she doesn't seem to get back to that high gear once she loses her momentum."

"Si," Camillo quietly responds.

As the twelve ladies complete their warm ups and head to the starting gate, I decide to step up the wagers a bit. I've been waiting for this moment, and I've been betting light today. Normally I'd go with a two-hundred dollar win and a two-hundred dollar place bet just in case she gets beat by a nose and runs second. But she's 6/1 on the odds board, and with twelve horses in the field, they should go fast enough early that she should get her chance to close in and pass them all late.

"Five-hundred to win on the seven," I call out to the teller.

"Five-hundo on the seven," the teller says, never making eye contact until finally wishing me good luck after he hands over the ticket.

I make my way towards the apron, but due to the long line at the betting windows, the race starts before I'm even out from under the grandstand.

"They're off! Sister Susie and Blank Check head out to the early lead," the announcer calls. I see Mondatta taking up her regular spot at the back of the pack as the field moves toward the first turn.

"And Mondatta is last and already some thirteen lengths off the lead. She'll have to make up thirteen lengths in the final seven furlongs if she wants to win the Matriarch."

I look to the infield tote board and see that the fractions are fast early on. Blank Check, who is a hopeless long shot, is pushing Sister Susie.

"They come to the quarter pole and Sister Susie is still in front. Hurricane Jane starts her move three wide, and now, here's Mondatta starting to roll on the far outside."

In what literally seems like just a few steps, Mondatta catapults past several tiring rivals as the field enters the stretch. Standing at the top of the apron with a panoramic view of the action unfolding in front of me, I see her poetry in its absolute purest form. Her legs move with such fluidity, she and Camillo look as though they are one. Mondatta inhales each of her eleven rivals, and as she enters the final sixteenth of a mile, she draws away from the competition. By the time she hits the wire she's alone. She's now a Grade-1 winner, getting a victory at racing's highest level.

Nearly forgetting about the $3,500 I'm about to get back for my bet once the race goes official, I pump my fists in the air and immediately head to the winner's circle to watch my new favorite filly get dressed in the red-rose blanket she just earned.

"C'mon in Ryan," Mahoney says as he nods to the gate attendant, who promptly opens the gate and smiles at me as I enter the winner's enclosure.

"I had five hundred to win on her John," I shout. "Did you see that move she made? She blew them away."

"I told you she was special," Mahoney says as he pats me on the shoulder. "I've been saying it for months now to anyone who would listen. Maybe now she'll get the respect she deserves."

The track photographer gathers all the folks in the winner's circle into a small group, as Mondatta and Jose Camillo return and join them for the winning picture. She's breathing hard, but you can tell she's not overly taxed. She knows she did well and she's still feisty, as Camillo dismounts and lays a big kiss on the side of her face. Her groom, Manuel, leads Mondatta back to the barn area, and I can't help but appreciate the fact that she is totally unaware of the magnitude of what she's just done. She's just beat out eleven of the best horses in her age group, and earned her owners a check for a hundred and fifty thousand dollars in the process. She's essentially paid for herself now. She's earned her keep and has earned enough for her after-racing life as well. And yet, all she seems to be intent on doing is getting back to the barn and having some dinner. Meanwhile, the owners, Mahoney and Camillo, are all shaking hands, giving hugs, and celebrating their newfound mini-fortune.

"Would you all care to join us up in the turf club to celebrate?" asks a well-dressed man who works for the track.

"I can't. I have a horse in the next race," Mahoney replies. "Ryan you want to head up there?"

"Naw. I'm more of a paddock and apron kind of guy," I reply with a smile, as I've always preferred watching the races from the apron down in front of the rail.

"Very good gentlemen, and congratulations on your big win," the man in the suit politely says as everyone goes their separate ways.

I go back to the same teller who sold me the

ticket and collect my winnings. The final odds on Mondatta were six point two zero for every dollar bet. So, thirty-one-hundred in profit, plus the five-hundred dollars I bet, and I'm flush with happiness and cash. Plus, Choctaw Nation still has to run.

Choctaw Nation ran a good second behind Rturntoserve in the Santa Anita Handicap, but his last start, earlier this month at Hollywood Park, left a lot to be desired, as he didn't have his usual late kick, and could only manage a fifth-place finish against weaker horses than he's facing today. He's 8/1 on the odds board as he parades in the paddock with all eyes still fixed on Rturntoserve, who's the heavy even money favorite. Essentially any amount you bet on Rturntoserve, you get back double that amount. Bet $100, you get back $200. Bet $1,000, get back $2,000. In a race like this, or in any horse race really, it's not a good bet, because anything can happen. But Rturntoserve is just so tough. I decide that Rturntoserve will be there at the finish, but so will Choctaw Nation, so I box them in a $200 exacta and throw another $200 to win on Choctaw Nation.

"They're Off in the Hollywood Gold Cup."

I'm playing with the house's money at this point, so while I'm heavily invested in this race, I have nowhere near the worry or stress that I had just a couple hours earlier when Mondatta was making her big rally from last place.

"Rturntoserve is not getting pushed at all up front and leads it by two. Choctaw Nation is still seventh and some ten lengths behind as the field turns into the homestretch."

Rturntoserve and Bernie Dalindo are simply too much for any of these horses, and when nobody goes up and pushes them, they essentially get to walk around the track and pick up a cool $300,000 payday for their troubles. Choctaw Nation spins his tires once again and finally gets going a little bit at the end, but can only manage a fourth place finish. It's a bittersweet way to end what has been a good day. With just one more week of racing left in Inglewood, everyone associated with racing in Southern California are setting their sights on Del Mar, which sits just an hour and a half south in San Diego.

After a shitty last week at Hollywood Park where I dropped back most of my Mondatta winnings, I head over to my pal Jon's place and collect my $12,500 and pair it with the $2,100 I have on me and get ready to head down the freeway.

"Have a good time in San Diego man," Jon says as we shake hands.

"I will. I'm excited. My sister lives down there so I'm going to see her, and hopefully pick some winners and get some sunshine. I've been living down here for going on three months now and I'm still white as a ghost."

"Alright brother, be safe," Jon says as I walk away.

"I'll be back after Labor Day," I say. "Breeders' Cup is at the end of September up at Santa Anita, you should come out."

"I'll think about it," Jon says.

14

WHERE THE TURF MEETS THE SURF

There can only be a few drives between two major metropolises as quick and easy as the one from Los Angeles to San Diego. There are only a few miles that aren't just extended suburbs from one or the other. Maybe the best part is driving by those two round buildings that look like boobs, the ones you see in the Naked Gun movie. I know San Diego well as my sister has made it her home for the last five years. She's a couple of years younger and works as an accountant for a big firm in town. She's done well, and somehow has managed to keep her head clear and out of trouble with the loss of our parents. We don't talk much, however we do share a common sense of humor. One that finds great joy in making fun of movies, trends, and television shows from our childhood.

"Afternoon everybody," I say as my sister answers the phone.

"Ryyyyyyyyyyyyyy," she replies. It's an ode to Cheers when lifetime beer drinker Norm would walk into the bar and make his grand entrance for a night of drinking and witty repartee with Cliff the mailman. Our uncle insists on doing that when anyone enters a room, and we just kind of picked it up.

"Are you in town yet?"

"I'll be there in a few minutes, I'm just passing by Del Mar right now," I say.

"Okay, just take the downtown exit. My place is literally the first building off the ramp. It's called the Delux."

"I'll see you in a few."

After I hang up, I spend a couple of seconds gazing over at old Del Mar Racetrack. From Interstate Five, a road I've now covered in its entirety, Del Mar sits just a mile or so to the west, right along the crystal blue of the Pacific Ocean. It's an old building, but has been kept up immaculately, and looks every bit as glorious as everyone's told me it is. I've never been, but that will change on Wednesday, when I attend their traditional opening day card.

"Hey big brother," Angela says as she greets me when I pull in. "Just park on the street, pay the meter, and we'll go to dinner."

As we hop in her SUV and get back onto the freeway heading south, we talk about how my trip is going, what I've been up to, and other small and unchallenging topics. We haven't seen each other since our mom died, and other than a quick few phone calls regarding her stuff, our relationship hasn't exactly been tight.

We pull into the trendy Gaslamp Quarter, San Diego's version of Portland's Pearl District. The main difference is the ocean breeze hitting your face, and down here people get to wear shorts nine months out of the year, instead of being bundled up in layers of black, green and brown.

We sit down at a nice steakhouse and Angela offers to treat for the meal.

"So what happened with work? How come you didn't get to stay up there for the off-season?" she asks.

"Same old shit you always hear — budget cuts, and only keeping on essential workers."

"That sucks. Are you getting unemployment at least?"

"I did for the first few weeks, until they realized I wasn't in Portland, and I wasn't looking for a job," I say with a laugh.

"Any news on mom's house?" she asks.

"Naw. Things are slow up there. Apparently the balance on the mortgage is right about what we should get for the place, so we might make a couple thousand or lose a couple. I haven't looked into it that much. Kind of don't want to know the truth, ya know?"

"Yeah, I understand. I just want it all to be done with," she says. "I don't suppose you brought down her dishes. Did you?"

"Those fucking dishes," I say as we both laugh. "I didn't. But I should have. We could have thrown them off the cliffs into the ocean."

"These hippy liberals down here would fine you for pollution," she says back with a quick retort, as she's one of those hippie liberals I like to mock.

The dishes in question were our mother's fine china dishes, which were a big source of squabble in our parent's divorce. They were one of three things mom asked for in the divorce, with the main one being her business, and the other, a family piano. Dad's divorce attorney, a miserable old woman who must have been jaded by her years of dealing with miserable people, decided at the last minute to move the dishes back over to our father's side of the assets ledger. Our mom went ahead and signed, and a year or so later, she had Angela bring the dishes over to her house, thinking they were rightfully hers. Well, dad blew his stack, and yelled at both Angela and me about how "those were his," and how dare we take them to her, even though he didn't intend to ever use them. It just went to show the petty, bitter things that divorce can do to a family. And to two people who once loved each other.

"You want to come out to opening day at Del Mar?" I ask.

"It's Wednesday at 1 p.m. Most people work at that hour," she replies, mocking my present employment status.

"How's the anxiety and depression stuff been?" Angela asks, figuring that coming off a joke was as good a time as any to make a serious inquiry.

"Eh. I've been doing better, I suppose," I say, as I cut through my steak. "I was kinda depressed the last few weeks before the season ended at Portland, but it never got that bad," I say, when in fact my anxiety had flared up several times since.

Sometimes it's strange to look across the table at her, sitting there as an adult with feelings, passions, and goals. For most of our lives, she was just the little annoying kid that lived down the hall. At some point, I left home, and she stopped being the little annoying kid.

She drops me off at the Motel Cardoza, a classy fifty-nine-dollar-a-night place I found online.

"Let's hang out again soon," she says. "I only live ten minutes down the road."

"Sounds like a plan," I say. "Goodnight Ang. I love you." I hadn't said that to her since dad died almost a decade ago.

Opening Day at Del Mar is, aside from Breeders' Cup Day, the most exciting day of racing in Southern California. There aren't any big races per se, but the simple fact of how many people come out, and how beautiful those people are, make it a destination on the racing calendar. The most beautiful, wealthiest people in San Diego all take the day off and come out to Del Mar dressed to the nines, as though they were going to an elite socialite party as opposed to a day at the horse track.

Walking into Del Mar for the first time, I'm in awe of what stands before me. The old stucco looking building is in nearly immaculate condition for a facility that's over seventy years old. Palm trees seem to pop up from out of nowhere in different spots around the building, adding a touch of color to the bland, sandy brown color of the grandstand. What the grandstand lacks in flashy color, the Pacific Ocean more than makes up for. From any grandstand seat in Del Mar, the bright blue Pacific is just a few hundred yards to the left, ebbing and flowing, in and out, second after second.

Del Mar opened to much ballyhoo when Jimmy Durante, Charles Howard, who owned Seabiscuit, and the great singer Bing Crosby, all teamed up to inaugurate the facility. Crosby greeted fans at the front gate when the track opened in 1937, and to this day, his song "Where the Turf Meets the Surf" is still played before and after the races.

An hour before the races kick off, I stroll through the front door in khaki shorts, a white button-down shirt, brand new Oakley sunglasses, and a smile as wide as can be, as Bing's words fill the air. Gorgeous women abound at Del Mar, but as the music stops, over the loud speakers, Maria Martinez begins to discuss her analysis of the races. I immediately head to the paddock area, where she's on the television set with Bob Ayala, a long time Del Mar handicapper. She is a showstopper in her white sundress, and unlike all the beautiful girls gathered around the paddock, Maria's the only one I'll look away from my *Racing Form* to see.

"Hey, Portland. You're not busted yet?" she asks once she spots me in the crowd after her paddock show.

"Believe it or not, I'm still hanging around," I say. "Hollywood was a little bit rough, but I'm looking forward to being down here. Where's the good place to go after the races? You got a Firecracker restaurant down here as well?"

"Is that a question or a date proposition?" she asks.

"Both, I think," I say with a smile. We've been keeping in touch throughout the Hollywood Park meeting, mostly by text messaging, as she lives over an hour's drive from Hollywood Park. Plus, she's been here in San Diego for the last few weeks getting ready for the Del Mar season.

"I'll tell you what, if it's just a question, go to Federico's down the street. If it's a date proposition then I'll see you at Don Tomito's after the races."

"Federico's it is then," I say as a wisecrack.

"Fine. Enjoy your dinner alone," she says as she starts to walk away.

"Wait! I was kidding. Where's Don Tomito's

at?"

"You got an iPhone. Google it," she says.

"Done. Now give me a winner in the first if you'd be so kind? I think not having your picks is what killed me at Hollywood Park," I say.

"You heard the show, I'm on the five horse, Yucca Ducca Ya Ya," she tells me.

"What a horrible name for a horse, but I'll put him in my early Doubles anyways," I say with a chuckle.

As I walk to the front of the apron and down to the rail, soaking in the horses for that first race as they stroll across the track, I turn around and stare back at the grandstand. The rafters are filled with people out enjoying horse racing. This is where I want to be announcing someday. Working at a track where the races are a big deal. Sometimes when announcing at Portland Meadows on a cold Tuesday with three people on the apron, I often wonder when and if I'll ever get a shot at a big time track. To be part of a track where people are clamoring to come out and watch the races. I'll probably always be a minor league announcer, but I can still dream.

"And there's the roar from the Del Mar crowd as the field is off in the opener. Bankroll and Teresita Mama head out to the front with Yucca Ducca Ya Ya in the third spot early, in a perfect spot under Martin Dominguez."

I'm going after some big money early, and Yucca Ducca Ya Ya is the key to my early Daily Doubles.

"They turn to the top of the stretch, and now Yucca Ducca Ya Ya takes command and starts to pull clear."

"C'mon you stupid named prick," I say under my breath. The comment is hardly audible, as the 50,000 other people screaming drown out any of my utterances.

"And Yucca Ducca Ya Ya draws clear to win by three."

Off and running, I complete my first twenty-dollar Daily Double when Master Monti scores in the second race, and within the first thirty minutes of the Del Mar season, which only lasts seven weeks, I'm already up three-hundred-and-fifty bucks. By the time the rest of the day is over, however, I've given back that much plus another three hundred, as my Pick 6 and Pick 4 tickets both got blown up when my single Gibbles, the heavy favorite in the Oceanside Stakes, failed to even hit the board as the biggest favorite of the day. In fact, only one person pieced together the Pick 6 today, and it paid more than one hundred and eighty five thousand dollars.

I didn't even make it through the last race of the day. After the debacle in the Oceanside, I retired to my car and decided to distract myself with a few dozen rousing games of solitaire on my phone. After about thirty minutes, I notice the masses of humanity starting to pour out of the track, signaling the last race must be over. Attempting to beat the traffic, I follow my phone's GPS system directions to Don Tomitos. It's maybe ten minutes from the track, and unlike the Firecracker in Los Angeles, Don Tomitos is an amazingly gorgeous Mexican restaurant with water fountains, and gorgeous murals all over the walls and even on the floors. I check my phone and see a text from Maria notifying me she's going to be about twenty more minutes.

"I need a table for two. Is it possible to get one out on the balcony?" I ask the young girl at the front desk.

"Certainly sir. It's about a twenty-minute wait right now. Is that ok?

"That's perfect. I'll be in the bar," I say.

I stroll into the bar, which is starting to fill up with folks who appear to also be coming from the track.

"Can I get a cranberry juice please?" I ask the bartender.

I drink water almost exclusively, as I've found that alcohol or sugared drinks tend to exacerbate my anxiety, and make me jumpier and more on edge than I already am. However, I've always felt guilty making a bartender, a person who makes all his or her money via tips and selling drinks, have to serve me a free ice water and not get a tip. At least with the cranberry juice, I get to give the guy a courtesy fifty cents or a buck.

"Hey Portland. Whatcha drinking?" Maria

says as she sneaks up behind me.

"Vodka and cranberry, hold the Vodka," the bartender quickly answers as he walks around to give Maria a kiss on the cheek."

"How are you my dear? How was the first day?" the bartender asks.

"It was great. Only picked two winners the whole day, but we had a great crowd, and the betting handle was up for the day. I want you to meet my friend Ryan McGuire from Portland. He's the announcer at the track up there."

"Nice to meet you Ryan. I'm Maria's cousin Raul," the bartender says extending a hand.

I look at her, smile, and feel some déjà vu from our initial dinner back in March.

"Do you only go to restaurants where you're related to the people who work there?" I ask.

"I like to eat, and see my family and friends. Is that so bad?" she replies.

Raul escorts us out to the balcony where we sit down to have our meal, with just the ocean as the accompaniment to the food and conversation. The warm July sun is in its final waning stages of the evening, making for one of the most picturesque ways to spend an evening with Maria.

"So, do you make a habit of going out with race track degenerates?" I ask her.

"Well they are the only kind of guys I seem to meet," she says.

"Do you have someone you see, I mean like a boyfriend," I ask.

"You really think I'd be eating a dinner with you tonight if I had a boyfriend I was going home to? I was dating a guy for a while, but we split up back in March, actually just a few weeks before I met you up at Santa Anita. You probably know him."

"Don't tell me he's a jockey," I say with a laugh.

"Jose Camillo," she says with a shy smile.

I let out an audible laugh for a few reasons. For one, Maria is probably seven or eight inches taller than the young Peruvian jockey. Secondly, it was Camillo on board Delirious Laughter that led to my first big score in Southern California. Thirdly, he rides Mondatta, my other favorite girl in California.

"Is that why you seemed so upset when I said I liked Delirious Laughter that day?"

"Maybe," she says with a wry grin.

"So you're a jockey jumper then?" I ask her, referring to the girls who make it a habit to bone jockeys. No matter what track you go to, whether a big track like Del Mar or a small one like Portland Meadows, jockeys always seem to have a group of devoted girls willing to date them or sleep with them. Of course, all of these girls are all at least five foot seven.

"No! We dated for like five months. But he started screwing around with Mahoney's gallop girl, and it was Mahoney who actually let the cat out of the bag," she says.

"So that's why you don't bet Mahoney's horses then?"

"I like Mahoney just fine. He wasn't the one who screwed that little girl," she says. "I've only had a couple of serious boyfriends since college, and they've both been people from the track. I always tell myself I shouldn't date race-trackers, but I just don't seem to meet anyone who isn't involved in it. Maybe I need to take up some other hobbies or something?"

We continue to talk over the enchiladas, prawns, and other delicious items that Raul brings out for our consumption. The bill comes and I grab it. But Maria insists on splitting it.

"You won't let me treat you? What kind of date would I be?" I ask.

"I know you're on a fixed income," she says with a smile.

"I wish it were fixed. It's been going backwards the last few weeks. I hit that early Double today and couldn't hit another bet all day. I'll get it back tomorrow though. One of the beauty's of this game is there is always another day."

We walk out of the restaurant and Maria quietly leads me over to a little walkway that goes around the back of the restaurant and down to the beach. Maria gets to the end of the walkway where the beach starts and removes her shoes.

"Take your shoes off," she says.

I kick off my flip-flops and we head down to the water. The mighty Pacific Ocean crashes into the sand, as it always does. And yet, each time you visit you can't help but still be in awe of the power and scope of it.

"When does Portland start back up for you?" she asks.

"The weekend after the Breeders' Cup. I miss announcing already. It seems that by the time the meet closes, I'm usually ready for a break, and to enjoy the off-season. But this year, once I found out I was getting laid off for the summer, I swear I missed it right away. I know it's a silly job. I mean, really, it's not like we're doing anything to save the world or anything. But I love it. I really do. There's something in the adrenaline rush and getting to describe the horses that really gets me off."

"I know what you mean," she says. "I think part of it is just being involved in something bigger than yourself. And part of something people remember."

"I totally understand," I say. "Sometimes I think the best part of the job is knowing the fact that even ten years from now, the owners are going to have a video of that race. And it's my voice and words that adorn the moving pictures of their animals in motion. Long after the purse money or bets they cashed from those races are gone, the memories, and those videos, will still be there. I mean it's a pretty damn cool thing."

As we continue down the beach, walking in the first couple of inches of water as the tide starts to move out, I finally decide to make a move, and instead of just grabbing her hand and taking it, I use my patented move of casually bumping my hand into hers and seeing if she moves it. When she doesn't move it, I know I'm in, and I interlock my fingers with hers. She looks over quickly and gives a small smile. For someone as beautiful and social as Maria is, she actually seems kind of shy at this moment. It makes her just that much more attractive to me.

"We should probably turn around," she says, realizing we've walked twenty minutes up the beach and Del Mar is actually back in view.

As we continue back towards Don Tomitos, the conversation steers back to our parents and family. The thrill of being able to talk to a girl who works in racing and not talk about racing is something I relish. As much as horse racing has been my life, it's also good to remember there are other things besides gambling. We reach the restaurant and Maria drops her shoes onto the pathway. But before she puts them on, I give a small tug at her hand.

"Hey. Come here," I say nervously.

I lean towards her and her eyes start to close. She leans into me as well and our lips greet. It's as good a place as any for a first kiss. I put my hand on her shoulder and we kiss gently. The entire time I'm obsessively wondering if she's just wanting to take it slow, or if I need to test the waters and really make my tongue more of a pronounced part of this occasion. I elect to keep it simple, because she doesn't need to be on the receiving end of a big sloppy kiss at such a perfect moment.

"We should do this again sometime," she says.

"I'm available tomorrow," I quickly retort, thrilled at her initiating more time together.

She laughs it off, mentions that I know where I can find her, and we part with a final kiss before heading to our respective vehicles.

"I really do want to keep seeing you Maria," I say.

"Good. I'll see you at the track tomorrow."

15

RTURNTOSERVE

I get to Del Mar early on Saturday morning and head out front to watch the horses train. Sitting up in the bleachers, I spot my pal Mahoney.

"How are they running, John?" I ask.

"Everything's kosher my man. It's a tough living having this as your office each day, but I do my best," Mahoney says as we both chuckle. The crisp wind off the Pacific Ocean offers up a scent that isn't found at many other racetracks in the world. Instead of the smell of hay and horse shit, Del Mar is blanketed with the smell of the ocean. That great mixture of salt and fishiness from a distance teases your nostrils, luring you to come closer to the magic waters.

"How do you like Mondatta's chances today?" I ask.

"Man, she's just tearing down her stall," Mahoney says. "She's been so good. I think she's coming into her own. She's going to be real special."

"Yeah. The race came up pretty light today for a Grade 1," I say.

"Yeah. That filly that Kaiser trains could be tough. But if Mondatta gets some pace to run at, she's going to be double tough."

The first Saturday of the Del Mar season is the first of many huge weekend cards during the seven weeks. The biggest race of the season, the Pacific Classic, is not for a few weeks, and that's the final big prep for the Breeders' Cup events that will be coming up at Santa Anita just a month or so later.

"Can anybody beat Rturntoserve in the Pacific Classic this year?" I ask.

"You know, he just seems to get a perfect trip each time," Mahoney says as he sits up in his chair. "I thought Choctaw Nation was going to get to him. But Rturntoserve is tough. I think Mondatta would beat his ass if she hooked him sometime."

"You really do believe in her don't you?" I ask.

"Keep this between us, but I'm thinking about running her in the Breeders' Cup Classic if she keeps improving."

"You're fucking nuts," I say.

"Hear me out. This filly hasn't had to go more than a mile and one-eighth, and if you watch her races, she just keeps accelerating the further she goes. The Breeders' Cup Distaff is at a mile and one-eighth, and while I think she has a decent shot in that race, the Classic is worth $5,000,000. I think she can catch even the best horses in the country going that long, and I don't think Rturntoserve wants to go that far."

"He got beat by a damn nose in that race last year, and he's won at that distance three times. I respect you but, c'mon," I say, knowing that all trainers think their horse is better than they really are.

"You just watch."

The Breeders' Cup Classic is open to all horses, be they male or female. A female horse hardly ever tries to run against the boys. Occasionally you'll see it. But for the most part, the boys run against the boys and the girls run against the girls. It's not quite like throwing a gal into an NBA game, but it's still definitely tough for a girl to beat the boys.

Mondatta comes into the paddock for the Grade 1 Clement L. Hirsch Stakes in her typical fashion. She's boorish, and not sitting still as her groom tries to put her red saddlecloth on her back, as she'd drawn the number-one post position for the race. I smile when Jose Camillo comes into the paddock, because just some fifteen feet away Maria is talking about each of the horses and giving out her selections.

"Number one is Mondatta. She's coming off a huge win last time out in the Matriarch, and very well could improve again today. She's trained by John Mahoney who is coming off a career meet at Hollywood Park and she's a deserving favorite in this spot."

Conveniently Maria doesn't give a mention to Camillo in her analysis, but she often will not mention a rider, so maybe it was just coincidence. Either way, she gives out Mondatta as her top selection and puts Freeway Gal as her second pick.

Freeway Gal is expected to go to the lead under jockey Frankie Tarphe, who's a Seattle-area native like me. Frankie's a third-generation rider, as his dad Basil and grandfather Franklin were both riders. Franklin Tarphe rode in the 1954 Kentucky Derby and finished fourth in the race. He was a successful rider in the Midwest during the fifties and sixties. He finished his career up at old Longacres in the seventies. His son, Basil, eventually dominated the Seattle oval during the eighties when he started his career. Frankie was born in 1980, and he didn't even bother sticking around the Northwest. When he was just sixteen years old, he took out his riding license and was on his way to a lucrative career. He was the Apprentice of the Year his first year, and each year since he's probably made between two hundred and five-hundred thousand a year. He's best on the lead with a horse like Freeway Gal who should be gunning right from the very start. Whether or not she can stay there is the question that bettors will have to decide. And, right now, she's at 7/1 to do so.

"And awayyyyyy they go. No surprises here,

Freeway Gal goes bursting right out to the front and takes command early. Alphaville sits in the second spot, and it's already three more lengths back to Marsh Landing in the third position. Dante's Pink is back fourth, then comes Radiatorre, and it's three more lengths back to Cherry Piper and Mondatta is last, already spotting the leader Freeway Gal about twelve lengths."

I've elected to bet Mondatta hard, even though she's the 8/5 favorite. My confidence in her and Mahoney's words this morning had me feeling so good that I put a thousand bucks on her to win. It's my biggest bet since I lost that thousand-dollar tilt bet back at Hollywood before I punched the wall on Gold Rush Day.

"The field runs toward the far turn, and it's still Freeway Gal who continues at an easy beat up front, with Alphaville applying token pressure. It's now seven lengths back to Dante's Pink, and now Mondatta is starting to kick in her move. She's up to fourth and is moving well on the outside."

This race is looking like the Matriarch at Hollywood Park last time, as Mondatta's big move is looking more like she's a true monster runner. She's inhaling all the horses, and I start to go to my patented right-handed *Form*-to-hip whipping motion.

"C'mon Mondatta, keep coming baby."

"They turn into the homestretch and Freeway Gal keeps finding on the lead. Alphaville is being pushed along in second, and here comes Mondatta down the far outside."

An audible groan from the crowd suddenly roars down from the rafters and I quickly turn my attention to the infield video board to get a better look at the race.

"Alphaville has lugged out and tripped Mondatta, who nearly fell at the three-sixteenths pole. Freeway Gal now in front by four, Mondatta has gotten back into stride as Alphaville is fading fast. Freeway Gal trying to make a final furlong now, but Mondatta has her sights set on this leader and is gathering her up with every stride. Final one-hundred yards, and here comes Mondatta. What a miraculous filly! She's overcome nearly falling down and will win the Clement L. Hirsch by a length. Freeway Gal held on for second, just ahead of Dante's Pink who ran third."

Mondatta has not only earned her stripes by winning her second Grade 1 race, she's proven that she can overcome trouble and still win. She has more than just talent. She has heart. She has athletic ability. She's pretty much everything you'd want in a racehorse. She's also put $1,700 in profit into my pocket this afternoon and continues to be my new favorite horse. I watched the race from about a hundred yards up from the finish line, so I rush my way through the crowd to head to the winner's circle. Mahoney has his hands on his knees, as it appears his heart had made a serious attempt at fleeing his chest when Mondatta stumbled at the top of the lane.

"You better get your ass in here, you're her good luck charm," Mahoney shouts from the winner's circle. I join the group, and high five and shake hands with Mahoney as well as Mr. Warren, who owns the horse and is beaming as he enjoys the fact that he has the kind of horse he's been searching for during his twenty years in the game.

Mr. Warren made his fortune selling

hardware. Raised in Los Angeles by a stay at home mom and a dad who worked for McDonnell Douglas, Mr. Warren took a job at a hardware store when he was sixteen. He worked there through high school and paid his way through college by working in that same shop in Pacoima. Upon graduation, he and his father bought the place after the owner decided to retire. The store continued its success and they soon opened new locations all throughout the San Fernando Valley. By the time he was thirty-five he was a millionaire, and had grown his group of stores into the largest chain of hardware stores on the West Coast, before Home Depot and Lowe's came around of course.

"Congratulations Mr. Warren," I say as I extend a hand.

"Thank you young man. I hope you bet her."

"I bet a thousand to win on her. She made me seventeen-hundred dollars," I reply with a smile.

"A thousand dollars? Jeez, I only bet a hundred," Mr. Warren says with a laugh, as the owner's share of the purse just pocketed him a hundred-and-fifty-thousand dollars.

We start to walk out of the winner's circle as Mondatta once again makes her way back to her thirteen-by-thirteen-foot stall on the backstretch. But Maria grabs Mahoney and Camillo to get their post-race comments on their big filly's performance.

"I'm standing here with winning jockey Jose Camillo, and winning trainer John Mahoney. Mondatta overcame a horrible stumble at the top of the stretch to win the Clement L. Hirsch Stakes. Jose, I know you have to ride the next race, so we'll start with you, tell us what happened at the top of the lane when you guys bumped with Alphaville?"

"Mondatta was starting her big run. That other horse was getting tired and just came out into my filly," Camillo says still catching his breath. *"I thought I was going down, but she's such an athlete. She recovered and didn't miss a beat."*

"Alright, thanks Jose," Maria says as she turns to Mahoney. *"John, this filly just keeps on improving doesn't she?"*

"She really has, Maria. She has more ability than maybe any other horse I've ever trained," Mahoney says standing with his arms crossed,

somehow managing to look jaded even though he just pocketed around fifteen thousand for his trainer's share of the purse.

"*What's next for her John? Maybe the Yellow Ribbon Stakes?*" Maria asks.

"*I think the Yellow Ribbon Stakes is the logical next step for her, and then onto the Breeders' Cup, if everything goes as planned.*"

I laugh, because other than Mahoney and probably Mr. Warren, I'm the only other person that knows Mahoney was referring to the Breeders' Cup Classic and not the Distaff.

Mahoney and Mr. Warren exit with me right behind them. We're quickly ushered upstairs to the exclusive Turf Club, where we get to sit in the Jimmy Durante Room, a room reserved for the owners, trainers and families of horses who win the big stakes races on a given day. Surely, we will later be joined by the winning connections of the Bing Crosby Stakes, which is run later on. There's a good chance that Rturntoserve's connections will be up here later on, as he's the heavy favorite in the Crosby Stakes.

The Jimmy Durante Room is exactly what I expected it to be. An amazing spread of food, loaded with charcuterie, cheeses, fruits, and nuts, as well as a cook slicing prime rib by hand. The walls are adorned with oil paintings of past champions who competed at Del Mar, including Seabiscuit, and more recent Pacific Classic winners like Best Pal, Skimming, Tinners Way, and many others. The host guides them over to a large table overlooking the track, conveniently located right at the finish line.

"Let's order some champagne for the table," Mr. Warren directs towards the host.

"Because of your spectacular win this afternoon Mr. Warren, the Del Mar Thoroughbred Club would be pleased to offer you complimentary champagne as well as access to the food platter," the host says as he takes that typical humble host posture, slightly bowed with his hands clasped in front of his lap.

We sit and reminisce about Mondatta's performance, and how she was somehow able to overcome that stumble and still win.

"Mr. Warren I'm going to have to head back

to the barn to make sure she's ok," Mahoney says. "I saw a little bit of blood on the back of her front left leg. It didn't look serious, but that was a big stumble and I just want to make sure she didn't do any more damage."

"I'll go down with you John," Mr. Warren says as he starts to stand up.

"Well we can at least wait for the champagne," Mahoney says as the table all laughs.

As if it was on cue, the waiters come with six champagne flutes filled with the golden, bubbly elixir. Everyone in the group grabs their glasses and looks to Mr. Warren, knowing it's his money and his horse that has afforded us this opportunity.

"To Mondatta," Mr. Warren says as he raises his glass.

"To Mondatta," we all echo his words.

"May we give thanks for her heart, her speed, her magnificent musculature, and her warm soul, that has brought us all together to enjoy our success on this wonderful day. To Mondatta," he says as he raises his glass even higher. We all sip our champagne before Mahoney and Mr. Warren set their glasses down and put their sports jackets back on. I stay back with Mr. Warren's two children, who are both around my age, as well as Mahoney's gallop girl Robin, a pretty twenty-something from New Zealand.

"Well, who do you guys like in the Bing Crosby?" I ask to break the silence.

The Bing Crosby Stakes carries with it a $400,000 purse, is open to all older horses, and is run at a mile and one eighth, shorter than the Hollywood Gold Cup and the Pacific Classic, which will be run a few weeks later at a mile and a quarter. A mile and a quarter is the same distance as the Breeders' Cup Classic. It's the shorter distance that makes Rturntoserve that much more dangerous. And he's only facing seven rivals today, one of them being Choctaw Nation. I have been on Choctaw Nation twice in a row, and twice in a row he's failed to beat Rturntoserve.

Everything on paper says that there's no reason the outcome will change this afternoon.

Rturntoserve has become far too tough for any of these rivals. He's 4/5 on the odds board, which means if you bet five bucks, you only get four bucks profit back for a winning bet. That's how sure people are that he is going to win.

Maria comes over the loud speakers and television sets giving her analysis of the Bing Crosby, and like ninety percent of the people in the building, she's readily admitting that Rturntoserve looks all but unbeatable. He prances around the paddock with the same intimidating look that Mike Tyson had before a fight. It's almost as though he wins his races before they are even run on the track. He prances like an equine dignitary as the summer sun in San Diego shines down upon his gorgeous dark bay and brown colored hair. He is a truly majestic creature and the kind of horse that draws photographers from around the state every time he makes his way out to the oval. His jockey Bernie Dalindo waits in the paddock along with Rturntoserve's Hall of Fame trainer, Bobby D'lorio. While it may look as though they are talking strategy, and how the race will unfold, the conversation is anything but.

"Did you see the set of cans on that blonde in the red hat over there?" Dalindo asks as he nods towards the woman in question. "Fucking unbelievable rack on her. I love this place. I fucked some gal the other night after me and Javier went out to this club. She had to have been a foot taller than me," Dalindo says as they share a laugh. Jockeys are notoriously horny little creatures, and Dalindo is not an exception. Even though he's been married twice already, he's engaged to a girl half his age who works as a gallop girl. You'd think she would know the probability of a jockey staying faithful is about as good as the probability of one playing in the NBA. But the fact that he's making high six figures a year, gets to eat at the finest restaurants in town, and has a certain degree of fame, at least in some circles, seems to be enough for her.

"Have a safe trip around there Bernie," D'lorio says as he gives Dalindo a leg up. D'lorio has saddled over three thousand winners in his career, including two Kentucky Derby winners. He's won almost every big race that the country has to offer, including some international races like the Prix de l'Arc de Triomphe over in Paris with his great grass runner Medallion. The Breeders' Cup Classic would be the final addition to his already impeccable resume and Rturntoserve will undoubtedly be the favorite in that race this year, barring any injuries, or unforeseen loss of talent or desire on the horse's part.

Rturntoserve is holding steady at 4/5 on the odds board while Choctaw Nation is up there at 11/1. I'm licking my chops thinking that Choctaw Nation should rebound and run better. Similar to last time, I put a big exacta box on the two runners, $500 each way, and sit back in the Jimmy Durante Room to enjoy the race with a panoramic view that few others ever get to enjoy.

"And awayyyy they go in the Bing Crosby. Rturntoserve and Alexie Mattosie go right for the early lead, and these two hook up in the opening stages. Motorcycle Mike content to drop in behind them in the third spot with Sporty Spicer right to

his outside. Then we come back two lengths to Seattle Diner who races alone in the fifth spot. He's two in front of Macklemore. And it's three more back to a line up of three: Choctaw Nation, Dancing Dimple, and Mercurio all share the back."

No surprises as Choctaw Nation sits at the back of the pack, but the big surprise is not only how fast Alexie Mattosie is going up front, but that Rturntoserve is going right with him. They engage in a cutthroat battle for the first half-mile and have pulled six lengths ahead of their rivals. I start to worry that, while the race is setting up perfect for Choctaw Nation and the other come-from-behinders, it might be too taxing on Rturntoserve.

"The field comes to the top of the stretch, and Rturntoserve has now put away Alexie Mattosie, and he draws off by three lengths. Motorcycle Mike and Macklemore are both starting to close in, and Choctaw Nation is starting to wind up, but he's forced to go out four wide into the stretch."

Rturntoserve somehow continues to muster up speed and courage, and just keeps on going. Even though Alexie Mattosie forced his hand

and took so much from him early on, the big horse just keeps on finding more on the lead. Meanwhile, Choctaw Nation is really kicking in, and with a hundred yards to go, my exacta bet is all but safe as Choctaw Nation gets into second. However, it pays probably five times more if he can get up and beat the big-hearted favorite.

"Rturntoserve just keeps on holding his lead, Choctaw Nation's going to be second best, but it's Rturntoserve, the more they asked, the more he gave, he wins the Bing Crosby Handicap by a length and a half. Choctaw Nation finished second, Motorcycle Mike was third."

Within five strides after the wire, Choctaw Nation blows past Rturntoserve, who's exhausted after his early battle. Maybe Mahoney was right. Maybe Rturntoserve doesn't want to go the extra eighth of a mile that the Breeders' Cup Classic will ask him to go. Maybe Mondatta could beat him. Heck maybe Choctaw Nation could.

By the time Rturntoserve's back in the winner's circle, I've made my way over here to watch the proceedings. Bernie Dalindo looks as much relieved as he does excited, because he knows he's taken a lot out of the big horse.

"Why the fuck did you duel with Alexie Mattosie?" D'Iorio says to Dalindo with a laugh, even though his question was dead serious. "His horse was 40/1! Just let him go and pass him later." D'Iorio is all smiles now that the race is over and in his favor. However one can imagine that when that :45.25 seconds for the opening half-mile went up on the board, D'Iorio was anything but happy or thrilled. It's likely that the word "fucking" and "midget" were used multiple times in reference to Bernie Dalindo, probably used together.

The two-dollar exacta returns fourteen bucks. So, my five-hundred-dollar winning exacta puts another $3,500 in my pockets and puts me up over $4,000 for the day. I'm sitting on nineteen thousand and change, plus I still have the ten grand left in my bank account. I'm down only a grand or two for the whole trip, which for a gambler of my magnitude is damn near even. Plus I've paid for living expenses for nearly four months, as well as food, the emergency room visit, the gun from the Hollywood Park motel, and a couple of massages, one legitimate and one from some Asian parlor in Inglewood.

It's been a great day at the windows and on the track, and I head down to the paddock to watch Maria do her last race analysis, and see what she's up to for the evening.

"So, my selections for the final race are seven, three, and four. Good luck players, and thank you for joining us on this Saturday at Del Mar. We hope to see you back with us tomorrow. Don't forget that racing gets underway at two. Everyone drive home safely and have a pleasant evening. We'll see you tomorrow, where the turf meets the surf, at Del Mar."

Maria clicks off her microphone and sees me waiting near the paddock exit. After the feature race, a nice chunk of the folks have started to leave, so the paddock is nowhere near as full as it was earlier in the day. The final race is often called the "Get Out" race, or "Getaway" race, for a number of reasons. If you're winning, then it's your last chance to get away with another winner. And if you're getting your ass kicked, then it's your final opportunity to try and get back some of the money you lost.

"How's your day been going?" Maria asks with a smile. I respect the fact that, even though we've been seeing each other, it's not professional for her to hug or kiss me in the open. After all, part of her job is giving the illusion that she's available, and that the gamblers actually have some miracle shot at getting her.

"You know, I knocked 'em dead today," I say, feigning humbleness. "I'm up about four."

"Hundred or thousand?" she asks with a smile and look of curiosity.

"Four grand," I say. "I clobbered both of the big races, I was all over Mondatta, and hammered the Rturntoserve exacta with Choctaw Nation."

"Well then I suppose dinner is on you tonight?" Maria replies.

"Come to think of it, dinner's always been on me. How about this time, I pick the place and you pay," I ask.

"You just made four-thousand dollars in about five and half hours and you want me to pay?" she asks me as she smacks me in the ribs with her program.

"That's right! And I know just the place to go!" I say.

First things first, though. I want to go check on Mondatta, check in with Mahoney, and see how she's doing after her stumble.

"Can we get back to the barn area with your press pass or do we have to call Mahoney to get back there?" I ask Maria.

"I can get us back there. The guard is a good friend," she says.

We head back to the barns, which reside on the backstretch, just beyond the outer fence of the Del Mar oval. We walk to the far end of the race track, and the security guard is nice enough to give us a ride on his golf cart to barn eighteen, where Mahoney has his horses stabled while he's at Del Mar. When we arrive, Mr. Warren and Mahoney are talking out front, and judging by the smiles on their face, my initial worry that she might be injured quickly evaporates.

"Hey, how's our girl?" I ask the owner and trainer.

"She's good," Mahoney replies. "She ate up all her food right away and she's in good spirits. She just scratched her ankle on that other horse's shoe. We'll just give her a couple of days off to recoup and she'll be good as new. We're just going to run her on Pacific Classic Day and then again in the Breeders' Cup."

16

BORDER

Maria and I leave Del Mar in her car and I direct her to head south on the I-5, through downtown San Diego, and past the Gaslamp district exit. As we near the city limits, she speaks up.

"Where the hell are you taking me? Tijuana?"

"Actually, yeah," I say, giving her a stone cold look, and trying to hide the smile that lies underneath.

"You're not serious. They don't let white guys in there after dark," she jokes.

"I'm totally serious. I haven't been to Tijuana in forever. I thought it would be fun."

Maria pulls quickly off the freeway at the next exit, and I worry that she is not to keen on the whole plan.

"What are you doing?" I ask.

"We're going to need passports you dork," she says. I hadn't thought of that.

We headed back to the track so I could get
my passport out of my car, and then stopped by
her apartment to grab hers. It was a bit of a
delay, but she seemed sporting to the idea as we
pop back onto the freeway.

"Let's park near the train station and take
the train down. The lines at the border for cars
are always super long."

"Good idea. Plus that way we can drink," I
say with a laugh.

"I thought you don't drink."

"I don't. But I will tonight. I mean shit, it's
TJ."

We pull up to the train station just north of
the border, and board the next train that
arrives. We're pleased to spot two empty seats
next to a nice young couple. The man looks like a
military guy, and with the naval bases in San
Diego, it's a good chance that he is.

"You guys going down for the evening?"
Maria asks the gal.

"Indeed we are," she replies. "We're going to
go bar hopping and dancing. We come down
every couple of months. We're both up at the

Coronado Naval Base."

"You're both in the Navy?" I ask. "That's awesome. I'm Ryan and this is Maria."

"I'm Carly and this is Chris," the young lady says.

Chris looks like so many military guys do. He has short, cropped, sandy blonde hair, a chiseled face, and muscular arms that stretch the limits of the black t-shirt he's wearing. Carly is much shorter than all of us, with short blonde hair and naturally bouncy curls.

Carly and Chris have been married for two years and met in the service. Chris joined immediately after high school in 2002, while Carly, a few years his senior, joined in 2003 after finishing college on a ROTC scholarship. She was obliged to four years of service in exchange for the Navy paying for her education at the University of Colorado in Boulder. Chris was from Arizona and was happy to be stationed somewhat close to his home, and when he met Carly three years ago, he knew he had found his match. She's a family oriented woman, and like him, somewhat conservative politically. They hadn't yet had children, but kids were definitely part of the plan in the coming years.

Maria and I talk with Carly and Chris for the few minutes we are on the train, as well as for the next twenty minutes as we stand in line at the walk-through border patrol. Carly and Chris know nothing about horse racing, which makes them even more appealing to chat with.

"Do you guys want to join us for drinks once we get into town?" Carly asks. "Always good to keep safety in numbers down here."

"I'm game for it," I reply, looking at Maria for her approval on the matter.

"Absolutely. Where are we going?" Maria asks.

"The Avenue Revolución," Chris says.

With still a couple hours of sunshine left, I notice the stark difference in pretty much everything as you cross the border from the United States to Mexico. The four of us arrive at a small mall area that's loaded with shops. Viagra and Ativan are available, as is almost every other pill known to man. We walk into a small cantina that looks like any other store in a mall only it's a bar.

"Let's get a bucket of beer. Dos Equis okay?" Chris asks.

"I want to get a seven and seven on the rocks," I say, as like most unseasoned drinkers, I can't stand the taste of beer.

"You never get mixed drinks down here," Maria says.

"Why the hell not?" I ask her.

"Because of the ice," Maria says. "You know how you always hear about you're not supposed to drink the water in Mexico?"

"Yeah, so?"

"Well, what do you think ice is made of?" Carly interjects as the three antagonists all start cracking up.

"Fine, beer it is," I say, throwing my hands up in the air.

The server brings out a bucket of cold Dos Equis beer, with the aforementioned ice surrounding the bottles and keeping it cold. They also provide a complimentary shot of tequila with the beer. They pour the agave nectar into a small plastic cup, like the kind you would use to shoot your mouthwash before you rinse.

"You shouldn't drink the tequila either," Maria says with a smile.

"Why not?" I ask.

"Just abide by the old axiom that if it isn't bottled, and if you didn't open it, then you shouldn't drink it," Maria says as we all open our initial libations.

"Here's to new friends and a fun night in TJ," Chris says as he raises his bottle.

We kick off our evening with that bucket of beer and a discussion about where we all grew up. Carly and Chris just bought a home in East San Diego out by the football stadium where the Chargers play, and they've started to decorate their house. Chris's parents are both realtors in the Phoenix area and did quite well over the last twenty years, as that city had turned into the monstrosity in the desert that it is today. Upon finishing those last refreshing yet bitter Mexican beers, we head back out into the mall.

"Do you know where we're going?" I ask Chris.

"Yeah, just follow us. We go over a big

bridge, walk a few blocks more, and then we're downtown on the Avenue Revolución," Chris says as he takes the point and position of navigator for this evening's journey southbound.

As we walk over a long bridge that goes over the Tijuana River, all of us look down at the mini valley where a river apparently used to flow. All that remains is about a four-foot wide stream with a hundred feet or more on each side of dried out riverbed, and cement.

"Is that a dead dog?" I ask as I point down into the dried out river valley. Below is what looks like the carcass of some man's former best friend, and as we get directly over it, all four of us can see that a variety of bugs and flies have already gone to eating the flesh of this once proud creature. The dog has probably been there for a few days, as his ribs are already visible. The combination of baking sunshine and bugs seems to have spelled the end of his fur and skin on the exposed side.

We continue over the bridge, and as we reach what appears to be Tijuana proper, we're greeted by a few kids selling gum and trying to hustle money out of the tourists who cross into the country.

"Chicle, chicle," a small boy repeats as he holds up the gum for purchase. He's no more than three-and-a-half-feet tall, but he's a persistent little bastard who doesn't seem to want to take all of our negative answers to his offerings.

"The big stop light up ahead is the Avenue Revolución," Chris tells the group.

The Avenue Revolución has always been the center for US tourists looking to come down to Tijuana and have some fun. The street is laden with cantinas, restaurants, dance clubs, street food carts, and of course, titty bars. When the four of us turn onto the Avenue, the amount of scenery to take in isn't quite what it used to be. I remember coming down with a buddy back when I was nineteen and the street being alive with people and lights, and the bars hopping with tourists. On this summer Saturday, however, it's kind of awkwardly quiet. The four of us were hoping for a fun night of partying and dancing, however it seems that other than a handful of locals and some older tourists, nobody else got the memo. Within a few blocks of walking on the Avenue Revolución, a guy outside trying to hustle people into his particular establishment hollers and gestures that we should come inside.

"Hey guys, we got dollar beers," the man says, instantly drawing everyone's attention. "And big titties," he says as he holds his hands in a cupping position in front of his chest, which is probably a small C cup.

"Hell yeah. Let's go in," Maria shouts with a big grin.

I'm shocked, but excited at Maria's apparent unhampering of her inhibitions. I nod, as do Chris and Carly, and we stroll inside. The bar has no door, and once we walk in, we see a desolate room with many empty tables. In fact, every table is empty. The paint scheme is green and white, with the green on the dark side and the white more on the brown side of the color spectrum. The place smells as if body odor had been preserved in a spray can and liberally applied to the air.

Up on the stage, three women in their late thirties or early forties are dancing in what appear to be nighty type dresses. These gals look as though they're not very interested in their work, or in life in general for that matter. Each has long dark, ratty hair, as well as huge breasts and an accompanying huge gut. The music playing is the traditional Mexican music that you hear at any Mexican restaurant in the States. However, these women are moving much slower than the number of beats per minute that the timpani and bongos are putting out over the speakers. They're simply shuffling around the stage, taking tiny steps, and moving back and forth as if nothing matters to them. Upon sitting, we order up some of the one-dollar Dos Equis and after the gentleman leaves to go to the bar, we all look at each other in dread.

"We can't stay here," I say.

"Why not? This place is great!" Maria quickly retorts. "Maybe you can get a lap dance from one of the gals up there? Sign says ten bucks!"

"I'm going to go pee, God help me as I go

find a bathroom in this shit hole," I say as I push in my chair.

I saunter to the back of the bar area, walk down the narrow hall, and finally get to the bathroom, or at least what appears to be the bathroom. There is no "Senor" or "Senorita" signs on the door. Apparently the Mexican health department isn't as stringent as Portland's. There are no urinals, but rather just open stalls with no doors, and toilets that look as though they were installed sometime during the nineteen seventies, which also appears to be the last time they had a toilet brush grace the inside of the bowl. I unzip my fly and begin to commence the emptying of the remnants of the two beers I drank just thirty minutes ago. As I'm finishing up and shaking off the last of my piss, I hear some soft steps coming into the bathroom. I turn my head and all I see is the top of a woman's head, with some ratty black hair that looks all too familiar. As quick as I can, I put everything back in my pants and start to exit the stall. Unfortunately, though, I'm greeted by one of the dancers, the fattest of the three, who puts her arms on each side of the stall to keep me trapped in.

"Hi honey how are you?" she asks in a voice as deep as I figured it would be.

"Fine. I need to get back out to my friends," I say trying to hint to her the fact that I want her to drop her arms and let me the fuck out of here.

"I'll do it for twenty dollars," she says as she makes a motion towards her mouth and gives the international, language barrier-breaking sign for a blowjob.

"NO!" I scream as I now aggressively walk through her arm and knock her grip loose from the stall. Hurrying out to the table, I see the beers have arrived. Unfortunately, so have the other two dancers. Chris is talking to one of them in a flirty way, while Maria and Carly are literally in hysterics laughing. One of the dancers puts her hand on Chris's leg and starts to rub it up towards his crotch. This married man's wife is sitting six inches from him, and laughing at the fact that her husband is about to get a rub down from a two-hundred-and-fifty-pound Mexican whore.

"You guys we gotta get the fuck out of here," I say, refusing to sit down. "Pound your beers and let's go!"

"Oh chill out. Sit down and relax," Maria says in the midst of her laughing fit.

"I just had a three-hundred-pound senorita offer to blow me on a disgusting germ filled toilet with her herpes laden mouth. I think I'm ready to leave," I say as I look straight at Maria.

"Fine. Let's pound them and go," Chris says, passing around the dollar beers that came in miniature eight ounce bottles.

Back on the streets of Tijuana, and heading deeper down the Avenue Revolución, we come across a Senor Frogs looking bar that appears much safer and more appealing than the previous haunt. The outdoor patio actually has some customers, some of whom even look like they might have made it past the seventh grade, which compared to the last place sounds like a winner to me.

We take our seats and order up another bucket of Dos Equis, as well as some tacos. The waitress drops off the huge green bucket full of suds as well as the tequila shots, which appear to be a standard bucket beer-drinking accompaniment. Maria and Carly immediately reach for the tequila shots and proceed to pound them back like true professionals.

"What happened to all that 'don't drink the tequila' bullshit from the other bar?" I ask.

"Fuck it, we're in Mexico," Maria says as her and Carly both let out an audible "whooooo."

The tacos are brought to the table, and they are exactly what I had hoped for—street tacos with beef and pico de gallo. They're fucking delicious. Something the Travel Channel's Anthony Bourdain would spend half a show gloating over. As happens with alcohol and good food, Maria and Carly have instantly become best friends and are bonded forever, while Chris and I seem to have an appreciation that if our ladies are happy, then all is well. Happy wife, happy life. When the waitress brings the tab over, Maria politely asks where the good dance clubs are.

"The best one in town is just down the next block. And it's tourist friendly," the server says with a smile.

We head towards the aforementioned club, which has a big overhanging sign that reads Las Pulgas Disco Club. But Chris notices weaponry being sold on the street and immediately halts our path. Laid out in front of him are knives and blades of all kinds. He immediately asks Carly for some money, and points out his two intended purchases. A butterfly knife and a switchblade knife. They appear to be of decent quality for the twenty bucks he hands over.

"How you going to get those across the border?" I ask.

"Dude, I'm a fucking Naval officer. You think they're going to give me any crap at the border? Half those guys are former Navy. The border patrol guys I mean."

Chris spends the rest of the walk to the club opening and closing his new butterfly toy, trying to do it as quick as possible each time. There's something about new knives and alcohol that gives men the exuberance and enjoyment seven-year-olds get from new toys.

"Bienvenido a Las Pulgas," the man at the door of the club says. He's wearing a white suit with a button-down black shirt that isn't buttoned at all. His hair has just shy of the amount of oil required by a new Ford Excursion, and he's wearing a cross around his neck that resides smack in the middle of his exploding garden of chest hair. I can't believe a guy like this really exists, because up until now, I thought they only existed in Will Smith cop movies, or as lampoons of Tony Montana.

The Las Pulgas Disco Club consists of a number of different rooms with various types of music. Maria leads us to the Salon Rancho, which features an upbeat salsa groove blasting over the sound system.

Maria and Carly hit the dance floor by themselves as Chris and I sit at the table. I feel like one of those beaten down husbands who sit all alone at the mall, waiting for his wife to finish her fun. Halfway through the first song of their dance I see a couple of guys dancing towards the girls. One's tall and one's short, and both have their shirts only buttoned up halfway, which appears to be a trend in this place. The girls still have big smiles on their faces as they talk with these guys, however, the tall one keeps inching toward Maria. He puts his hand around her waist, and she kind of looks back to me, as she keeps dancing. I'm not thrilled about this, but as long as they are just dancing, I suppose it's fine. Then it happens. He kinks his neck to the side, and quickly buries his mouth into the soft part of her neck, kissing her quickly, and from the looks of her reaction, biting her.

I spring up from my chair and start to walk over to them. She immediately recoiled back and out of his grasp, as he continued to put on a cocky smile. As I'm about five or six steps from him, he finally notices me walking in a straight line right at him. This is about the same point that I start to think, "what the fuck am I doing?"

"What the fuck's your problem asshole?" I say to him, more a statement than a question.

He just stands there, trying to look tough,

and confused all at the same time. I signal with my finger for him to come here, and I whisper into his ear.

"Ella es mi novia. Please leave her alone."

I knew how to say, "she is my girlfriend" in Spanish, but the whole "leave her alone" part I just couldn't remember.

"Si," was all he said as he walked away.

I didn't want to fight this guy. I don't want to fight anyone. I'm terrified of getting punched in the face. Not the pain per se, just worried it would shove the nose cartilage up into my brain and kill me, or something like that.

"What did you say to him?" Maria asks after the guys are far enough away.

"Don't worry about it. He won't bother us anymore," I say confidently, even though my heart is jumping out of my chest. I want her to think that I told the guy I'd kick the living shit out of him if he ever looked at her again. But, if I told her that I'd begged him to leave us alone, I might not look too tough.

"C'mon Portland. Time to show me what you got," she says as she extends an arm to me.

I fucking hate to dance. My dancing knowledge involves either a slow-dance shuffle, or the hip-hop-grind dance kids do nowadays. Nonetheless, I join Maria in the center of the dance floor, and give it my best effort. She's truly a remarkable sight. With the lights shining down upon her glistening skin, I'm completely infatuated with not only her beauty, but also her strength. This woman has been through some serious things, and has come out the other side with strength and grace. We continue to dance, and when I nod my head to go back to the bar and catch my breath, a slower song comes on.

"C'mon, one more, we can go slow," she says grabbing my hands.

"Fuuuucck," I whine. "But next beer's on you."

"This whole night is supposed to be on me you cheap ass," Maria zings right back at me.

As we slow dance, whether I've finally worked up the courage or because the six beers I've drank are finally settling in, I start to kiss Maria on the side of her neck as we dance cheek to cheek. She responds by turning her head away, exposing the light brown hue of her soft neck even more. The skin where her neck meets her trapezius muscles might be the softest skin I've ever kissed. The tiny bit of sweat on her skin coats my lips. As I continue to kiss her neck, she clutches my shirt, in my mind, giving complete permission to continue. Within a few more seconds, I kiss my way to her ear, then her cheek, and then finally to her mouth, where she responds, and kisses me right back. The drunken dance floor make out is a situation nobody would be proud of if they were a sober spectator of the event, but in the hazy moment as a participant, there might not be anything better. Even inebriated, I still keep my eyes part way open, not allowing myself to fully be enveloped in the moment with my girl. Rather, I must keep constant eye on the door, on the other people who may be watching, and anything else that may arise. Can't leave my anxiety at the border.

When the clock strikes eleven, Carly initiates our return to San Diego. The trains back to the States run until just after midnight, and we have a twenty-minute walk back to the border, plus any line at the border to wait through. The entire walk back, Chris, who has become the drunkest member of the quartet, plays with his switchblade knife. He repeatedly pushes the blade back in, then hits the button to release it, each time pointing it at an imaginary bad guy saying "What bitch? You want some of this bitch? C'mon bitch!"

Upon arrival at the border, everyone's happy to see that the lines are short. Just a few people deep at each stall. I get there first, and I'm greeted by the customs official with his usual batch of questions, examination of my passport, and then a simple "go on through."

Chris and Carly, despite carrying deadly weapons, and being approximately thirty-two sheets to the wind, go right on through.

"What's your name and destination?" the customs agent asks.

"Maria Martinez. I'm going back to my apartment in San Diego."

"What was the purpose of your trip?" the agent asks.

"We came down as a group of friends to have

dinner, drinks, and to walk around Tijuana."

"Are you intoxicated Ms. Martinez?"

"Yes I am. Is that illegal?" she asks.

"Are you getting smart with me?" the customs agent responds as he takes his eyes off of her passport and directs them to her.

"No sir. I was just worried by the way you asked that I was somehow violating a law," she says calmly.

The agent continues to ask her questions, far more than any of the three of us were asked, with the irony being that Maria is easily the most well-behaved and non-drunk of all of us. But her last name is Martinez, and she has brown skin. She warned us on the walk over that she'd be quizzed more than anyone else. And they certainly did. Finally, the customs agent allows her to pass and we head back to the train.

"How are we gonna get home?" I ask Maria. "I'm too drunk to drive, and I think you are too."

"We'll just take a cab," Maria says. "We can come get my car in the morning before the races. Ugh. I haven't even looked at the *Racing Form* for tomorrow."

We get off at the first station where we're parked, and being as it's a Saturday night, and we're just a mile from Tijuana, there are three cabs ready and waiting. Maria and Carly hug, Chris and I shake hands, and we exchange numbers to maybe hang out again. Maria's tone has changed as we hop in the cab and head to her apartment. She's gazing out the window when I gently grab her hand and ask if she's okay.

"Yeah. It's just that fucking dick at the customs desk," she says. "It's annoying. I know it's going to happen, and I know I'm going to get through, but just once I want them to just let me through without a grand inquisition."

"I know sweetie. I'm sorry."

"You actually don't know," she says.

"You're right. I don't," I respond.

We hold hands the entire way back to her place, and I guiltily pay for the cab, as this whole trip was my idea. We exit the cab and head up to her place, which is small, and sparsely decorated. It's a temporary place where

Del Mar puts up many of their seasonal employees.

She heads into the bathroom while I head to the kitchen to pour myself a glass of ice water. When she comes out, she's changed into an oversized t-shirt, and while I had been thinking of what might happen later in the evening the whole night, I'd resigned myself to the probability of no sex after the border debacle and ensuing cab ride home.

"Come lay with me," she says as she plops onto the queen-size mattress on the floor.

I take off my shoes and shirt, but leave my pants on, just in case "come lay with me" is literally code for come lay with me, and that's all.

"I had fun tonight," she says as she embraces me. We lay face to face on the pillows. She runs her fingertips up and down my forearm, gently stroking all the hairs and nerves along that path. I lie in a perfect bliss of tired, drunk, and content. It's a rare moment of peace.

"You're fun, even though you can't dance," she says, laughing.

"What are you talking about? My moves are deadly."

"That's a good word for them. They can kill a mood, that's for sure," she laughs.

I playfully tickle her in response to the jab, and start kissing her. The tension that was building up on the dance floor, and over the past few weeks, immediately comes rushing back into the room as we kiss harder, firmer, and deeper. I slide my hand along her side and around the curve of her hip. Maria cuts a curvaceous shape, with her hips jetting up into the air away from her waist. I run my hand up onto her back and pull her in closer, pressing her face into mine to the point where it's almost painful. My cock is taut against my pants, begging for release. I grind it into her leg, and as soon as she feels the rounded point, she wastes no time and reaches down. After she wrestles to open my belt for a few seconds, I reach down and pop it off. I even undo the button on my jeans. No sense in making her work for it. She grips me firmly, almost viciously. I tilt my head back, delighting in the moment. I just as quickly grab at the waistband of her underwear and try, unsuccessfully, to slide them off of her left side. She lays on her back, arches her hips up in the air, slides them off, and somehow manages to look even sexier by throwing them as far away from the bed as possible.

"Do you have a condom?" I ask. It's amazing how that question can interrupt the whole experience, even when one is only a couple feet away in the nightstand.

She points to the top drawer. I sit up on my knees to grab it. She lies back as I put the rubber on, and I dive down onto her. I kiss her on her lips, as I take my hand and guide myself into her. She immediately breaks the kiss and cocks her head straight back into the pillow as I thrust.

I generally spend ninety-nine percent of my day worrying about something. It could be my health, money, family, or just having another panic attack. But for the few minutes I'm with Maria this evening, it all goes away. The worry subsides, as we kiss, touch, and thrust. With so many of the girls I've been with over the years,

I gave little thought to their enjoyment, or to my performance. It was get in, get off, and get out. With Michelle, it was different. And now, with Maria it's different as well.

"I like you," I whisper in her ear before again kissing the side of her neck.

"Who do you like in the seventh race tomorrow?" she asks.

17

PACIFIC CLASSIC

The summer at Del Mar has been a wonderful experience on a number of levels. Aside from enjoying the races at Del Mar in the afternoons, the sunny California weather, and of course, evenings with Maria at the beach or in the bedroom, Del Mar has become the highlight of not only my trip, but of my year. With just two weeks left in the Del Mar meeting, and just a few more weeks after that until the Breeders' Cup World Championships at Santa Anita, all the horses are making their final pushes towards the world championships. Back East, the top horses on that coast are preparing at places like Saratoga, Belmont, and Keeneland. Horses in the Midwest are getting ready at Arlington Park in Chicago, and Churchill Downs in Louisville, while the best in the West are all at Del Mar.

The Pacific Classic is the biggest event on the racing calendar at Del Mar, and features a $1,000,000 purse for the owners, trainers, and jockeys to go after. The race is at a mile and a quarter, and features the best older horses on the left coast, with Rturntoserve and Choctaw Nation now headlining that cast. Mondatta is running in the Playa Del Rey Stakes for older fillies and mares at one mile and one eighth, and she's become the queen of her division.

It's the Wednesday morning before the Pacific Classic, which is going to be run on Saturday, and I'm sitting in the Jimmy Durante Room upstairs with Mr. Warren and trainer John Mahoney at a table with a bountiful breakfast of huevos rancheros, bacon, and fruit, getting ready for the post-position draw for the big races. I feel my pocket vibrate. I reach down, look at the screen, and see it's my boss from Portland on the phone. Since our table is in the back, I quickly put my napkin on the table and answer the call as I walk out to the foyer.

"Hey Keith. How are you?" I answer.

"Ryan. I'm doing well. I'm just getting things

in line up here for next season. That's why I'm calling. I wanted to let you know we've set our opening day on the Saturday after Breeders' Cup. We're going to run Saturdays, Sundays, and Wednesdays at 1 p.m. each day. But we're only running sixty days this year."

"Sixty? Yikes."

"Well, we just don't have the money to run the normal eighty days, and the horsemen are on board. I wanted to give you a heads up, and formally ask you back to call the races again."

"Sounds like a plan. I'll see you then," I say, feeling kind of conflicted. Walking back to the table, I feel relieved knowing I have employment coming back in just under two months, but bummed that I'm losing about twenty five percent of my workdays. Many people at the track who work seasonally aren't paid per hour or on salary, but rather get a day rate. The guys on the starting-gate crew, the outrider, the announcer, the placing judges, all get a per-day rate. I know there's no sense in asking for more money because of the economy. And the economy of horse racing being what it is, there's no shot at a raise. Any demands would probably lead to my boss going out and finding some young kid who would work for half the money. Where else can you find a job where you make a few hundred bucks a day for sitting around talking about horse racing, with twenty-minute breaks every half hour?

"In the Playa Del Ray Stakes, number one will be Barameter," the racing secretary calls out, as they start the draw. *"Number six will be Mondatta."*

Mr. Warren and Mahoney both nod in approval knowing that with Mondatta's deep, come from behind style, it isn't going to matter where in the field of seven she breaks from.

After the drawing for each race, Maria stands at the podium off to the side and interviews the trainers and owners of the main contenders in each race.

"Can we have the connections of Mondatta come up and join us," she says looking in Mr. Warren's direction.

Mr. Warren sends Mahoney up to discuss Mondatta's chances. She beat the best in her division the last few starts, so she's already the favorite at Playa Del Ray. Plus her main competitors, Freeway Gal and Sister Susie, are electing to pass on this race and just train up to the Breeders' Cup Distaff.

"John Mahoney, the trainer of Mondatta, is joining us. John, your gal has come into her own this year. She's really become a monster," Maria says as she points the microphone towards the big trainer.

"She really has Maria," Mahoney says somewhat cautiously. *"She just keeps getting better and we couldn't be more happy with her."*

"Surely the plan with her is the Breeders' Cup Distaff at Santa Anita?" Maria asks.

"We are definitely pointing her towards the Breeders' Cup, but we'll see how she does on Saturday."

"Thank you John, and best of luck to you and all the competitors in the Playa Del Ray on Saturday," Maria says as she turns the draw back over to the racing secretary and track president.

The draw continues with the racing officials

trying to make a bigger deal of the Pacific Classic than it probably should be. With only five horses entered for the race, Rturntoserve stands out, with Choctaw Nation looming as the obvious second choice. The other three runners have a big disadvantage in terms of their class and ability. It's questionable they can handle the mile and one-quarter distance. I'm excited about the Pacific Classic because one of the three horses, Alexie Mattosie, is not expected to win. He was the long shot that dueled Rturntoserve early, and almost caused him to get beat by Choctaw Nation in the Hollywood Gold Cup. With this race, they'll each have to go another eighth of a mile. Those factors point to Choctaw Nation being a great bet. He's going to be the second choice, but should be a much higher price than Rturntoserve. The Pick 6 is guaranteed at a million bucks on Saturday, and I'll be taking a big swing at it. Especially since my two old favorites, Mondatta and Choctaw Nation, are almost surefire winners. Granted, Rturntoserve will be tough, but at a mile and a quarter, and with Choctaw Nation improving, Saturday could be his day. It could be my day as well.

18

PICK SIX

The sun comes up just as it should on a late-August day in San Diego, rising over the hills to the East. I'm sitting on Maria's back porch reading the *Racing Form*, which we spent the entire previous evening dissecting, and writing down my selections and plays for the big Pick 6. My ticket is going to be expensive, because outside of the two singles I'm using, Mondatta and Choctaw Nation, the other four races all feature full fields and wide open groups, where literally any of six, seven, or eight horses can win. My Pick 6 ticket will look like an upside down pyramid. I've spread wide in the first four races of the sequence, and then use only Mondatta in the eighth race, and only Choctaw Nation in the ninth.

Race 4: 1, 3, 5, 6, 7, 9
Race 5: 4, 5, 6, 7, 8

Race 6: 2, 3, 9, 10

Race 7: 1, 2, 3, 4, 5, 6, 8, 9, 12, 13

Race 8: 6

Race 9: 3

All those numbers are the horses I'm selecting for the Pick 6, with the total ticket costing me $2,400. Almost ten percent of my entire net worth is going towards this ticket. Even if the favorites win each of the races, with Choctaw Nation beating Rturntoserve, the payoff will be plentiful no matter what. There's going to be over a million bucks in the pool, and if I can hit a long shot or two, and beat Rturntoserve, then I will be taking up residency in fat-bankroll city.

"What are you up to out here?" Maria says as she sits down on the other rickety porch chair, her cup of coffee steaming into the chilly summer morning air.

"You still think Rturntoserve can go that far today?" I ask.

"Yeah. He did it in the Big Cap and he's not facing anybody tough today," she says, fully knowing I'm all-in against him.

"You just watch," I say.

"How much is your Pick 6 play gonna be?" she asks as she sips her coffee.

"Twenty-four hundred," I say confidently, even brashly.

"What?" she says, nearly spitting out her coffee.

"What do you mean what?"

"That's a ton of money. I knew you were playing big and doing well, but isn't that a lot of money to be putting up on a bet?"

"Yeah, it is. But I've been doing alright, and I'm going to stop gambling again once I get back to Portland," I say confidently, knowing it's probably total bullshit.

"You don't have to stop. Just tone it down maybe?" she replies. "But you strike me as more of an all or nothing kind of guy when it comes to that kind of stuff."

"Yeah. I used to play way too much, so I took a few years off to collect myself and put things in perspective," I say as I set the *Racing Form* down in my lap, for the first time really hinting at telling her what a real problem it was.

"Did you have a problem?" she asks.

"I wouldn't say it was a problem. I was just spending too much time doing it."

"Okay. I just don't want you to overdo it," she says, as she puts her hand on my knee. "I've seen a lot of people go broke in this game. It gets ugly. And to be honest, it scares me a bit to see you betting so much."

"I only took out of the bank what I could afford to lose, and four months into this trip, I have only two grand less than when I came down here. Two grand for four months of food, lodging, and fun is pretty God damned good. And if this bet today loses, then five grand for four months of fun, food, and lodging is pretty damn good, too. I mean, no matter what happens today, or for the next week, I'm up for the gambling part of things."

"All right, all right, don't be so sensitive. I was just making sure," Maria says.

Maria and I drive to the track a couple of hours before the races start, so she can go meet up with the television crew and map out their plans for the day. I make my way out to the apron to get a good table to set up as my home base for the afternoon. I've brought five-thousand dollars with me for the day's races. It won't all fit in my wallet, so half the cash is in my right hip pocket. I can feel it press against my leg with each step. With the early races being so open and competitive, I figure it's as good a time as any to really go after some serious money. I shoot Mahoney a text to see how the big girl is doing, knowing that Mahoney isn't the most immediate replier in the world.

"How's Mondatta? She gonna win?" I ask.

I grab a fresh sliced roast beef sandwich from the carver station downstairs, and as I head back to my seat, I can feel my hip vibrating from the phone. Sitting next to me on the apron are a couple that I've seen numerous times over the summer and I say hello to them as I sit down with my lunch.

"Who's gonna win the Classic today?" I ask.

"Rturntoserve," the guy says of course.

"Yeah, he looks pretty tough in there. It's going to take something special to beat him," I say. In horse racing, the other gamblers are your competition, because it's a pari-mutuel game. The more money that's bet on a horse, the lower the odds. So there's rarely any sense in telling your competition that you like a horse, especially when it's not the favorite.

I grab my phone, casually look, and find an immediate response from Mahoney.

"She should," the message reads. Even more confidence to add to my impending big bet.

The day starts off on a sour note for me, and for most of the betting public at Del Mar, as Lesley's Rib scores a huge upset in the first race, knocking me, and probably ninety-five percent of the patrons in the building, out of our early Pick 4's and Daily Doubles. I spent a hundred and forty four bucks on my early Pick 4, and another hundred on Daily Doubles, and that money is now gone. I drop another two-fifty in the second race when I bet on the favorite, who runs like he is towing a Mack truck down the homestretch. Race three continues the pain as I doubled down my efforts, betting two hundred to win and place on my top pick Menacing, who got the lead early, hit the wall late, and finished fifth. So far, the speed horses are all having a tough time of it, which bodes well for me later in the card, as both Mondatta and Choctaw Nation are deep closers.

I head to the window early as betting starts for the Pick 6 in race four. The last thing I want is to get shut out, or have a teller mistype my ticket and not be able to change it. I find the hundred-dollar window, where you're only allowed to make bets of one-hundred dollars or more, and start rattling off all the numbers in my Pick 6 play. The teller prints out the ticket and exchanges it for twenty-four crisp one-hundred-dollar bills. After losing almost a thousand to start the day, and now in for another twenty-four-hundred dollars, I check my bankroll. It still has girth, but it's definitely smaller than I'd planned on it being at this point.

The Pick 6 sequence starts in probably the most perfect possible way for me when the 12/1 shot, Swiss Exploit, rallies from off the pace and gets up in the final yards to beat the favorite. I had both of the top two runners in my Pick 6, so it wasn't as though I had to sweat out the finish. However, with Swiss Exploit winning, it immediately knocked out well over half of the tickets, and ensured that even if the favorites win from here on out, I'll still be getting a huge payday.

I mosey on back to the paddock to watch the horses warm up for the fifth race of the afternoon, and the second race of the Pick 6. I have five runners in the next race, with all five of them being the five outside runners in the field of eight. The number two and number three runners haven't much of a chance. However, the horse down on the rail, Mystacallie, is 4/1 on the morning line, and not without a chance. My opinion, however, is that Mystacallie is a speed horse. She's a runner who has to have the lead all to herself to run her best race. Something she won't get today. Mystacallie, like a number of speed horses, seems to only run her best if there are no other horses looking her in the eye. Horses have different running styles, some are closers, some are speed horses, and some stalk the pace setters. But when you boil it down to hundreds of years of breeding, horses are pack animals. Some of them just want to run with the pack, some want to be leaders. Mystacallie is one who only wins if she is on the lead early. In any of the races where someone challenged her early on, she was always toast. And with a couple of other speed horses in the race this afternoon, it doesn't look like it's going to be her day. Maria on the other hand, disagrees.

"Number one is Mystacallie," Maria says, as her voice blasts over the in-house sound system. *"She's been running in longer races, and needs the lead to win, and I think that it's something she might not get today. However, I spoke with her trainer Darrin Saul who said he has been training her in the morning to pass horses, and that she's responding well. I think it could be her day."*

"What the fuck?" I think as I walk over to the paddock gate where Maria will exit when she's done. When we went over the ticket and my selections this morning, she hadn't said a fucking thing about Mystacallie. So why now, after my bet was made?

"Mystacallie? What the heck?" I ask when she comes walking out.

"I talked to Darrin an hour ago, and he's really high on this horse. He said he's been doing everything he can in the mornings to train her to come from off the pace and be able to pass runners. That combined with her fitness she has from routing, and he really thinks she should win."

"You know I don't have her on my ticket, right?

"Yeah, I know," she says with a smile.

"Well, she sure as shit better not win, or dinner and rent will both be on your tab," I say flustered and storming away like a child. Maria stands there in shock, befuddled by what seemed like a light moment and ended with me marching away.

I'm pissed at Maria, not because she's done anything wrong, but because she represents the possibility that my ticket might be garbage in the next five minutes. Of course, if I had received that same inside dope, I'd probably have added Mystacallie to my ticket. But once your bet is in, and the first race of the sequence has been run, then as they say, all bets are off.

"And awayyyy they go. Mystacallie broke sharply, but so did Razzle Dizzle, and Razzle Dizzle is going to take the lead. Mystacallie is going to sit in second early on, with Chip's Gold right in behind them in third. It's already three and a half lengths back to Star Harbor and Fiddlers Afleet, who race fourth and fifth, with Dr. Disco and Gallant Fields. And Hout Bay is the trailer."

If this race would have been run ten minutes ago, then I would be feeling like a million bucks as Mystacallie wasn't able to get the early lead. However, given her new training that Maria mentioned, I'm just hoping that Mystacallie will go back to the usual pattern that she's had in her previous races.

"The field turns to the top of the stretch, and Razzle Dizzle digs deep and finds more. Mystacallie, still plugging away in the second spot, is guided off the rail by Jorge Virgo, and now is starting to rally on this leader. Hout Bay is starting to fly from the back."

I switch my view between the race itself and

the huge television board out in the infield to get a better judgment of how each horse is moving. My heart pounds incessantly, as Mystacallie starts to inch up on Razzle Dizzle with just a final hundred yards to go. Hout Bay is closing but isn't coming fast enough, so it's all up to Razzle Dizzle to somehow hold off Mystacallie.

"Razzle Dizzle trying to hold on, Mystacallie is closing and closing fast, here's the wire, and it's gonna be — a photo finish!"

A massive groan comes from the crowd as the two fillies hit the finish line at nearly the exact same time. In the old days, there would actually be a few minutes to find out who won the race, because they took a photo and had to develop the film. Now it's all done by a high-speed camera, which zooms in very far, within millimeters, so that the stewards can accurately judge who the winner is.

Before the results are posted, they show a slowed down television shot of the photo finish, and I let out a huge sigh of relief, as it appears via the television shot that indeed Razzle Dizzle did hold off her oncoming rival.

A cheer goes up as the numbers are posted on the tote board.

"The winner is Razzle Dizzle. Mystacallie second, and Hout Bay finished up in third."

An audible groan pours out of my mouth to go along with the fist pump, as I realize that, even though Razzle Dizzle was the favorite, I'm still alive and moving onto the third leg. I head back to the paddock. I have a date with Maria to vent and yell at her for putting me through ten minutes of torment.

I'm moving on to the third leg of the sequence where I have five runners. In the fourth leg, I have ten of the twelve runners. Now that I've passed this hurdle of a race, it should come down to Mondatta and Choctaw Nation.

"I didn't know if I'd see you after that one," Maria says to me, spotting me before I saw her. "Now you can apologize for snipping at me before the race."

"Son of a bitch," I say with a smile. "I'm sorry. I was a dick."

"I was going to call down to first aid, cause I figured you might have gone into a mild stroke," she said.

"I was freaking out until I saw the replay and could tell she'd hung on. I call photos for a living ya know," I say to her with some playful sarcasm, mocking the fact that I've miscalled several photos in my young career.

"Well, keep the train rolling. I'm pulling for you," she says. She gives me a wink and heads back to her position in front of the paddock camera.

I sail through the third and fourth legs of the sequence, beating the favorites in both races, but not winning with big long shots either. For the fourth leg, I went ten horses deep, only leaving out two hopeless 50/1 shots. And, of course, my top choice, a 9/2 runner named Marvelous Marv won easily. My ticket would have been just two-hundred and forty dollars if I had singled out just that runner. But it's too late to turn back now. With the big upset in the first leg, a couple of decent prices, and with Choctaw Nation hoping to upset Rturntoserve in the finale, this ticket will still pay very well if I can get it home.

Mondatta comes strolling along into the paddock with her groom Manuel, looking every bit as beautiful as she ever has. She probably weighs a hundred pounds more than when I first met her in the barn at Santa Anita back in March. She's filled out and come into her frame. Her musculature is ripped, and the small veins around her muscles show themselves through her thick hided skin. She prances on her toes as she enters the saddling area where she continues to bob her head around. She's figured this game out and knows that when she comes over here, it means that soon she'll be running.

People often ask whether horses know if they are in a race. The answer is that the good ones certainly do. It's not enough to simply have speed or breeding. If that were the case, then the most expensive, best-bred horses would win the Kentucky Derby every year. More so, it's about heart. Horses with the hearts of champions seem to find a way to gut it out against their blue blood rivals. While Mondatta was certainly not cheap, and while she's certainly well bred, it's her heart that's gained her the wins and accolades she's earned on the track. She'll be going a mile and one eighth, what has become her usual distance, in this afternoon's Playa Del Ray Stakes. Her owner Mr. Warren, and his lovely wife Mrs. Warren, are in the paddock along with two of their children, a couple of family friends, and, of course, Mahoney. Mahoney is dressed in slacks and a nice button-down shirt. A far cry from his usual attire of jeans and flannel or collared shirts.

"She's on her toes," Mahoney tells Mr. Warren, assuring him that his barn star is in perfect running shape and attitude.

"I'm confident in her," Mr. Warren says, while gently smacking his program in his hand, trying to get rid of some of the palpable anxiety that comes before a race like this.

Mondatta will be breaking from the number six post position. Mahoney and the groom move to tie the black and gold saddle towel around her girth, and Mondatta rears up slightly, as if to remind them who's in charge.

As she and her six rivals come out into the walking ring to get examined by the patrons, many of the bettors check their programs and Forms, jot down notes, and finalize their ideas for wagers while watching the horses. One of the horses, Maria's Monsoon, is sweating profusely, and appears to be having a mild anxiety attack while forty-thousand people at the track, and hundreds of thousands across the country, watch on simulcast television, or on one of the many online wagering platforms. As Jose Camillo gets a leg up from Mahoney, he shows calm and reserve well beyond his youthful age.

I decide to watch the race with Mr. Warren and Mahoney from up in the grandstand, where Mr. Warren has a couple of private boxes rented for the day. The crowd is abuzz and everyone's enjoying the sun. Mr. Warren is busy talking with his kids, and guests, while Mahoney sits with his eyes fixed on Mondatta through his binoculars. Most people give little thought to watching the horses warm up. But Mahoney likes Mondatta to get a good, solid warm up to get rid of some of her nervous energy before the race commences. Mahoney puts down his binoculars as the field approaches the gate, and as they start to load, he looks over to Mr. Warren and offers his hand for a shake.

"Mr. Warren, good luck my friend," he says.

"Thank you, John. Let's hope she does well."

Mr. Warren sits down. And being the polite and attentive gentleman that he is, he pats Mahoney on the back, as it's clear, the trainer is the most nervous person in the box. The money isn't as important to Mr. Warren as the horse's safety, and the possibility of having a great filly to go into the Breeders' Cup. Gentlemen like him revel in having a great horse. It's not just something to brag about, it's a living thing of beauty, something that lives, eats, and breathes. She's truly majestic.

"And awayyyy they go in the Playa Del Rey."

Mondatta and Jose Camillo break cleanly, and as expected, she drops back to last and to the rail.

"Maria's Monsoon bursts right out to the front, and within a couple of strides she's two lengths in front. Battle Worn is up into the second spot with Nitro Girl in third. They've pulled two and a half lengths in front Sister Sierra and Mama's Maid.

Lavender Blue is sixth, and as expected Mondatta is the trailer."

As the field starts their run down the backstretch, everyone in the box is silent, but definitely pleased, as the opening quarter-and-half-mile times on the board are very quick. Maria's Monsoon, who was acting up and nervous in the paddock, is using that nervous energy to go fast early and force a quick pace.

"The field heads into the far turn. Maria's Monsoon is still in front by three, but she's gone very fast to get that lead. Battle Worn continues a perfect trip in behind her, and is another length in front of Mama's Maid who starts an early bid. Sister Sierra is fourth, while Nitro Girl comes under a ride at the inside. Mondatta is still last and about nine lengths off the lead, as they are midway on the turn."

Camillo is keeping Mondatta on the inside and saving all the ground, as if he goes to the outside on the turn, then he'll be running further than he has to. Mahoney starts to twitch in his seat as they approach the quarter pole.

"They come to the top of the stretch and Battle

Worn takes over the lead. Mama's Maid starts her rally into second. Nitro Girl and Maria's Monsoon both start to back up. Mondatta is trapped and has nowhere to go!"

As the field comes into the stretch, both Nitro Girl and Maria's Monsoon are retreating on the inside paths. Camillo, thinking he will find a way through, decides to stay down on the rail. As he tries to navigate his way through traffic, Mondatta's increasing speed, and those two runners backing up, force him to rear back on the reins to get Mondatta to slow down, and not trip over the hind legs of the horses in front of her. When Camillo tries to get outside, he's trapped, as Sister Sierra is right to his outside. And since the rail is to his inside, he has nowhere to go. He's forced to slow down and try to get Mondatta outside of Sister Sierra once he lets her pass.

"Get her out!" Mahoney screams. "Get her the fuck out of there! God damn it!" Mahoney smacks the front railing in their box and swiftly kicks the chair next to him.

"Battle Worn has kicked away by three lengths,

Mama's Maid is in second, and let's see, Mondatta is still in some bother and is some eight lengths behind."

Mondatta finally gets loose, but it's far too late. Battle Worn is long gone. And Mama's Maid is five lengths ahead in second with only a furlong left to go.

"And it's Battle Worn to pull the upset and win the Playa Del Ray. Mama's Maid was second, and Mondatta finally got going late to finish third."

I plop down in my seat, a padded steel chair that's only about two feet from where Mr. Warren and Mahoney are standing.

"What the hell was he thinking?" Mr. Warren asks Mahoney. He's as confused as the other thirty-thousand people at Del Mar who had placed their hard earned money on Mondatta.

"Mr. Warren, I have no idea what he was thinking," Mahoney says with his arms on his hips. "He's fired. Trust me, that little shit just isn't ready to ride a horse like this in a Breeders' Cup race."

Mahoney shakes his head in disbelief as he starts to head down to the unsaddling area to check on his horse and talk with her rider. Mr. Warren follows him out as the Warren kids and me sit perplexed. I hunch down in the chair with a sense of numbness that usually I would have given anything for, given my anxiety. But this numbness involved the wind being completely kicked out of me. I feel my phone vibrating in my pocket, and hoping it's a good distraction of some kind, I check and see that it's a text from Maria.

"That was brutal," is all the text says.

"Unreal," I reply.

As the results are posted official, and Battle Worn strides into the winner's circle along with her owners and trainers, I grab Mahoney's binoculars, and scan down to see him and Camillo's meeting as the young rider hops off of Mondatta, who actually looks pissed off and irritated herself. It's as though she realizes that she lost and wants to get another crack at those horses she probably would have passed if she'd had a clean trip, and not had to slam on the brakes. I can see Mahoney talking to Camillo, but from a distance, it doesn't appear that he's yelling at him or berating him at all. Mahoney even cracks a smile at some point in the conversation.

"What the fuck Mahoney?" I think to myself.

It's now twenty minutes until the Pacific Classic, the biggest race of the season at Del Mar, and with just a field of five, it's clearly a two horse race. Rturntoserve is 2/5 on the board, a huge monumental favorite if there ever was one. My top pick, Choctaw Nation, is 5/2 while the other three are all above 10/1 in the odds. I have seventeen hundred bucks left in my wallet and head immediately to the windows. There's no need to go to the paddock, or listen to Maria's analysis or even see the horses on the track. I walk straight to the window, and ask for fifteen-hundred to win on Choctaw Nation and a two-hundred dollar exacta with Choctaw Nation over Rturntoserve. At a small track like Portland Meadows, a fifteen-hundred-dollar win bet would have a drastic effect on the odds, sending Choctaw Nation's odds and eventual win payoff plummeting. However, at Del Mar, on a day like Pacific Classic Day, when there's probably about eight-hundred-thousand dollars in the win pool, my wager doesn't force down the odds a single click.

The one consolation I have is that the Pick 6 does payout if you have five out of the six races right. Fifty percent of the pool is divided amongst the winners who have six out of six. Twenty-five percent goes to the house, as that's how the track makes their money. So, essentially, they don't give a shit who wins. They just want the most amount of money bet, so they can get a bigger piece of the pie. The final twenty-five percent of the pool is divided amongst the players who have five out of six. Five out of six, with a couple of huge favorites beaten, including Mondatta, will pay a couple thousand. I actually could still make some money. Plus, if I do get five out of six, that means Rturntoserve will have lost, meaning very few, if any, will even have five out of six, let alone all six.

"The five equine athletes in the paddock are competing in our most prestigious race, the $1,000,000 Pacific Classic at one mile and one

quarter," Maria says as she starts her analysis. *"This race is a Grade-1 event, and our signature race, so let's take a look at the contenders."*

Maria goes through the five runners, spending a bulk of the time talking about Rturntoserve and Choctaw Nation, as everyone realizes that they are two deserving candidates. Rturntoserve and Choctaw Nation both look amazing in the paddock, and the two athletes appear primed for the event. This is their final prep for the Breeders' Cup Classic, which is now just four weeks away. The winner's share of the Pacific Classic is six-hundred-thousand dollars, and even second place takes home two-hundred grand.

The bugler gets behind the microphone in the winner's circle and starts to play the call to post. The horses come out from the tunnel that leads from the paddock to the track, and Rturntoserve and Choctaw Nation are the first two to come out. Their three other rivals, Alexie Mattosie, Dial Me Up, and Indianwarpaint follow them out as they parade in front of the grandstand. My bets are in, but as time passes,

I'm half tempted to head back to the windows, cancel the wagers, and get out of here with at least some of my money in my pocket if Choctaw Nation doesn't win. If Choctaw Nation wins, I still get my five of six correct in the Pick 6, which will easily pay a couple of thousand dollars, so it's not like I don't have anything riding on the race. But I know I can't cancel a bet. The "what if" would be so much worse than the possibility of losing the money. Every gamblers worst nightmare is to throw away the winning lottery ticket. And if I cash in these tickets and Choctaw Nation wins, and Rturntoserve finishes second, then I'm throwing away probably five grand or more. As the field starts heading towards the gate, Mahoney and Mr. Warren arrive back at their box.

"Well that was certainly disappointing wasn't it?" Mr. Warren rhetorically asks.

"I'm sorry pop," his oldest son says.

"Don't be, Brad. She ran her heart out, and just had some bad luck. That's horse racing. That's just how it goes sometimes."

"She's doing fine," Mahoney says

interjecting. "We're gonna head back to the barn after the Pacific Classic just to make sure she eats up, but I didn't see anything wrong. She just got a horrible ride from that fucking kid."

I'm listening, but passively so, as I take my wallet out, and check and then double-check my tickets. Whenever I have a bet down, especially a big bet, either by habit or paranoia, I will always make sure I have the right horses on my ticket. I learned this the hard way back in 2006 when I was visiting Churchill Downs in Louisville, Kentucky. I had played a Pick 3, trying to pick the winners of races four through six that afternoon. After hitting a nice 8/1 shot in the first race, I went on to hit another good price in the second leg. I had three horses in the third and final leg, the three logical favorites, and sure enough, one of them won. I was sitting in the historic bleachers at Churchill Downs — where people sat watching all of the Kentucky Derbies, as well as numerous Breeders' Cup events — when the big red OFFICIAL sign lit up, and I saw a Pick 3 payout of four hundred and twenty eight dollars. As I walked over to the teller line, I took the ticket out and waited behind a couple of other lucky bettors who were cashing their winning plays. When I gave the ticket to the teller, the gentleman put the ticket into the machine and little computer screen displayed the words "ticket not a winner." The teller looked at me and callously said, "I'm sorry sir. It's not a winner." I grabbed the ticket and double-checked it. Sure enough, in the second race, when I had called out the two, four, and six to the teller, the teller punched in two, three, and six. One stupid little mistype of the key. Of course, the horse the guy mistyped proved to be the one I needed for the win. I went from up four-hundred-and-twenty-eight dollars to down fifty-four bucks just like that. And, of course, the track isn't going to reimburse the patron for an error, as they get out of being liable by having signs everywhere that read, "please check your tickets. We are not responsible for errors."

For the Pacific Classic though, my wagers are exactly as I thought them to be.

"Who you got in here Ry?" Mahoney asks.

"Well my Pick 6 is dead now," I say, brashly

hinting that I had only Mondatta in the last race. "I can get five out of six if Choctaw Nation wins, plus I bet some money for him to win and an exacta with Rturntoserve."

"He can't beat Rturntoserve," Mahoney says.

"We shall see."

The horses start their walk down the long chute at the far end of the homestretch to begin this long race. The odds board hasn't moved an inch since I laid down my seventeen-hundred bucks, with Rturntoserve still the huge favorite, and Choctaw Nation the clear second choice.

"All in and locked up. The gates open, and there's the roar of the Del Mar crowd as they're off in the Pacific Classic. No surprises here as Alexie Mattosie goes right to the front. Rturntoserve going to sit back in second early on, as Bernie Dalindo opts to rein in his runner in the early stages. Dial Me Up is in the third spot, no more than three lengths off the early leader, while Choctaw Nation is closer than normal today, only five lengths behind, and he's just in front of Indianwarpaint."

The field runs by the crowd with one circuit left to go, and the hopeless Alexie Mattosie is on the lead with Rturntoserve breathing right down his neck. The layperson can't necessarily see the difference between the two horses as they are about the same size and color. But seasoned race watchers like myself, Mahoney, and many others in the crowd can see just how easily and relaxed that Rturntoserve is traveling early on, and how much more work per stride Alexie Mattosie is putting in. It's like watching a nice new Chevy, which is beautiful, and a great car, driving alongside a brand new Bentley, which travels with such smooth grace and strength that its power and class over the other vehicle is obvious.

"They wheel onto the backstretch, and it's still Alexie Mattosie, travelling well enough, and leading it by a length and three quarters. Rturntoserve is steered just to that rival's outside in the second spot. Here's Dial Me Up now, making an early bid as he comes right to the outside of Rturntoserve. It's now six lengths back to Choctaw Nation and Indianwarpaint who share the back."

I love seeing Dial Me Up making that early move, as Rturntoserve has enjoyed a garden trip thus far, and maybe, just maybe, Dial Me Up will force Bernie Dalindo's hand, and he'll make a move too early. Making a move too early in a mile and one quarter race could spell disaster for a horse like Rturntoserve, who isn't necessarily a horse that loves going that far.

"They start their run towards the far turn, and now Rturntoserve and Dial Me Up are coming right after Alexie Mattosie, who is being ridden along to keep that lead. Choctaw Nation is starting to get underway. He's drawn to within five lengths of the lead, and Indianwarpaint is ridden along at the back and not gaining any ground."

I take my eyes off the live race and start to watch on the small television monitor in the box, as the pan camera gets me in closer to the action when they are on that far turn. I can tell that Choctaw Nation is starting to pick up his stride, and as the field reaches the top of the home stretch, his jockey Gary Golo kicks him to the outside so he doesn't get blocked or run into any traffic.

"They turn for home, and now Rturntoserve takes over. Dial Me Up trying to stick with that rival, but

he's fallen a length back. Choctaw Nation is starting to warm up to the task, but still has three lengths to find."

I stand up and start going to a vigorous right-handed whip of my own, beating my folded *Daily Racing Form* against my right hip, as I cheer on Choctaw Nation.

"C'mon Gary, c'mon Gary, turn him loose!" I scream.

The crowd roars as the runners come into the final hundred yards, and the screams start to increase the closer they get, because it becomes more and more apparent that their horse, the favorite, the horse most people have bet on, Rturntoserve is holding sway.

"C'mon, God damn it," I scream, praying for a miracle, but knowing that it's not going to happen on this day.

"And it's Rturntoserve, who is just too good for them. He has a date next month in the Breeders' Cup Classic. He wins the Pacific Classic by a length and a half. Choctaw Nation ran his heart out to get second with Dial Me Up in third."

"Fucking cocksuckers," I shout as I kick the

empty chair directly in front of me, sending it flying.

Mr. Warren turns around and gives me a disapproving look, while Mahoney taps his owner on the shoulder and suggests they head back to the barn area. They quickly, along with Mr. Warren's children, get up and start to organize their things to head back.

"You going to come back with us?" Mahoney asks me.

I decline the invitation, knowing that Mr. Warren probably doesn't want my company after the temper tantrum I've just thrown. Plus, I'm in no mood to go pet Mondatta and feed her carrots, especially considering I'd blown through five grand in the last five hours.

"Naw, I'm going to go home. I gotta get out of this place," I say.

As I head for the exits, I can hear Maria come over the loudspeakers talking in the winner's circle to the connections of Rturntoserve.

"Another amazing performance by this horse, Bernie Galindo, I think he proved his detractors

---

wrong today about the distance?" she asks the veteran rider.

I'm quite sure that Maria's question was immediately referencing me, as just eight hours earlier we were on her back porch talking about the race, with me telling her I thought Rturntoserve couldn't go that far and win again.

"He really did Maria," Dalindo says between taking breaths. "I've ridden some great horses over the years, but this is absolutely the best one I've ever ridden."

"Now Bernie, you've said that before," Maria says as they both laugh.

"I know. But this horse just keeps on going, and has the heart of a champion. I can't think of any other horse I'd rather be on in four weeks at Santa Anita. This year is our year."

"We shall see," Maria says as she looks back at the camera. "We will all find out in four weeks at the Breeders' Cup."

19

SIN CITY

As the final weekend of the Del Mar season is upon me and the rest of the folks who spend their time at the track, my luck has truly gone south. After the bad day yesterday with the Pacific Classic and Mondatta going down in defeat, I decided to take today through Thursday off and venture over to Las Vegas. It isn't as much the destination, ok maybe it is, as the desire to get out on the open road and try to put some space between the me and the racetrack. A normal person would have just gone to Disneyland, but a single thirty-something guy going there alone kind of reeks of weird-o-ness.

Upon arriving in Vegas, I get a room at Luxor hotel, in the pyramid, where you can step out of your room and see all the suckers down below losing their money playing blackjack, craps, or any of the other table games. Mostly, I just wanted to get the fuck out of San Diego.

Thankfully, Maria's apartment is paid for by the track, and she's letting me stay with her for free, so I can watch my money. But I figured I could set aside two-thousand bucks and get away for three days to try and relax. While I want to gamble, I don't want to watch a single horse race. It has been years since I've played cards, and poker was actually my first gambling love. When I saw the movie Rounders with Matt Damon in college I became hooked. The idea that I could win money off of my wits, and do something that didn't require hard work, sounded great. I played cards for a year after college and did pretty well. In fact, I made money that year. However, my love of the horses, and of food, women, and all the other leaks that a gambler's bankroll can spend money on, eventually led to the well drying up and forcing me back to school. It was either that or get a job. I certainly didn't want to work.

After checking into the hotel, I immediately head for the pool. I've never been one to sit and relax in the sunshine, or relax at all for more than about twenty minutes. However, I know it's in my best interests to spend more time relaxing and less time at the poker tables. Upon arriving at the Luxor pool, I'm greeted by families, kids running around, girls relaxing in small bikinis, and a one-hundred-and-three-degree sun getting ready to fall over the western hills.

I order a drink and put a towel over my face. I put my MP3 player on, and lie back to enjoy the baking sun on my skin. With Bob Dylan's *Nashville Skyline* record gently pulsating in my ear, the effect of the drive and the exhaustion of the big loss yesterday allow me to enter a relaxing and much needed sleep. I wake up and "Country Pie" is playing, so after pulling the towel off my head and getting my bearings, I realize I've been asleep for damn near an hour.

"Can I get you anything else to drink?" a cocktail server asks as she sees I'm out of my comatose state.

"No, I think I'm fine. But thanks for asking," I say as I collect my things and head back to the room to shower. When the hot water hits my skin I quickly realize that my pasty white belly might be a little bit burnt.

"Mother fucker," I scream as I turn the shower knob back closer to the big C as fast as I can.

After putting on some lighter fitting clothes, I head downstairs and out to the cabstand. When I first started coming to Vegas back in 2002, the Mirage was where I spent eighty percent of my time. The poker room at the Mirage was where many of the biggest games in town were for a number of years until the Bellagio, which is now owned by Mirage and MGM, came along and essentially became the capital of poker in Vegas. I always played the 6/12 limit hold 'em games when I came, and when I'd get on a heater, I'd make my way up to the 10/20 games. On this evening, after looking at the big board for what games are open, and how long the waiting lists are, I can see there are six 10/20 games going and just six people on the waiting list, as opposed to a list a mile long for the 6/12 games.

"Can you put me up for the 10/20 game please?" I ask the floor man, a tall kid about my age who oversees the poker room in a cheap black suit.

"Absolutely sir. What's your name?"

"Call me Whites," I say with a smile.

My friend from high school, and my best poker-playing buddy, was my pal Frankie Corcoran. Frankie had some weird condition where his fingernails had a strange white color to them. He must have told me seven times what the condition was called, but I can't remember. Maybe it was calcium deposits or something. Anytime me and Frankie would go play cards up in Seattle at any of the poker rooms, or on some of our trips to California, Frankie would play under the name Whites. In fact, even when we'd play together online, his handle was Whites. Frankie was an amazing card player. He was one of those guys who were gifted at pretty much everything in life. He was an all-state football player, and played baseball with me for our high school and on the summer Babe Ruth league team, which my dad coached. We would always play quarter games when we were on road trips for baseball, or just Saturday nights at our friend's houses. Stupid games like Three-Five-Seven or Guts, or any of ten other games that were part of our weekly rotation. Frankie would regularly win the games, as he just always seemed to have a good sense about cards and what hands people had. He went onto play football and baseball in college, and upon graduating, followed in his father's footsteps and went into the Navy. He had taken officer training in college and decided to try out for the Navy Seals. Just like everything he did in his life, he was a success, and the best at what he did. Frankie joined the Seals, and during his second trip to the Middle East back in 2007, he was killed by sniper fire when they were on a special mission. I was working in Dayton when Frankie's body arrived back in the States, and I was unable to attend one of my best friend's funeral. "Whites" was the only name I could think of for getting into any poker game.

I headed over to the bar adjacent to the poker room with a small beeper that they gave me that would vibrate when my seat was ready.

"Can I get a Shirley Temple please?" I ask.

"Of course, Sugar," the bartender replies.

"Hey, I know you," says an older gentleman sitting to my right. "You're the announcer up at Portland Meadows."

"Yeah. How on Earth do you know who I am?"

"I live up in Seattle, and I go to the track up there all the time," the man says as he extends his hand. "I'm Ron Grayton."

"Ryan McGuire," I say as I shake the man's hand.

"I knew your dad. He used to hang out in Tina's Bar with me and Big Nose Mark," Ron says as he steers his body more towards me. He's probably about as old as my dad would be if he was alive, fifty-three or fifty-four. He looks like a horseplayer too, with his old, collared polo shirt and slacks. His hair is unkempt, and he's rocking the comb-over as though it somehow hides his baldness.

"You knew my dad?"

"Yeah. I knew him well. He would sit at Tina's bar with us every weekend and would bet. He talked about you quite a bit, about what a good baseball player you were. I must have offered to buy him a beer a hundred times over the years. But he always only drank Coke."

"That's because was a recovering alcoholic," I say. "He quit drinking when I was nine, and other than a relapse on my eleventh birthday, he never touched a drink again as far as I know."

"No shit. Wow. He never told us he had a drinking problem," Ron said. "Well, can I buy you a beer?"

"Actually, I'm going to play in the card games tonight, so I don't want to drink. Gotta keep my wits about me, ya know?"

"Well, maybe someday I'll run into your sister, so I can at least buy one McGuire a beer. I mean, with a fucking Irish name like that, I figure you'd all be drinkers," Ron says, and we share a laugh.

"You know Ron," I say before taking a sip of my beverage. "I'll never forget after dad died, I was cleaning out his house, and under his bed I found a bottle of whiskey. It was unopened and the receipt was there with too. It was dated June 24th. I sat there for a second, and then realized that it was only a month or so before he died that his doctors told him that there was nothing left for them to try, and that he should simply go home and die. He died on July 24th, and I figured that he probably stopped at the liquor store on the way home and bought that bottle. He probably figured maybe it would be just easier to drink himself to death than to sit and wait for the nodules of cancer in his lungs to eventually take away his breath. And for some reason, he never took that step. I tell you, I wouldn't have fucking blamed him in the least if he would have. But I found myself somewhat strangely proud of him. I know how tough addiction can be, at least, how tough I picture it to be, and once he quit, he quit for good."

"Well, here's to your pop," Ron says as he raises his glass.

"Do you play the horses?" Ron asks.

"You know I didn't for a few years. But I've been staying down in Southern California for the spring and summer, and have been playing the races at Santa Anita and Del Mar. Got my tits kicked in on Saturday," I say as I take the cherry off the spear in my drink.

"Yeah, I'm going to go play some of the races tomorrow in the sports book, and then we fly back up to Seattle on Tuesday," Ron says.

"Nice," I say as I sip my grenadine-laced beverage.

The vibrator in my right pocket starts to shake and I stand up quickly, grabbing my drink.

"Mr. Grayton it was really cool to talk to you. Maybe I'll meet up with you in the sports book tomorrow," I say as I shake the man's hand again.

Sitting down in the 10/20 game, I buy in for two racks of red chips, an even thousand dollars. I don't plan on playing long enough to lose that much money, but I've always been a believer in buying in for a large chip stack to at least give the other players the impression that, not only do I mean business, but that the money isn't an object to me. The games on a Sunday night are always a lot tougher than the games on Fridays or Saturdays because all of the tourists who come down to Vegas for the weekend have flown home. Sunday you get the old snow birds and Vegas residents, poker pro's, and some California folks who are going to head back to Los Angeles in the morning. After a few hands, I realize my table is full of tight players who would rather have you pull out their teeth than give you their money via a poker hand.

Within forty-five minutes, I've already donated a couple hundred to the game before I get myself involved in a big pot. It was raised a couple of times before the first three cards came down. And I had three of a kind right off the bat, when the two queens in my hand found their third sister on the flop. The pot was bet, raised, and raised again before it got to me. Sitting on "the nuts" and having your bet raised is a great feeling. Fourth Street brought a second club, but there were no real straights on the board, and if the board pairs, I've probably got an unbeatable hand. After a round of betting and calls, there's probably about seven-hundred dollars in the pot. A three of clubs comes on the last card, and while it brings the possibility of a flush out there, I'm pretty sure I still have the best hand. I bet the limit of twenty bucks on that round, and just two people to my left, an elderly man in a flannel shirt and a red Colorado Belle Casino hat, raises the bet to forty dollars.

"Fuck," I say as I drop my head.

"Sir, please watch your language," the dealer says looking in my direction.

"My apologies. I call the bet."

The old man as expected turns over an ace and a seven of clubs to make a flush, which beats my three of a kind. The old man scoops the pot that has to be somewhere in the neighborhood of eight hundred bucks, with probably two hundred and fifty of it my fucking money.

"I gotta get out of here," I say as I pack up my remaining few stacks of chips.

I head out to the Let it Ride table, which is essentially a poker game where you play against the house. There are two people already sitting there when I join the game. One an older man in his sixties, the other a forty-something-year-old Persian guy with one of those thin pervy mustaches.

"It's a ten-dollar table sir, and a five-dollar

optional bonus play," the dealer says. The dealer is probably one of the more friendly dealers you'll find around. Gregarious and quick with a witty joke, or observation, he's essentially the polar opposite of any racetrack teller I've ever made a bet with.

"Well, you gotta play the bonus right?" I rhetorically say to the table.

"Eh. I never play bonus," the Persian guy says looking down at his remaining chips.

Within a few hands, I'm down sixty bucks, and looking for my first winner, when I grab my three dealt cards and see a nine, ten, and queen of hearts.

"I'll see one card," I say as the dealer leaves my first bet out on the table.

An eight of hearts comes down, giving me a flush draw, a straight draw, and a straight flush draw if the one remaining card to come out is a jack of hearts. With my three ten-dollar bets out there, and the five-dollar bonus play, I take a long look at the dealer who gets ready to turn over the final card.

"Jack of hearts would be nice," I say.

"Oh yeah?" the dealer says with a smile.

He reaches into the dealer's shoe and pulls out the final card, turns it over, and I immediately see the red corners. The flip of that card probably took half a second, but once I saw red, it seemed to move in slow motion. The more he kept turning the card, the more I noticed lots of paint in the middle of the card. The jack of hearts hits the deck and the table erupts.

"Hell yes!" I say as I stand up in excitement.

"What you get? Flush?" the Persian asks.

The dealer grabs my three cards and exposes the fact that I just hit a straight flush, the second highest possible hand a player can get. My eyes dart straight towards the odds placard on the side of the table, and I see 50/1 next to the words "Straight Flush." Fifty-to-one on thirty dollars is fifteen-hundred bucks, plus five-hundred-to-one on the five-dollar bonus bet is a total of four thousand bucks.

Trip paid for.

It took about fifteen minutes to get all the IRS paperwork sorted out before I finally get handed eight pink $500 chips. I leave after tipping the dealer two-hundred dollars in cash, and head to the cashier's cage to collect my winnings. As I'm riding in the cab back to the Luxor, I see a few missed texts from Maria.

"Hey. How's Vegas?"

"Give me a buzz if you get a chance."

"Hope you're having fun!"

Upon getting back to the Luxor, and plopping down on my bed, I call Maria.

"Hey sweetie. How were the races today?" I ask.

"Hey. They were fine," she says sounding half asleep. "Vinny Shyster had three winners today, so that tells you what kind of day it was."

"Crazy shit happening at the track, huh?"

"Yeah, I suppose so. How was your day?" she asks.

"You know, I had an amazing day. I got here, fell asleep by the pool, and, I look like a lobster from the neck down. But I made some money at the tables. Enough to pay for the trip."

"Well, you still have a couple days to blow that money back," she says.

"You smartass," I reply laughing, fully knowing she's a hundred percent right. "Get some sleep. We can talk more tomorrow. Okay?"

"Goodnight, Portland."

20

THERAPEUTIC PROVIDERS

I spent all day Monday walking around Vegas, visiting the mall at Caesar's Palace, and stopping by the sports book at the Mirage to visit with Mr. Grayton for a few minutes. The Mirage sports book is one of my favorite places in Vegas. All the odds for every game, and every sport, are up in lights on the wall. There are literally hundreds of screens with every game going on. I decided against any gambling today, and instead chose to treat myself to an in-room massage. Most people would call the spa downstairs, or look online for a masseuse, but I go to the "Therapeutic Providers" section of my trusty Craigslist.

Relaxation in your Hotel Room—$100

I click the link, and am greeted by a picture of a lovely woman. A bit older than the thirty-five years she claims in her posting. She's a voluptuous looking lady with a large bust. I'm hoping that her therapeutic services will include some hand-to-penis therapy. I dial the number and she answers after the first ring.

"Yeah, I wanted to see about the massage service," I state in a quiet voice, as if the people in the next room can hear what I'm saying. Sometimes I think the shady part of these interactions is half of the turn on.

"Sure, sweetheart. Where are you at?"

"I'm at the Luxor. Room six nineteen."

"Okay. I'm right down the street. How long do you need? I can be there in ten minutes," she says.

"I'm ready when you are."

As I hang up the phone, I'm greeted by the background picture on my phone's screen—a shot of Maria and I posing together on the beach. Even though I'm dating the most beautiful girl I've ever been with, my desire for cheap companionship always seems to win out. Even when there's just a couple of days to get through. Sometimes I think I get off on fucking up my life. Failure has its own addictive quality.

A soft knock at the door comes just fifteen

minutes later, and I spring to my feet to answer. A woman much larger than the one in the picture, but facially resembling her, is standing in front of me. I don't hesitate to have her to come in.

"So, it's one hundred for the massage, and are you wanting to provide a tip?" she asks as she sits on the bed.

"Yeah, I suppose, I thought it was all inclusive," I say confused. Funny, I figured a hundred bucks for probably thirty minutes of work was a pretty damn good tip.

"Well, for an extra sixty I'll do a hand finish, eighty and I'll take my top off for the finish, and for a hundred it's a blowjob with a condom."

"Let's do the eighty-dollar tip," I say as I start to get undressed.

"You make yourself comfortable. I'm going to go use the bathroom," she says.

Sitting on the bed with an awkward boner, waiting for the naughty massage lady, is quite an uplifting and self-esteem enhancing situation. Or not. I'm tempted to be an asshole, and ask her to clap her hands while she's in the bathroom, so I'll know she's not stealing anything. She stays in the bathroom for what feels like an eternity, even though it's more likely about a minute and a half. When she comes back out, her top is off, and her massive cucumber, toothpaste-tube looking breasts are hanging out. She sits down on the bed, straddles me, and begins to give me probably the most amateur back rub in the history of $180 back rubs. Within probably fifteen minutes, she asks me to turn over. She begins to tease my inner thighs, and all the area around my exposed, quickly engorging, self. She gently dips one of her pontoon breasts down into my face, so I can take her nipple into my mouth. She begins to stroke me, and pulls back quickly to grab some of her massage oil. Within about two minutes of performing her right-handed task, she takes a deep and annoyed breath.

"Are you gonna cum, or what?" she asks.

"Sorry. I take a while," I reply. Pardon me for not being a two-pump chump with such an eager and hot mess of a masseuse.

"Well, if it's more than another minute or so,

you'll have to do it yourself," she says. Her jaded perspective, and lack of customer service, isn't exactly a great way to conduct her illegal business. In a place like Vegas, however, where ninety percent of the customers are out-of-town folks, she really doesn't have to worry about repeat business. About forty-five seconds later, she stops and grabs her shoulder as if it's sore from the taxing duty she'd been contracted to perform.

"You're on your own sweetie," she says as she sits there, waiting for me to commence my self-gratification.

"You know what? Just leave. I don't want someone with such a shitty attitude around me," I say as I sit up.

"What the fuck is your problem?" she says as she puts her shirt on.

"My problem is I just gave you a hundred and eighty fucking dollars, and you're acting like it's a fucking chore to jerk my dick for three fucking minutes. Get the fuck out of here."

She grabs her stuff, grabs her money, and heads out of the door. It's likely many of her work endeavors have ended in similar style. But she's off to do whatever it is that a back and whack masseuse does in their free time with their newfound cash.

I spend all of Tuesday and Wednesday walking around Vegas, playing some small money blackjack, and even going to a movie at the Rio Hotel. I did sit back in the 10/20 game for a while on Wednesday afternoon, but the daytime crowd during the week in Vegas consists of a bunch of rock players. Weekend poker in Vegas you play against drunks, tourists, and guys who've been watching poker on ESPN, and think they are ready to take on the pros of Las Vegas. They aren't. I'm certainly no pro, but I fancy myself a decent enough card player, when I'm not on tilt. Patience has never been my most redeeming quality, and unfortunately for me, in poker, patience is an absolute must. Within a few rounds of playing, I take a tough beat on a good size pot, and find myself calling with bad hands looking to get even. As if by divine intervention, my phone begins vibrating. It's Maria calling. I fold my shitty cards, get up, and walk away from the table to take her call.

"Hey sweetie," I answer.

"Hey. How goes Vegas?"

"It's going well. I went and saw that new Tom Hanks movie last night. It kind of sucked," I say.

"Yeah, it looks pretty bad. But he's so cute and sweet."

"So, what's up?" I ask.

"Nothing. Just bored, and wishing you were here. This apartment is kind of depressing. Plus, I have to start packing up my stuff and getting ready to go back to LA on Monday," she says. "Are you going to stay with me in LA?"

"Well, I had planned on just going back to the Motel 6 next to the track again," I say. "I mean, I have to leave for Portland right after the Breeders' Cup. Like literally the next morning, because I still have to find a new place up there."

"Oh. Okay," she says with surprise and disappointment in her voice.

"I mean, I'd like to, and I will, I'd just figured it was kind of temporary, since Del Mar was so short, and it wasn't your actual house. I don't know. I mean, I really like you, and I'd love to keep seeing you, and talking with you. It's just going to be tough when I live in Portland six months a year, ya know?"

"I'm not asking you to marry me or anything like that," she says. "I just figured, since we've been staying together, that we could keep doing it."

"Well, I'm down for it as well. I just need to make sure I really dedicate a lot of time to the races, and towards the Breeders' Cup. That's going to be my chance to make some big money."

"So, you're telling me that you're more worried about gambling then hanging out with me? If that's the case, then I can leave you alone," she says, clearly irritated.

"No, no, that's not what I meant," I say scrambling. "I just need to focus. So I don't want to be distracted."

"Don't you think that if ever there was a girl who'd understand the need to handicap races, it would be me?" she says.

"Good point," I say, laughing. "Well, let's

give it a try. I'll just meet you in Los Angeles, though, because I think I'm going to stay here an extra day or two. And honestly, Del Mar can kiss my ass!"

"Well, let's give it a try," she says.

"See you then," I say.

21

CAL EXPO

Upon returning to Los Angeles, I stop at the In-N-Out Burger on Radford Street to enjoy a Double-Double before heading to Maria's place. I've been living out of big garbage sacks that I brought from Portland, and other than my laptop, and some books I bought over the summer, I haven't added a lot of stuff to my list of personal possessions. Most of my stuff is still in a storage locker in Portland, from when I moved in with Michelle.

September in Los Angeles is like July or August in Portland. It's eighty degrees most days, and people walk around in shorts and flip-flops. I pull into Maria's apartment, grab my plastic bags and backpack, and head into the building. It's a two-story apartment building, with a small gate and talk box for visitors who need to be buzzed in. She already gave me her code, and as I walk in, I admire the well-kept grounds and bushes that adorn the front entryway. After passing through a small tunnel, there's a pool and sunning area surrounded by another small gate to keep the unsupervised children from drowning. Maria's located on the ground floor, number 12, adjacent to the pool. Her door is slightly ajar and music is coming out of the apartment.

"Hello," I say as I knock and push the door open.

Maria is standing at the sink finishing up some dishes. She's wearing yoga pants and a tank top, and her tall, curvy figure cuts an amazing profile.

"Hey," I say a little louder, trying to cut through the music.

"Hey, baby," she says, turning her neck and smiling, as I walk behind her and plant a kiss on her cheek.

"Did you have a good drive?"

"I did. But I'm friggin exhausted. What are you up to for the rest of the day?" I ask.

"Well, I have to finish the laundry, and then my friend Cara has a bachelorette party tonight, so we're going out to dinner, and then dancing. I shouldn't be out too late. You can just hang around here or whatever. The extra key is in the junk drawer over there."

Cara works at the track in the television department, and there's an old saying in racing —Monday is Saturday. Racing's one of the few industries where most of the people working in it look forward to Mondays. Cara's isn't the first Monday night bachelorette party I've heard of.

"Honestly, I'll probably just stick around here tonight, and start looking at Santa Anita's opening day," I say.

With Maria out of the house for the evening, I spent the afternoon napping, and then broke open the *Racing Form* to start looking at Santa Anita's opening day card for Wednesday. Upon flipping around Maria's television channels, I settle on TVG, which is an all-horse-racing channel. Since it's a Monday, there isn't much big-time racing going on, just some harness tracks, as well as Mountaineer in West Virginia and Delta Downs in Louisiana.

The host is a young guy named Johnny who's

a very thinly built, excited young man. He's got an Eddie Munster type widow's peak spiked hairdo and displays a big smile during the entire broadcast. I've met some of the TVG guys from my previous trips down to Los Angeles. But Johnny is one I haven't had the pleasure of chatting with.

One night at Los Alamitos, which is the Quarter Horse track in Orange County that's on the same street as Disneyland, I hit a Pick 6 bet. I went on TVG before the races as a special guest along with the hosts, Ron and Joe, and we talked about my race calling and the races in general. Before I got off the set, they asked me for my picks for the night at Los Alamitos, and I told them that I was going after the Pick 6. I was going to play a twenty-four-dollar ticket, and TVG even posted it online, similar to how they do for their other talent who give out their Pick 6 or Pick 4 plays. By the time the night was ending, I had nailed the first five races, and returned to the TVG set to brag and watch the final race of the night. When another favorite came back, the payout after the race went official was seventy-six dollars. We all had a good laugh at the entire situation, and the TVG crew busted my chops for being a chalk hound, someone who picks a lot of favorites.

I decide to do something I've managed to avoid all summer as well as for the last two years. I head to www.betthehorses.com to play the races online, and deposit three-hundred bucks into my old account. I'm off and running, playing the races at Mountaineer and Delta, and based on Maria's recommendation, I ordered a pizza from Tortelli's down the street.

Within an hour, the pizza arrives, and most of my initial deposit is gone. One of the problems with the online betting for me is that there aren't the distractions of chatting with other people, visiting the paddock, or any of the other fun things you can do at the track. I go to the account services section of my online account and pump another three hundred in there. Instead of wasting time chipping away at the first three hundred I lost, I immediately put a hundred bucks on a horse named I Must Geaux at Delta Downs. I Must Geaux breaks slowly, can't overcome that early trouble, and finishes fourth as the favorite. With just two minutes until the next race at Mountaineer, Johnny has been touting the number-five horse for the last couple of minutes, and is even singling that horse in his Pick 4 at Mountaineer. I click the "Wager Now" button and put my remaining two hundred to win on the five, who's named Snowbound Hero. He's 2/1, so a win would put me back at about six hundred in the online bankroll, which is exactly where I started.

"They're off and racing. And, oh, there's a stumble at the start, and Snowbound Hero has unseated jockey T.R. Irwin."

I'm irate but simply drop my head between my legs as I sit on the couch. For a horse to be eligible for a win, horse and rider must cross the wire in front as a team. So, with T.R. Irwin sitting on the ground in front of the starting gate, and Snowbound Hero continuing on running without his rider, my bet is toast.

"Are you fucking kidding me?" I say out loud, shaking my head.

Instead of taking a break or quitting, this is

where my compulsivity creeps in, because there is no going back from here. I go online and put in five-hundred dollars this time, and immediately look for the next race going off. It's getting late and there are only three tracks still running. Delta has one left, Mountaineer still has three races left, and Cal Expo Harness, the track I visited in Sacramento a few months back, is just beginning their program.

I've been on tilt while playing online far too many times to count. About three years ago, just before I met Michelle, I was down in Redding, California, of all places to visit a girl. I met the girl on Craigslist, of course, and after chatting and e-mailing for a few weeks, and talking on the phone for several hours each night, we decided to meet up. She lived in San Luis Obispo, California, and Redding was halfway between the two of us. I rented a room at the Super 8 motel just off the Interstate Five — classy, I know — while she was going to stay with a friend who lived just outside of town. She came to the hotel just before dinner, and we shared one of those awkward hugs people have when they first meet from off the computer. I remember her pictures all showing this outgoing, dare I say "ruckus" girl. And yet, she stood before me meek and scared, albeit donning black leather and lace. We went out for dinner, and then wandered around downtown Redding, the bulging metropolis that it is. We eventually made our way back to the hotel and banged deep into the night. Because she was staying at her friend's house, she had to go home, even though it was well past midnight. I remember driving out into the middle of fucking no where California, thinking this was probably where my life comes to an end, because these are the roads that slashers prey on.

The next morning we were going to meet for lunch before hanging out for the rest of the afternoon and evening. I got up early and started playing the races from Aqueduct, Gulfstream, and all the other big East Coast tracks that run during the morning on the West Coast. Within a couple of hours, I had blown twelve-hundred dollars, and I was so pissed off and angry, I lied to the girl, and said I felt sick and needed to go home. I left this poor girl sitting alone at IHOP. After driving four-hundred miles to meet her, and having a great time with her, I was so disgusted with the idea of having to be happy, and wanting to enjoy her company, that I just left and drove back to Portland. I did of course grab an In-N-Out burger before heading back.

Continuing playing the races on TVG, I just keep firing and missing. I drop three hundred more before getting down to my last two hundred of the night. There are no more races left at Delta or Mountaineer, so it's just Cal Expo left. The good news is that, at worse, I can only lose every thirty minutes now, instead of every five or ten when the other tracks were going. It's getting past nine thirty when Cal Expo's late Pick 4 starts, with a guaranteed pool of twenty-five-thousand dollars. I put together a one-hundred-and-ninety-two-dollar ticket with four horses in the first three legs, and three horses in the last event. The first leg of the sequence I hit a 3/1 winner, and I'm off and running. My account is tapped out, so from here on, I have to sit back, and just watch and wait. Leg two brings with it a huge upset, when an 18/1 runner named Al B. Fit gets up and wins after the big favorite broke stride in mid-stretch.

"Now we're fucking talking!" I say as I get up to refill my ice water. Sometimes sitting down and letting the adrenaline flow through me, without getting up, can lead to the adrenaline taking over and sending me over the edge into a fit of panic. I've learned to try and get clarity away from the computer and the gambling. As I stand, I feel a little light-headed, so I go outside to get some air. Sometimes, in the midst of a gambling rush like this, it's easy to not read the signs my body is telling me—that maybe this isn't the best idea, or that I need to take it easy. Plus, I can rest in forty-five minutes after I hit this bet. I've noticed my anxiety disorder flaring up more often in recent weeks, but I seem to be able to calm myself by getting some fresh air, taking a walk, or just laying down.

Upon collecting my breath and heading back

inside, I sit down to watch the third leg of the Pick 4. I've got four runners in it, the top four favorites in the race. I didn't handicap the sequence at all, just picked a couple of morning line favorites, and a couple of decent price horses in each leg. The fact that I hit Al B. Fit was strictly luck, as the morning line maker had him at 6/1, and he floated all the way up to his long shot price of 18/1. If he had been 15/1 or 20/1 on the morning line, then I would have never even given him a second look.

The horses sprint out from behind the gate, and as they reach midway down the backstretch, the lock on the door shimmies and Maria walks in.

"Hey, sweetheart," I say, taking my eyes off of the television screen for a split second to at least give her the courtesy of some eye contact with my greeting.

"How's your night been?" she asks with wide grin.

"Oh fine. You were right. That Tortelli's is fucking great pizza. I ate more than half of it. There's some left if you want it, in the fridge."

Maria rushes over and lays a kiss on me. But not just any normal "Hey. How ya doin? Haven't seen you in five hours" kiss. She buries her tongue into my mouth, and I can immediately taste the tequila from the margaritas she's probably been pounding all night with her girlfriends.

"Well, to what do I owe that?" I ask, smiling, as she stumbles back to an upright position, and I lean back on the couch.

"I have to pee," she says as she heads into the bathroom.

"And it's Downtown Bound who wins it by a nose."

It was the seven horse that won the third leg, and at 6/1, he was the longest price horse of the four runners I played. Now I know this ticket is going to pay if I can get one of these final three horses home in the last leg. It was going to pay well regardless of who won the third race because of the big long shot earlier, but this just knocked out a number of the remaining live tickets.

Maria comes back into the room and plops

down on the couch with me, her head in my lap, as I gently stroke her hair and listen as she talks about the party. Maria gently rubs my leg as she tells of the dancing, and how her friend Cara, who is the one getting married, got so drunk that she fell doing a spin on the dance floor. I'm trying to do my best job of fake listening, as I'm really trying to keep an eye on the odds board at Cal Expo. Maria starts to creep her hand up my leg until her long fingers grace my quickly engorging self. Please don't get hard. Please don't get hard. Just wait till this next race is over. Shit.

"Let's go over to the bed. I want to play," she says.

"I don't know sweetie, I'm kind of tired," I say, hoping to put it off for at least eight more minutes until the race starts. But the rigid rocket in my shorts is a dead giveaway that this is happening.

"Please, I really want you right now," she says.

Knowing it's probably in my best interests to give in to her request, I reluctantly agree. At least some common sense part of my brain gave me the proper instruction that a fucking hot sweet girl wants to ride me right now. We rush over to the bed. Maria immediately takes off her dress, and leaves on her bra and panties. Her ass. I love her ass. She's what people would call voluptuous. I just call her perfect. I lie down, and she quickly whips my pants down and begins to go down on me as I lay my head on the pillows. Looking as much over her shoulder towards the television as I am looking at the top of her head as it bobs up and down, I'm thinking, maybe she'll keep doing this for ten minutes till the race is over. Damn, here she comes. She kisses her way up my stomach and plants one on me. It's always strange when one partner is really drunk and horny, and one is sober and moderately distracted. Inevitably, the drunk person is going to get a lame lay. But the good news is they are usually so hammered, and horned up, that any fucking will suffice.

She climbs her way up on top of me. Because of some of the anxiety medications I take, achieving orgasm, even with someone as sexy as

Maria, isn't always a two pump and done situation. I can't tell you how many times I've wanted to just scream out loud at myself to "hurry the fuck up." Three minutes into her riding me, I can hear Johnny, the third member of this little threesome, in the background on the television.

"Let's go out to Brad Earline with the call of the final race from Cal Expo. Good luck if you're one of the lucky few still alive in that Pick 4."

Even though I've spent my career memorizing the names of horses, I didn't get a chance to see what the names are of the horses I'm live to on my ticket. In an act of desperation, or maybe quick thinking, I suggest that Maria get on her knees so I can enter her from behind. I know that is her favorite position, and her eyes light up at the suggestion. She immediately slides off of me and gets on all fours.

I get up on my knees and gently grab her hips with my hands. Aside from this allowing me to give her the pleasure she wants, I've put myself into a position to watch the race, which is now halfway over. Two birds. One stone. I'm live to the three, four, and seven. And the three is out on the lead going well. The four is second, and the seven is fourth but doesn't look to be in any kind of trouble. As the field turns into the stretch, my first two horses, the three and four, both take off for home. My Pick 4 bet is looking better and better with each and every stride, but as the field nears the final one hundred yards, the eight horse starts to rally up from third. I fixate on the eight who starts to run after the three, and it's going to be desperately close as the finish line looms. Most players will try and will their horse to the finish line. All I could think of in that moment was how badly I wanted the eight to stop gaining ground. Just get tired you son of a bitch. In my haste, I stopped any pumping action towards Maria, and within about three seconds of me limping up inside her, she turns her head around without saying anything, and sees that I'm only concerned with the television.

"What the fuck are you doing?" she says as she looks at the television, realizing I'm watching the race.

"Are you fucking serious?" Maria says as she leaps forward and off of the bed.

"What? Sorry, I just looked away for a second," I plead.

Maria looks two hundred different shades of pissed. Add into the mix that she's enjoyed a couple of cocktails, and I know this isn't going to play out especially great.

"Cal Fucking Expo!" she shouts at me. "You'd rather bet on Cal Fucking Expo than fuck me. You are fucking sick."

"I didn't even have a bet down," I say as I sit back on the bed, taking a very defensive position.

Maria walks over to my computer and touches the mouse pad, which turns off the screen saver and reveals that my online wagering platform is indeed logged in, and that the odds board is fixed on Cal Expo. Motherfucking MacBook, and motherfucking me for not setting a security password. That stupid computer has fucked me more than any girl recently.

"What the fuck is this then?" she asks.

"I bet the Pick 4, and that was the last leg. I wanted to watch the race," I say. Maybe being honest will fetch her understanding.

"Well, how about maybe, 'Hey Maria, I'd like to watch this race. Do you mind?' Get the fuck out of my house. You make me sick. You're a fucking degenerate gambler. I should have known the first day I met you. Who fucking thinks they are going to make a living betting the horses. Get the fuck out of here. Grab your shit and leave, you sorry-ass motherfucker."

"You're overreacting sweetheart," I say trying to reason with her.

"No, I'm not," she says. "Please just leave. I don't want you here right now."

"You're going to break up with me for betting? What the fuck?"

"I just don't want you here right now," she says as she puts her shirt back on. "Time and time again you've shown you care more about betting than you do about anything else. And I can't play second-fiddle to a fucking game. Because, I know how this game is going to end. Please just grab your shit and leave."

"Can we at least talk about this? It was stupid," I say as I close my laptop, because staring at that fucking Cal Expo betting menu that just told on me is like salt in an open wound.

"Just leave. Go back to the Motel. We'll talk about it later. I just don't want to see you right now."

"Fine."

I grab my clothes that are still resting in my garbage sack, fire the computer in there, and head out. In the background, I can hear Johnny giving out the results from Cal Expo.

"And look at that Pick 4 at Cal Expo with the three just hanging on. Thirty-five-hundred bucks for every dollar wager."

My frustration over Maria's reaction is somehow slightly relieved by the fact that I just got back into the black for the day, up now twenty four hundred after being stuck eleven hundred just an hour and a half ago.

"I really think you're overreacting," I say as I come to the door with my bag in hand. "I think you're drunk, and you're overreacting."

"Maybe I am. But, you make me feel bad. And I don't want to be around someone who makes me feel bad."

22

ATIVAN

Driving away from Maria's house with only one place I can think to go, I head east towards Santa Anita to the Motel 6. I flip my satellite radio to the Howard Stern channel, trying to distract myself from what I'm feeling. Confused, irritated, and pissed off to be frank. Maria overreacted. All I was doing was stopping for five seconds to watch the end of the race. She works in horse racing. She should understand the importance of a bet, especially one where serious money is up for grabs. That thing paid over three-thousand bucks. How can she get mad at me for paying attention to the final one-hundred yards of a race that was going to yield me what most Americans make in a month?

Upon arriving back at the Motel 6, I'm pleased to see the same young lady working at the counter who had been there during my first stay. With just three weeks left until the

Breeders' Cup, and until I have to leave, I book the room until the day after the Breeders' Cup, which will be the end of my time down south.

"You'll be in room 207, that's up the stairs and around the back," the young desk clerk says.

"Do you have anything on the first floor?"

"Not for tonight, but we will tomorrow if you want to move in the early afternoon."

"Yeah, I'll do that," I say as I sign the receipt.

I decide to leave the thirty-two hundred that I won earlier in the evening in my online account. I figure I'll play a little bit online, make some bets on there, and not bring as much cash to the track. Since I've got about fourteen thousand in cash left, I figure if the three grand in my online account can last me for the rest of the trip, then I can head back to Portland with that fourteen thousand, plus the eleven thousand still in my bank account. Twenty-five thousand would be more than enough to head back up north with. To be down only six-thousand bucks for five months of what was essentially a vacation sounds pretty good.

Jason Beem

I spend the night debating on what I'm going to say to Maria when I see her next. Other than "I'm sorry" about seventy times. Surely, I'm going to see her, as she's in the paddock area each race. However, I can avoid her easily if I just stay away from the paddock.

I got up early and head back to the barn area on my first morning back at Santa Anita. The atmosphere is a little different than I had remembered from the spring. With the Breeders' Cup just a few weeks away, many new trainers from back East are sending their best runners over early to get acclimated to the track. There are photographers from the *Daily Racing Form* as well as many other racing publications from not just around the United States but from the foreign press as well. I walk back to Mahoney's barn to check in with him and see how the big mare is doing. As I walk into the barn, I hear Mahoney singing along to an old Merle Haggard song playing on the stereo.

"Mahoney. How're you doing my man?" I say as I duck my head into the stall that Mahoney is mucking out.

363

"Ryan. Where the hell you been the last week? I figured after the Pacific Classic you might have headed home."

"You can't get rid of me that easily," I say. "I'm going to stick around for the Breeders' Cup, and then I'm out of here. Gonna head back to Portland. We're opening up the Saturday after the Cup races. Which race you gonna run Mondatta in?

"I thought I told you—the Classic," Mahoney says with a smile that I can't decipher as fake or genuine.

"Are you really going to run her against Rturntoserve?" I ask.

"Actually yes," Mahoney says as he puts his shovel down and starts to exit the stall. "She wants the longer distance, and with a big full field, I think someone is finally going to push that Rturntoserve. And we're going to be the one to pick his ass up and take home that three-million-dollar winner's share."

"Well, I hope you're right John. Where is the big mare? I want to go pet her."

"Just two stalls down," Mahoney says

pointing to the right. "But, don't give her any carrots. She still has to work this morning. She was supposed to go workout before the break, but that fucking agent Domino got his riders mixed up."

"Did you fire Camillo from the horse?" I ask.

"You saw that ride last time out," Mahoney says as he throws another bale of hay into the next stall. "I can't have someone making bad decisions like that when the big money is on the line. My share of the winner's share in the Breeders' Cup is three-hundred thousand. Three-hundred grand. That's enough for me to send both my kids to college and pay off my mortgage. Plus, I'd probably get some great new clients because I'd be getting my name out there. We're going to have Juarez ride her. He already knows we're going in the Classic, and he's the best rider available. I'm going to go nominate her for the Classic, and the Distaff, and we'll surprise them all on the morning of the draw."

"No shit. Well, I'm rooting for her, you know that," I say.

I walk over to Mondatta's stall and give her

a quick pat on the front of her face. She's got her warm-up saddle and headgear on, as she's going to be heading out the track soon, but she's not her usual fired up self. She's very sweet and loving. Far from her usual fired up way of being when she's getting ready to run.

"She seems kind of docile today, John," I say.

"You know, she's just getting a little sweeter as she gets older," Mahoney says. "I think this summer was big for her. She really figured out the game. Watch though, in ten minutes when she goes out, she'll be all business and fired up."

As morning turns to late morning, I spend a couple of hours back at the Motel 6, taking a nap before heading out to the races for the afternoon. I make some of my bets, including my large Pick 4 play for the day, a $450 ticket, on my online account. I'm still going to bring cash to the track just in case my online bets don't prove as prosperous as I hope.

Upon arrival for the races, I'm pleasantly surprised at the crowd that has chosen to attend the opening day of the Santa Anita Fall

Championship Meet. It's a weekday, and it's 1 p.m., so one would think most of the working population would be at their jobs. But it appears many took the afternoon off to come bathe in the Southern California sunshine and enjoy a day at the races.

Most of the horses who will be running in the Breeders' Cup have already ran their final prep races, so the Fall Meet is made up of mostly claiming races, and the occasional stakes event. Claiming races are the most common type of race, and each horse is for sale for the listed claiming price. It's a way of keeping horses against evenly matched competition. If you put a horse worth $20,000 in a race against $5,000 claiming horses, he's probably gonna win, but you're liable to have him get claimed, or bought, for $5,000.

I've already punched in my early Double and rolling Pick 3's online, and with the big Pick 4 ticket, I'm in well over a thousand dollars total for the day. My day gets off to a poor start when the favorite I wanted to beat in the opener proceeded to jump out to the front and never look back, destroying not only his competition, but my early Double and Pick 3 in the process. By the time the fifth race of the day rolls around, I haven't cashed a single ticket. I'm down over five hundred bucks and my Pick 4 is just about to start. I've been hearing Maria over the loudspeaker all day, but have yet to visit the paddock, trying to respect her wishes that she probably doesn't want to see me. I know that I'm going to eventually have to go back to the paddock to check out the horses in races I'm going to be betting big on, but for now, it's probably better to stay away.

The horses get ready to load for the fifth race, which starts the late Pick 4. I have four of the horses in the nine-horse field. As the horses begin loading into the gate, I stand against the rail, and suddenly have a quick, but potent, moment of worry and dizziness. As I snap my head around to the side and stand up straight, I feel a staggering wave of fear grip my mind, that something is wrong, and that I'm going to fall down. I grab onto the fence and think that I must now escape. Something is not right, and I feel like I'm losing my equilibrium. Fuck. Fuck. Fuck. I check my pulse to find that not only is it still beating, it's beginning to race and pound through my neck. The thought that maybe I'm having a heart attack keeps popping up, as I hear the bell ring to notify that the race is underway.

The urge to flee takes over, so I make a run for it, and get the hell away from the crowd. I take my bottle of water out of my side pocket and promptly dump it down the back of my neck. A little trick I learned once was that cold water on your neck creates a thing called the dive reflex, which is essentially a panic attack in reverse. I've experienced this panic before, and even though I know that simply finding a seat and breathing through it will make the worry and symptoms go away faster, the urge to flee wins out. As it always does.

I walk over to the sidewall of the grandstand and use it to brace myself, as I walk as quickly as possible towards the back gate to try and get to my car. Each step feels as though it's going to be my last and I'll fall down. But, somehow, I stay upright. I make it out back by the paddock, and I can hear the track announcer calling the final strides to the wire. I don't even catch who won the race, as all I'm focused on is getting the hell out of the track and to my car, where I can rest and try and compose myself. As I walk down the back stairs and along the far side of the paddock, I spot a bench next to the famed Seabiscuit statue. As I approach the open space with no wall to brace myself, I instantly feel my heart rate seem to jump up to 200 in a split second. I lunge at the bench, plop down, and try to compose myself and catch my breath. The panic attack is in full swing, and while sitting seems like a good idea at first, all it seems to do is intensify my worry that I'm still not at my car and something is still wrong. Plus, now just standing up again seems scary.

"Security, Security, someone please help," I scream near the top of my lungs. An elderly gentleman hears my calls for help and walks over to flag the security worker who stands near the paddock entrance.

"Please someone help me," I call out again,

feeling as though reality is now slipping from my grasp. Moving from my seat on the bench to the ground, I render myself helpless and out of control of my body. I've reached the point of no return. I'm now resigned to the fact that the medics are the only people taking me out of here. The adrenaline and cortisol are pumping so fast and hard through my veins that I've lost any ability to see straight or stand up properly.

"What seems to be going on sir?" the young security guard asks me as he kneels down to help.

"I think I'm dying. I can't catch my breath, and I can't move," I say in a fit of shallow, rapid breaths.

"Are you having chest pains sir?" the guard asks.

"No. Please get me some help. Call an ambulance."

"One twenty four to hawkeye," the guard says into his walkie-talkie.

"Go one twenty four."

"I'm at the West paddock entrance, and we have a patron complaining of shortness of breath, and requesting help and an ambulance."

"AMR is on their way, one twenty four," says a voice at the other end of the walkie-talkie.

Lying on the ground, I can see out of the corner of my eye that a few patrons have gathered around. I ask the guard if he can ask them to leave. I also see Maria approaching with a look of concern on her face. Great.

"Are you okay, Ryan?" she asks.

"Ma'am, please, just give him some room. He's fine," the guard says.

"I think I'm dying Maria," I say. "I can't breathe, and I can't seem to calm down. I got really dizzy and tried to walk out of the place, but I just couldn't make it."

"You're having a panic attack Ryan," she says as the guard takes out his blood pressure kit to check my levels.

"The panic didn't start until after the dizziness started," I reply, trying to convince her that I am indeed dying. This is it. For God sakes, at least say something profound Maria. "Please get the ambulance here soon. I can't take this."

Maria comes over to the bench I just dropped from, sits down, and rubs my shoulder, trying to get me grounded and to initiate some kind of relaxation. And it actually works a bit.

"I'm so sorry. I'm so sorry," I keep repeating, as my shame just keeps mounting.

"Don't be sorry. Just relax and breathe slowly," she says.

"I can hear the sirens now sir. The ambulance will be here in just a second," the security guard says. "Just keep trying to slow your breathing down. Everything is going to be okay, sir."

Five members of the Arcadia Fire Department, as well as two members of AMR, the ambulance company, walk up to me along with their stretcher.

"Sir, do you think you can stand up and get onto the stretcher?" one of the firemen asks.

"No, I don't think so. Just help me up please," I ask, my speech much more rapid than normal.

"Okay. Grab our hands sir," one fireman says as he offers his hand to me along with another officer. Fuck, this is gonna be bad. I can feel the head rush already.

"And lift," the guard says as both guys pull me up. I take two wobbly, impossible steps over to the stretcher and just plop down onto it.

After they put some ties around my legs, they put the blood pressure sleeve on, and start to check for that as well as my pulse rate.

"One fifty two over eighty. That's a little high. But it's probably the anxiety," the fireman says.

I'm loaded into the back of the ambulance, which is backed up to the track's main entrance. They slam the door shut, and the quiet is instantly deafening. My panic continues in the back of the ambulance, as they start to pull out and head to the nearest hospital. The ride consists of me trying to catch my breath and get some kind of calm restored to my body, while the AMR employee continually asks me questions and gathers my personal information.

"Do you have insurance, Mr. McGuire?" the medic asks.

"No, I don't anymore," I say.

"Okay, that's fine. We should be to the hospital in five minutes or so sir. Just try and relax. All your vital signs look good."

I know that my heart is alright. It's a panic attack. It's always a panic attack. It's another in a long line of freak-outs and runs to the hospital, only to find out that nothing is wrong. I'm honestly surprised it didn't happen sooner on the trip. These attacks seem to come out of the blue, and usually a couple times a year I will have a big blow up like this.

I'm wheeled into the hospital, and I feel about as pathetic as a thirty-two-year-old man can feel. All the young nurses are looking at me, while the oldest nurse of the bunch tells the medics to take me into room twenty-three. The doctor comes in, and after talking to me for a bit, agrees it's a panic attack and nothing else is wrong. They give me an EKG just to make sure that it's nothing serious like a heart attack. My chest hair has permanent shortages in the spots where they put those little sticky EKG things on, just cause it seems once every few months I'm getting one.

Within an hour of arriving, the attack from my adrenal glands seems to have fully dissipated. Thanks, Ativan. The inevitable anxiety hangover has set in, for as awful as a panic attack is, the post anxiety hangover is about as blissfully tired as a person can feel. While waiting between nurse and doctor visits in my room, I check my phone to see that the big Pick 4 ticket I played died a painful death in the second leg when a 30/1 shot somehow snuck in to win.

"Mr. McGuire, you have a visitor. A Ms. Martinez," the nurse says.

"Yeah, let her in," I say as I straighten my gown and cover my pale white legs with the blanket.

"How you feeling?" she asks as she comes in and sits down. "You scared the shit out of me."

"Why aren't you still at the track?" I ask.

"I told my boss that my boyfriend was at the hospital, and that I needed to leave," she says with a small chuckle.

"Boyfriend huh?"

"Well, I just needed it to sound serious

enough to get out of there. But I'm still not sold on the boyfriend thing right now," she confidently shoots back.

"I was just clarifying the situation," I say.

"Look, I think you're a good guy. You're usually quite sweet, and I enjoy being around you. But you have a serious gambling problem. I've dated guys with issues like this before, and I can't be a second fiddle. I can't be the fall back in case your gambling goes bad. I can't sleep with you, and worry that you're trying to hear the television, or you're worried about some bet that's still live. I can't do that. But I can be here to help you, and be your friend."

Fuck. My eyes are starting to well up a bit as Maria begins to show emotion of her own.

"So, did they say it was just an anxiety attack?" she asks.

"Yeah, it's always a fucking anxiety attack. My whole adult life has been a series of anxiety attacks. One after the other. Sometimes I just want to stop it all," I say looking down at my lap.

"Don't say things like that. You don't mean

that," she says.

"Can I show you something?" I ask looking back up into her eyes as she nods in approval.

I pull up my gown to show a scar that runs an inch or so on the side of my abdomen.

"Yeah, you said you had surgery for an appendicitis right?" she says, realizing now that I must have lied to her about that as well, because why else would I show it to her now?

"No. I stabbed myself," I say as I run my finger along the three-year-old wound.

"What?"

"I had been on a long gambling binge. I didn't sleep for a few days, and was just out of my mind in tears and loneliness," I say. "I drove to the hospital cause I wanted to get help, but instead I just sat out in the parking lot playing with my old roommate's knife while I cried. Finally, I made the decision I didn't want to live anymore, and I plunged it in as hard as I could. It didn't go that deep, and within a split second, all I could think about was my mom. I couldn't do that to her. I pulled it out, pressed my shirt against the wound, and sprinted into the hospital as fast as I could. Fuck, I even chickened out on killing myself."

"You have to stop with the gambling, get some help, and start being good to yourself," Maria says as she grabs my hand.

"I'm sorry. I know I fucked up," I say. "I'm going to quit. I've quit before and I'll quit again. I just needed a break this summer. I needed to unwind."

"You call this unwinding?" she asks. "Cause it seems like it's making things worse for you than it is making them better."

"I know," I reply. "The Breeders' Cup is in two weeks, and after that, I'm heading home, and going to go back to Gamblers Anonymous meetings, and back to work."

"Maybe it's best for you to go home now and just quit?" she asks.

"Yeah, you're probably right."

"I just don't want you to hurt yourself or lose all your money, you know?" she says. "I mean, you've said when you get upset you go on tilt, and start pissing your money away."

I nod my head in response to her comments. I

know she's right. But just knowing she's right doesn't mean I'm going to do that. It would be quite simple to just pack up and leave, and not gamble anymore. But I've already come to a firm conclusion that I'm staying. I can't leave just a couple weeks before the Breeders' Cup. It's been my final goal since I set out on this trip. Not to mention the fact that I could just as easily bet the races from home, or at Portland Meadows, or at an off-track betting parlor. It's going to happen. Once the train gets going fast enough down the tracks, you don't just stop it. And that's how it is with any addiction, be it coke, heroin, cigarettes, or gambling. Once you have the jones kicking, you're not stopping until you bottom out. Granted bottom and rock bottom are two different places. For some people, bottom can be as simple as realizing that they have a problem, and that it might be in their best interests to stop. For others, it involves an intervention from family and friends who have been negatively affected by the addiction. Most people's bottom usually involves reaching such a level of moral, financial, and emotional bankruptcy, that they cease to function as a proper member of society at large, let alone function as a husband, wife, son, or niece.

My worst bottom ended up consisting of tens of thousands of dollars in debt, inability to get any more credit, lying to family and friends, missing family events, weddings, and school to gamble, as well as pawning and stealing. I pawned so many of my possessions that by the time I did quit, the room that I rented consisted of a bed, a computer, some books, and my clothes. I pawned my drum set for four hundred bucks, even though it was probably worth double that on the open market, and triple that when they were new. But when you need to get a bet down, you're willing to take a bit of a loss to get back into the action.

I pawned countless other musical instruments, my iPad, my iPod, and worst of all, a TAG Heuer watch my mother gave me for my twenty-sixth birthday. I had never been a watch wearer, but because of the thought and price of the gift, and because of the personalized message, I always kept it on. It was something I thought I'd never part with. However, by the time I was nearing my bottom, and had run out of things to sell, I sold it to a buyer from Craigslist for a measly two-hundred dollars. Somewhere in Portland, Oregon, there is a kid whose dad bought him a watch that's engraved "To Ryan, My Favorite Announcer, Love Mom."

Maria stays with me while I talk with the social worker. I eventually get discharged with more Ativan and instructions to return if the symptoms get worse. Maria's kind enough to give me a ride, but she's quiet in the car.

"My car is still at the track. Can you drop me off there?" I ask.

"Yes, I will," she says continuing to look forward.

As we drive through the now empty Santa Anita parking lot, and park alongside my car, I start to gather up my wallet, keys, and cell phone from the hospital bag.

"Thanks for coming. I really appreciate it," I say.

"I'm always here for you. I just want you to find some peace and happiness," she says.

"I know."

23

THURSDAY

The Breeders' Cup is a two-day event that takes place on Friday and Saturday. The girl's races are all on Friday, while the boys all compete against one another on Saturday. It switches locations every year, and this year is being run for the sixth time in its twenty-six year existence at Santa Anita. The first Breeders' Cup was actually held across town at Hollywood Park. I spent the last couple of weeks preparing for the big event by talking to as many trainers as I could, hanging out with the private clockers in the morning, and of course studying the advance copy of the *Racing Form*.

I took the two days before the Breeders' Cup off of betting, as my wagers weren't exactly panning out in previous weeks. My cash bankroll is down to about eight thousand after dropping four thousand over the last week. I had to fight my desires all week. Knowing that I couldn't go into the Breeders' Cup with a small bankroll, I managed to distract myself by going to Disneyland each afternoon. I spent the mornings watching training, clocking workouts, and speaking to the many trainers I've become acquaintances with. Then in the afternoons, I headed down the freeway to Orange County, and spent my time at the ESPN restaurant watching baseball, or just walking around downtown Disney. However, with the Breeders' Cup starting up tomorrow afternoon, I know I must dedicate the day to being at the track. It's important for me to note any potential track biases going into the weekend. Sometimes the track surfaces get groomed a certain way to give favoritism to horses running on the inside, or outside, depending on which part of the track is firmer. I want as much information as possible, and I want to make one more trip back to Mahoney's barn to see how things are with Mondatta.

"John. How's the big mare doing?" As I walk into Mahoney's shed row, I see the trainer feeding his runners some grain.

"As good as can be," he says. "We're going to make some history on Saturday."

"I can't believe you're going to run her against the boys in the Classic," I say.

"She'll be just fine against those big boys," Mahoney replies as he starts to gently pet the horse in front of him. "I really think Alexie Mattosie is going to go early with Rturntoserve, as will Mission Accomplished. It's going to set up perfect, and all she needs is to run her race, stay out in the clear, and we'll be just fine."

"You know John, call me crazy, but I really do think she has a big shot," I say. "I'm going to use her and Rturntoserve in the Classic on my tickets. Especially in the Pick 6. I really love a couple of long shots earlier on in the card, so I think it could pay huge."

"Who you like in the races tomorrow?" Mahoney asks me.

"I've got a few choices, but I really think that Sister Susie is going to run huge in the Distaff. I mean Mondatta would be a huge favorite in that race, I can't believe you aren't running her in there," I say again.

"Well, Mr. Warren is a sporting owner, and I can think of five million reasons not run her in there and run in the Classic," Mahoney says as he pours grain into his horse's bucket. "Plus, second place in the Classic pays essentially the same as first place in the Distaff, and I think we've got a big shot at the top spot."

"I hope you're right my friend."

I take in the races on Thursday afternoon, but spend the afternoon casually watching while reading the *Form*s for Friday and Saturday. The track seems to be playing fair for the most part, as horses on Thursday are winning from on the lead or from behind. Some are winning on the rail, and some are coming down the outside. In between each race on Thursday, horses for the big races on the weekend can be seen coming over the paddock to school and get comfortable with their surroundings. Some of the European horses look like absolute monsters of horseflesh. Chiseled with muscles that look as though they were cut from stone, the European runners primarily come over for the grass races.

However, one of them, Mysteriano, will be in the Classic against Mondatta, Rturntoserve, Choctaw Nation, and many of the other top horses in the world.

I see Maria as I'm walking out, and when her eyes meet mine, I shoot her a small smile, but keep on walking. I know she's thinking that I shouldn't be here, so no reason to go have an awkward "stop and chat," or get a lecture that I don't want to hear. I know that I need to keep my emotions in check, at least for the next couple of days.

Upon arriving back at the Motel 6, I order in a pie from Johnny's Pizza in Arcadia and put on a movie. One of my traditions before big racing days is to watch the 80's horseracing movie *Let It Ride*. Usually I reserve it for the night before opening day at Portland Meadows, or before the Kentucky Derby. But these next two days will likely be the biggest betting days of my career. Plus, it's a story about a guy who has a really good day at the track, and ends up making half a million bucks when every race he plays, he hits. Here's hoping some of the magic will rub off. I feel strong with my selections and bets. I've allocated three thousand for Friday's races, and five thousand for Saturday's card. If I lose every bet then I'll be going home with nothing but the eleven thousand in my bank account. Truthfully, though, I never expected to head home with any more than that anyway.

As *Let It Ride* ends, I peer over at the digital clock on the nightstand to see that it's just shy of ten o'clock. Feeling a little cabin fever from being holed up the last few hours, I head out for a walk. I venture across the street and walk along the backstretch at Santa Anita. Taking a seat on a little hill behind the track, I sit, take some deep breaths, and admire the majesty of Santa Anita dimly lit from the moonlight. It's quiet now, and the serenity of the huge palm trees blowing in the breeze will all be erased in just a handful of hours, as nearly one-hundred-and-fifty-thousand people will pass through the turnstiles at the Great Race Place over the next two days. Over one-hundred-and-twenty-million dollars will be wagered through the betting windows. And one champion will be crowned

Southbound

Horse of the Year.

24

FRIDAY

I reserved a box for both Friday and Saturday, as with the massive crowds, I want to have a place to set up as my home base. I arrive at eleven thirty, about ninety minutes before the first race of the day. The Breeders' Cup consists of thirteen races over the two days, with six races this afternoon and seven races tomorrow. The feature this afternoon is the $2,000,000 Breeders' Cup Distaff, which has twelve runners going a mile and one-eighth. Mondatta would have likely been a big favorite in this race based on the tremendous season she's been having. But, Mr. Warren and Mahoney decided to give her a chance against the big boys and run for the big money. I'm toting my entire bankroll, eight thousand bucks, but only three thousand of it is designated for the bets mapped out for the day. With the horses parading in the paddock for the first Breeders' Cup race, Maria's voice comes over the public address system, echoing throughout the expansive grandstand.

"Ladies and gentlemen, welcome to Santa Anita, where we are pleased to welcome you to the Breeders' Cup World Championships. Our first race of the day is the Breeders' Cup Juvenile Fillies Turf event for two-year-old girls on the grass course." Maria goes on to describe each of the fourteen horses in the field.

I'm watching the horses in the paddock via the television in my box and I pay particular attention to Emperor's Queen, a European shipper making her first start in the States. When it comes to racing on the grass, European horses are generally regarded as the top horses in the world. Emperor's Queen looks magnificent and is on her toes.

I head to the windows to make my first wagers of the day.

"I'll take five hundred to win on Emperor's Queen, and a twenty-dollar exacta, Emperor's Queen with the 2,3,5,6,9."

The teller hands me two tickets in exchange for the six-hundred dollars I pass over the counter. With just seven minutes until the race, Emperor's Queen is taking some money, and is the 4/1 second choice in the big field, with the New York runner Bobby's Flay being the favorite.

"And awayyyy they go."

Emperor's Queen finds herself and her jockey, Frenchman Claude Lecomb, in the middle of the pack early on as the speedy runners go quick early. I stay seated and watch most of the race on the television, as it's easier to get a good idea of what's going on with the benefit of a zoomed in lens. Bobby's Flay is right behind Emperor's Queen as they start to come into the homestretch. The early leaders begin to tire, and a mad scramble for the lead ensues as they enter the final furlong of the race.

"C'mon Queen, get through," I say as I stand up to watch the final ten seconds of the race.

"Emperor's Queen crying out for room, as Bobby's Flay starts to move on the far outside," the announcer calls.

Lacomb uses Emperor's Queen's momentum and power, and tries to squeeze through a very small hole between two horses that are staggering in front of him. One of them stumbles over Emperor's Queen's back foot in the process and nearly unseats the jockey, who somehow manages to stay on.

"Emperor's Queen gets loose. But it's Bobby's Flay the leader, Emperor's Queen now bearing down on her in the final strides, here's the wire — Emperor's Queen to win it."

I smack my *Form* down against the railing of the box in celebration of hitting my first wager of the day. My five hundred to win at 4/1 will net me twenty-five hundred, and the twenty-dollar exacta with the favorite will probably tack on another couple hundred to that total.

"Ladies and Gentleman please hold all tickets, we have a Steward's Inquiry," the announcer tells the crowd.

I figured the Stewards would review the video, as me, and everyone else in the stands, saw the horse stumble. What I don't know is whether Emperor's Queen caused the interference. The head-on replay begins on the in-house television screens, and the first time I see the stumble in slo-mo, I know my wagers are in deep shit. Emperor's Queen clearly forced her way through and cut off the other horse, which, even though that other horse wasn't going to win, might have cost her a position, and will likely cause Emperor's Queen to be disqualified and placed behind the runner she interfered with.

The Stewards watch the replay several times before informing the announcer of their decision.

"*Attention race fans. We have a disqualification,*" the announcer calls out as the entire crowd roars. Many people are thrilled as the favorite Bobby's Flay has been put up to first, but many people are also infuriated, because they, like me, had their money on Emperor's Queen.

On Breeders' Cup Day, there's a forty-five minute delay between each race, and with me pissed off from the disqualification, I flip channels to the simulcast of some of the other tracks that are running across the country. Instead of being up a couple of thousand, I'm down six-hundred dollars. Happily, I notice there's just three minutes to the next race at

Emerald Downs, my former hometown track in suburban Seattle. I open my program and see that a friend of mine, trainer Len Smoot, has a horse in the race, and it's the second choice on the board at 5/2 odds. I dart from my seat, run up to the teller station, and put two-hundred dollars to win, and two hundred to place, on Len's horse Blumountainspecial, a speed horse.

Blumountainspecial comes out of the gate slowly, as he hops the minute the gates popped open. He rushes up to get close to the leaders, but by the time the field comes into the homestretch, he's tiring and fading back through the field.

"Motherfucker," I say with disdain as I'm now down a grand with five Breeders' Cup races left for the day.

I spend the next few races punting as planned, with Pick 3 tickets and Daily Doubles that all seem to fall short in one way or another. In horse racing, as in all gambling, there are ups, downs, and runs of good and bad luck. However, having them on your biggest days of the year is a killer to the bankroll, and to the ego. After losses like the ones I'm incurring today, a normal gambler would just sit back, chalk it up to bad luck, and wait until the next day. I don't do that though, as between each Breeders' Cup loss I continue to pound away at the windows on tracks like Emerald Downs, Golden Gate Fields, and whatever else is running on a Friday afternoon in the early fall.

With two Breeders' Cup races left on the afternoon, the Breeders' Cup Distaff and the Breeders' Cup Filly and Mare Turf, I check my ever-thinning wallet to find that my eight-thousand dollars has dwindled down to eighteen hundred. I had planned to only put three thousand through the windows and I've gone far beyond that amount. If I stop now, I only have enough money for about forty percent of my planned bets for the big day tomorrow. However, sitting here in this box, overlooking the massive infield at Santa Anita, and with just five minutes left until the Filly and Mare Turf, I get up and head downstairs.

"Fuck it."

I run down the steps and get in the teller line,

which is about eight people deep. I stand there with my feet bouncing, my fingers twitching and snapping, and my right hand nervously brushing my hair back, which is one of my many nervous ticks.

"Five-hundred-dollar Daily Double, four and seven in the Filly and Mare Turf with Sister Susie in the Distaff," I call out in a hurry as the horses begin loading in the gate.

"And, also, eight hundred to win on the four in here," I impulsively call out.

It was a wager I hadn't planned on making, but the idea of waiting around another forty-five minutes to get all my money in sounded undoable to me. In fact, waiting even five more minutes to get that kind of action seems like an impossibility.

"And awayyyyy they go."

I run out to the apron of the track to watch the race with my two horses in the Daily Double. Emeryville and Janie's Demon both close up early. Emeryville is my main selection and the one I put the additional eight hundred to win on.

398

"The field heads down the backstretch, and it's Timbers Army who leads the field by two. They're going at a slow pace out there, as Emeryville and Janie's Demon stalk the leader from second and third, just two lengths behind."

As the field runs into the final turn, I can see that Emeryville's jockey, Curt Lowder, has a hammerlock grip on his reins, signifying to me that he has a ton of horse left underneath him. Timbers Army has been winning her races this year going wire-to-wire, but none as far as this race.

"They turn to the top of the stretch, and Timbers Army kicks on for home with Emeryville chasing."

"C'mon Lowder, get her going," I plead as I start to whip my leg with my *Form.*

"C'mon Timbers Army," a small, older Asian guy next to me yells immediately following my request.

"C'mon Emeryville," I yell out.

"C'mon Timbers Army," the Asian guy says, laughing and enjoying this seemingly fun interaction.

"Timbers Army just keeps finding on the lead,

and Emeryville draws to within a neck with fifty yards to go," the announcer calls out.

"C'mon Emeryville," I say as I squat down, watching the infield television to get a better idea of the impending photo finish. However, there was no photo finish needed.

"And Timbers Army hangs on to win by a head, the more they asked the more she gave," the announcer says before clicking off his microphone.

"Yeah, Timbers Army," the Asian guy says as he holds up his ticket that I can see is a five-dollar win bet.

"Fuck Timbers Army, and fuck you and your cheap five-dollar betting ass," I say as I storm away. I can feel the sweat starting to bead on my forehead, and on the tips of my fingers. Looking at the clock on the tote board, I can see that it's now four-thirty-five in the afternoon. Without missing a beat, I instinctively start running out of the facility. I carefully run down the stairs before going to a full sprint through the paddock. Passing by the bench I sat on during that last panic attack, I burst through the entry gate and out to my car.

I hop in, and speed out of the West entrance and towards Huntington Drive. It's Friday afternoon during rush hour, and even though Huntington Drive isn't the freeway, it's one of the main arteries through town. Looking at the clock, I see that it's four-forty-four. By my calculations, I should be able to reach my destination by five. Within a couple minutes, I pull into the Wells Fargo parking lot. I'm making the same trip I made back in March, but this time, I'm taking out the remainder of my cash.

"I need to make a large withdrawal," I say to the woman at the counter.

"How large sir?" the kind, elderly woman asks.

"Eleven-thousand dollars, please," I say as I fill out the withdrawal slip.

"Okay. I'll have to get the manager to help you with this transaction," she says as she picks up the phone and dials to the back.

Out walks the same branch manager who gave me the twenty thousand on my first trip to this bank. I hadn't planned on going back for more. But at this point, it's my only chance to get back the money I've lost over the last few weeks. What started as a wonderful spring had turned into a better summer, and was now becoming a painful fall. The manager lays out one hundred and ten hundred-dollar bills, and after I nod with approval, she piles them all up and puts them in an envelope. It's now five o'clock and I have all the ammunition I'll need to attack the races on Saturday. I had five thousand dollars' worth of bets scheduled for tomorrow, and I know that I need to stick somewhat to that plan, as I need the money to get back to Portland on Sunday morning. I rationalize that six thousand or so, even if tomorrow I lose all five thousand dollars of my scheduled bets, is enough for me to get back to Portland and get back on my feet safely. With the Pick 6 on Breeders' Cup Saturday guaranteed at three-million dollars, I know that will be my best chance of having a monster score.

I come back to the Motel 6, where I study the

Racing Form again, and put together my Pick 6. I order another pizza, the third straight night I've had that for dinner, and then remember that I'm going to need enough money in my account for the Motel 6 bill that will be charged to my card after Saturday night. I've left seven-hundred-and-forty-eight dollars in my account, which I figure is about four hundred less than what my total bill will be, as I've been here more than two weeks now.

Circling all the horses I think have a chance to win tomorrow in the Pick Six, my newly constructed ticket comes out to eight-thousand dollars. Some of the earlier races, like the Sprint and the Juvenile, look to be wide open, with as many as ten horses having a chance to win.

My strategy is to just be alive going into the last leg, when I'm going to be using just two horses in the Breeders' Cup Classic. Rturntoserve and Mondatta. I've been watching these two win all summer and both are coming into the race well. Rturntoserve is going to be the big favorite and Mondatta will be a long shot, as she's taking on the boys. She's 12/1 on the morning line, which is the track handicapper's best idea of where her final price will be.

I had planned on trimming down my ticket for the Pick 6 to about four-thousand bucks, and having a thousand or so in other bets throughout the day. However, living with the regret of a life changing score not happening because I chickened out for a couple thousand bucks, is something I just can't fathom. With an eight-thousand-dollar ticket, I still have three grand for driving home and getting an apartment. Somehow, this rationalization all makes sense to me, and I start to construct my final ticket for what will be my final bet of the trip. Hopefully my final bet for a long time. Preferably—ever.

Upon finishing my ticket, and writing it down in succinct order on my program, I add up the total a few more times.

Race 5: 1, 2, 4, 5, 6
Race 6: 1, 3, 4, 6, 7, 9, 10, 11, 12, 14
Race 7: 3, 6
Race 8: 5, 6, 9, 10, 11

Race 9: 4, 6, 8, 10

Race 10: 3, 10

The two-dollar base ticket will cost exactly eight-thousand bucks. If you're going to make big money, you gotta risk big money.

25

SATURDAY

I sleep in on Breeders' Cup Saturday morning and decide to stay at the Motel 6 for a few hours instead of going to the morning workouts. I'm fucking exhausted after everything that transpired yesterday. I decide that with the big bet looming later this afternoon, maybe it's best to wait until the races start before heading over. I have my box reserved, but the idea of sitting there and waiting around for the Pick 6 to start seems like a bit too much. Plus, I'm just feeling depressed.

The toll of the last few weeks, Maria, and the fact that I have to go back to Portland and work, is finally catching up to me. Lying in bed, the blanket on top of me seems to weigh two-hundred pounds. Depression is a strange thing when it strikes. The idea of simply getting up and hopping in the shower, something that I do every day, feels like the equivalent of having to climb a mountain. I've had some severe bouts of it before, and I've found that the best remedy is to push myself up out of bed, get in the shower, and get moving around. Fighting that urge to stay in bed is the only way for me to move forward.

I finally get up and into the shower at ten thirty. I stand there with the water beating down on the back of my neck. I like a scorching shower that leaves my body bright red. I spend a few seconds looking at myself in the mirror. I place my hands on the cold sink and lean into the mirror, inches from the glass. As I stare into my hazel eyes, I try to think of something profound and righteous to say, but all I can muster is that my eyelashes are too long.

Even though it's a huge day at the track, and many of the patrons will be donning their best duds, I throw on a pair of jeans and a long sleeve t-shirt that I got at Del Mar this summer. I spend the next thirty minutes sorting through all my stuff and putting my clothes back into the garbage bag, as I'm planning on heading out of town first thing in the morning. While putting on my sneakers, I hear my phone let out a single solitary beep, indicating a text message.

"Hey. How'd yesterday go?" the message reads.

Seeing those words next to Maria's name on my phone, I instantly perk up and respond with a dramatic understatement. I type, "Eh. I lost a little bit. Who do you like today?"

I brush my teeth as Maria's response comes in. I peer down to the phone resting on the counter.

"I'm going with Choctaw Nation to pull the upset in the Classic," Maria had written.

I can't help but laugh, as I've spent the entire spring and summer chasing Choctaw Nation, who failed to win a race during that entire time.

"Ugh. I hate that horse, LOL," I respond. "I'm going with Mondatta and Rturntoserve for my Pick 6 play."

"How big a ticket are you playing?" she responds back.

"Five-hundred-and-eighty-eight bucks," I send back, hoping she'll believe my lie.

"Well, best of luck. Come and say goodbye

before you head back."

"Definitely. I'll come see you in the paddock," I respond, happy that she at least wants to see me off before I hit the road. My hope is that with some time off, and with me quitting gambling, maybe we could stay in contact during the Portland season. Even though she'll be in California the whole winter, maybe she could come up to Portland and visit, as Portland Meadows runs during the early part of the week when Santa Anita has off days.

I finally head over to Santa Anita at eleven thirty. The sea of patrons is visible from across the street at the Motel 6. Walking through the turnstiles, I go straight through the paddock and head upstairs to the Frontrunner Restaurant to have lunch. The races start early on the Breeders' Cup Saturday, and the first of the Breeders' Cup races is just twenty minutes away. The first race in my Pick 6 sequence is only an hour away.

"Good afternoon sir. Can I get you something to drink?" the waitress asks.

"Just an ice water and the charbroiled

salmon please."

Sitting there in the crowded restaurant, the buzz of the Breeders' Cup is sensational. People from all over the world come to Santa Anita for these championship races, including the folks at the table next to me. They have ownership badges in lanyards around their neck and are speaking French. It's ten minutes to post.

As the horses for the first of the Breeders' Cup championship races come onto the track, they're called to the post by the track bugler, a tall, thin man wearing a bright red coat, tight white pants, and a tall black top hat. He plays the call to post, and then follows it up with a little freeform playing. Though I'm tempted to get down to the race, I'm also content to just watch this event, the Juvenile Sprint. I feel a pit in my stomach. Partly it's hunger, but part of it also is the fact that I don't want to make any bets. I'm burnt out from the last few weeks, and yesterday was a traumatizing wake up call for how bad things could get. I lost eight-thousand dollars over the course of four hours.

The waitress brings the salmon to me as the

horses begin loading for the Juvenile Sprint.

"Anything else sir?" the server asks.

"Naw, just the check, I'm going to head out right after I'm done," I reply. Most racetrack restaurants have a habit of leaving the patrons sitting there waiting for the bill, because the longer they take, the more likely the patrons are to wager.

I watch intently as a long shot wins the Juvenile Sprint, coming from off the pace to win for trainer Paul Lucas, an old time veteran winning his first Breeders' Cup race after ten previous attempts. Each Breeders' Cup race features an expanded winner's circle presentation with a garland of flowers placed over the jockey's lap. Then, an NBC reporter interviews the owner, trainer, and jockey, and finally, a celebrity presents a trophy to the winning owner. In this case, it's a B-list actress named Mona Ford, who was popular during the seventies.

With thirty minutes until the start of the Pick 6, and with the Breeders' Cup Juvenile being the first leg, I want to look in the paddock before making my play. The advantage of the first race being a two-year-old race is that I can check if any of the horses on my ticket are acting up in the paddock or over-heating. Upon arriving there, Maria comes out over the loud speakers with her analysis as well as her top three selections for the race. Her top three picks are three of the five horses that I'm using in my Pick 6, and I feel confident that I have the only five horses that can win the race.

The juvenile's parade onto the track as I go over to check in with Maria before the race.

"What a crowd, huh?" she says as she approaches me at the entry to the paddock.

"Yeah, it's great. Biggest crowd I've ever seen at a racetrack. Then again, we did have four-hundred people at Portland on closing day," I say with a smile.

"I have to run up to the winner's circle, cause I'm helping the NBC reporter. But after the Breeders' Cup Sprint they're on their own, so my schedule will be more open later in the day. Come see me later," Maria says.

"Sounds good. I'll see you later," I say.

I like the way all of my horses look in the paddock, and I head upstairs to the restaurant to make my bets, as the lines down on the main level are twenty people deep. I arrive at the window and read off what will be the biggest wager of my life. The teller greets me with a smile, something I think is a good omen since tellers never smile.

"I want a two-dollar Pick 6 ticket," I say to her, then taking thirty seconds to call out the entire bet.

"An even eight-thousand dollars," she says.

I take the eight thousand from my wallet, as the teller waits. She won't print the ticket until it's counted and accurate. After counting the eightieth bill, she hits the print button, and the long ticket makes its way out of the machine.

"Here you are young man. Good luck," she says with an even bigger smile.

"I'm going to need it," I say.

I head down to my box to watch the first leg of the Pick 6 sequence. I'm happy that they gave me a different box than yesterday, as that one proved not to be the luckiest of seating assignments. Not that I'm superstitious, but I certainly don't wear the same shirt, shoes, or socks as yesterday, and I don't want to be seated anywhere near that same spot.

"And awayyyy they go. Middle Child heads out for the early lead with the big favorite, Lumber Jacker, in the second spot, and those two fly early. Red Star Ryan, Trapped In Vegas, and Motion Man are in the second flight with the European runner Austere in sixth."

The field is strung out early as the favorite Lumber Jacker, and long shot Middle Child, go out and duel on the front end. My horses are spread out throughout the group with the favorite on the lead, a couple in the middle of the pack, and two of my runners, Olie's Maze and Juggler's Hands both at the back.

"They turn into the homestretch and it's Lumber Jacker leading, but he's in deep water as the back markers start to run on. Here's Motion Man and here's Trapped in Vegas up to make a lineup of three on the front end. And now, from the back of the pack, here comes Juggler's Hands flying down the center of the course."

I feel pretty good. With just 100 yards to go, the four still in with a shot are all my horses. And Juggler's Hands, the biggest price at 13/1, is rallying fastest.

"C'mon Juggler," I scream. The echoes of the fans' cheers bang off the roof of the grandstand, and I can barely hear my own screams as they hit the sixteenth pole.

"Juggler's Hands and Malcolm Purcell have come from last to win the Breeders' Cup Juvenile," the announcer calls out at the wire.

"Alright, alright, alright," I say as I pump my fists and sit back down. I know it's far too early to get too confident. Pick 6 is a marathon, not a sprint. But I also know that with a 13/1 long shot winning the first leg, a huge number of Pick 6 players have already been eliminated. Feeling a vibration against my right hip, I pull out my phone to see a message from Maria.

"Hope you had that one."

"One for one. Let's keep it going," I reply.

"Nice work! Who've you got in the Sprint?" she asks.

"The 1, 3, 4, and 14," I lie. If I tell her I

actually have ten of the fourteen runners, she'll
know I spent far more than I told her.

"Good luck. I love the 14; just a tough post
position," she replies.

The horses break from the gate for the
Breeders' Cup Sprint. I try to stay relaxed as I
watch. The only horses I don't have are all over
29/1, so barring something goofy happening I
should be fine.

*"They come to the top of the stretch, and
Millerstown has been in front every step of the way.
Rolland's Winder starts to make up ground from
second, and on the outside now, here comes Super
Tanker."*

Super Tanker is the favorite in the race, and
the defending champion in the Breeders' Cup
Sprint. He flies down the center of the course to
get up and win in impressive fashion. I'm happy
to be moving on, but to go ten deep in a race and
end up with the favorite is a lot like kissing your
sister. Actually, it's not that bad. But you get
what I mean.

The Breeders' Cup Turf Sprint is the third
leg in the Pick 6 sequence, and maybe the race

that I'm most scared of. With thirteen runners sprinting down the hill on the Santa Anita grass course, it really is a total crapshoot. I only have two runners in the field. The two favorites. I would liked to have spread out more, but my incorrect assumption that the Sprint would end up with a bomber, forced me to pare down my ticket in the later races. As I'm looking over the *Form*, I hear Maria over the speakers giving out her selections.

"I'm liking the three, six, and ten in this race," she says before going on to describing each runner in more detail. I have the three and the six, Let's Celebrate and California Joe, so I immediately look at the past performances for the ten horse. I'm concerned now about that runner, as well as a couple of the others I couldn't put in my ticket.

"And awayyyy they go in the Breeders' Cup Turf Sprint."

Immediately, one of my selections, the favorite, California Joe, stumbles out of the gate and has to rush up to get into contention, which is never a good sign. Having to use up your horse early usually costs the horse too much in the final yards.

"They come down the hill and Wanton Chili has the lead, and flies up on the front end. Mouthful of Cavities is second with California Joe now up in third. Into the stretch now, and Mouthful of Cavities and California Joe go on with it. Wanton Chili drops out, while The Whammer and Let's Celebrate start to rally on the outside. Final sixteenth of a mile, and The Whammer and Let's Celebrate take over. These two are going to fight it out to the finish."

I have Let's Celebrate, but don't have 30/1 shot The Whammer.

"Here's the wire, and it's going to be—a photo finish," the announcer calls out as the seventy-thousand plus in attendance all let out a collective groan. At first glance, I thought Let's Celebrate might have had the nose down in front at the wire, but just like everyone else at the track, my eyes turn to the infield television. A fifty-foot by thirty-foot mega-screen shows the final strides of the race and slows it down as they come to the wire. They show the replay in

slow motion four more times, and each time the two animals hit the finish line, the crowd cheers, and each person shouts who they thought won it.

"And the winner is The Whammer," the announcer calls out as the number eight goes up in the top spot on the tote board. My heart sinks. I knew this race could be my undoing, but I never thought The Whammer would do me in. I sit here, knowing that I'm still alive for five out of six, which on a day like today will still pay in the low five figures. But knowing the chance for the big score, the life changing score, is not going to happen knocks the wind out of me. Putting up so much money on animals running around in a circle with a little man on top of them can lead to unpredictable endings.

I head down to the far side of the apron, and on to the top of the homestretch, to watch the next race. The Breeders' Cup Dirt Mile features eleven runners, and I have five of them on my Pick 6 ticket. If I can get a couple of price horses, and then Mondatta in the final leg, my five out of six ticket should pay tens of thousands of dollars. In fact, it's possible that nobody will have six out of six with a horse like The Whammer winning a race. If nobody picks all six of six, then all the people with five will split up the entire pool since it's a mandatory payout today. Minus the track taking their twenty-five percent of course.

The field heads toward the homestretch and one of my selections, the eleven horse, Flamethrowintexan, has the lead and is a big price.

"C'mon Tex. Keep going you son of a bitch," I say as the horses go flying by with nearly a quarter-mile left to go.

I try to hear the race call, but with the sea of people screaming their heads off, all I can hear from this far down is a faint echo of the speakers. I fast walk down the stretch, and as I get closer to the infield monitor and tote board, I see Flamethrowintexan's name and number in the first-place spot, at 11/1 odds.

I'm now three out of four in the Pick 6 with two races left to go. The Breeders' Cup Turf at a mile and a half, and, of course, the Breeders' Cup Classic later on. With three long shots in the four races, even though I'm still only eligible for five out of six, the five out of six is now going to pay a minimum of twenty or thirty grand. Just two more races and I'll be able to skip town with close to what I came with. I'm already planning how I'll put the money away and not touch it once I get home. The last time I quit gambling "for good," my Aunt was nice enough to help me out by starting a joint account where I couldn't take out cash unless she granted permission. Maybe she'd allow me to go back to that agreement in order to let me get back on my feet and help me control my finances. She doesn't know I've been down in California gambling. I told her that I came down to work at the tracks here for the summer, doing media stuff.

The field for the Breeders' Cup Turf only features ten runners, one of the smallest fields on Breeders' Cup day. The field is loaded with European runners, and three of my four horses in the race are Euros. The big favorite is a horse named Chamberlain Tower who was recently second in the biggest race in France, the Prix de l'Arc de Triomphe at the Longchamp racecourse in Paris. There's also the winner of one of the world's richest races in Dubai earlier this year, Cummings Plaza. The only American horse I've included is the old veteran Classy Mike, who's had a resurrection of his career at age seven. Classy Mike was a monster four-year-old, but injuries and lack luster races plagued him at ages five and six. Since he was a gelding, and unable to produce as a stallion, his owners brought him back for a seven-year-old season that's included some huge wins across the country.

I decide to watch the Breeders' Cup Turf race at the top of the stretch, where I watched the last race. I seem to have good luck when watching races from the top of the stretch, so I figure, why not?

"And awayyyy they go in the Breeders' Cup Turf."

The field comes down the hill as they start up at the back of the course, and then do another full lap to make the mile and a half journey.

"Classy Mike as expected goes right out the

front, with Cummings Plaza in the second spot, and Willy Will He is third. Chamberlain Tower, the Arc winner, is in the fourth spot early on as the field comes by the wire for the first time around."

My four picks are all up front early as they pass by, and I hear the announcer say the opening half mile was completed in fifty-one seconds, a slow pace, which is a big advantage for my front running foursome.

"They head onto the backstretch, and it's still Classy Mike who has the lead and is travelling well. But Cummings Plaza is now breathing down his neck on the outside, and Willy Will He continues in third. Chamberlain Tower is fourth, and here's an early backstretch move by Hotel Diego who moves up alongside of Chamberlain Tower."

These long turf races usually involve a mile and a quarter of the horses just galloping easily and then an all-out sprint for home once they get into the stretch.

"They hit the top of the lane, and Classy Mike and Cummings Plaza turn for home in front, with Chamberlain Tower and Hotel Diego just in behind them as the runners sprint for home."

I have three of the top four with Hotel Diego the only horse I don't have on my ticket. My other horse, Willy Will He, has already started to back out of the race and won't be of any consequence. The group blows past me, and the massive Chamberlain Tower looks like he just needs some room before he takes off. But Hotel Diego is keeping him boxed in behind Classy Mike, who's still battling and is still a nose in front.

"They hit the final furlong and Classy Mike is joined by Hotel Diego, and Hotel Diego puts the nose in front. Chamberlain Tower is crying out for room —and now he gets loose, but it might be too late. It's Hotel Diego the new leader, Classy Mike fights on, here's Chamberlain Tower who's rallying—but it's going to be Hotel Diego to win the Breeders' Cup Turf."

I somehow hear Bill Tomlinson's call at the finish line from down at the top of the stretch, and I feel as though I've been kicked in the balls by a pointed boot. I walk toward the fence and extend my arms out to grab the fence, dropping my head between my arms in anguish. Eight-thousand dollars evaporated the minute Hotel Diego hit the finish line in front. I drop down to my knees, turn around on my butt, sit with my back against the fence, and shake my head in disbelief. I had really thought that this time was going to be different. This was going to be the day that I got the better of the races. But it's not. I was back where I was just a couple of years ago, unable to control my gambling, unable to stop and damn near busted. I should have just stayed up in Portland and gotten another job this summer.

I sat there against that fence for fifteen minutes, sitting in total shock. Losing at the racetrack often features added insult to injury, because your competition, the other bettors, are around you celebrating as some of them just won.

"The horses are now parading in the paddock for the five-million-dollar Breeders' Cup Classic," Maria says over the loud speakers. *"These champions will go one mile and one quarter, and of course, the heavy favorite in here, Rturntoserve, looking to continue his perfect season and avenge*

last year's loss in this same race."

I finally get up and walk back towards the paddock to peek at the horses parading in the walking ring. A quick glance at the odds board and I see that Rturntoserve is the heavy favorite, while Mondatta is 13/1 and my old pal Choctaw Nation is 19/1. A big part of me wants to leave and get out of town right now. After everything going wrong over the past few days, and weeks for that matter, my feet feel like they weigh fifty pounds each. As I amble through the paddock, I see Maria. But can't muster the energy to face her.

Mondatta is doing her usual acting up in the paddock. She appears to be oozing confidence. She's on her toes, and she looks like she's ready to run. Mr. Warren and Mahoney are in the walking ring, both donning their best suits for the big race. Mahoney instructs the new jockey Luis Juarez before giving him a leg up. His advice to Juarez must have been something along the line of "Take her back to last early and blow by them all in the stretch."

The horses go out to the track. I decide to

stay back in the paddock and watch the race on one of the televisions that adorn the back walls of the track. With the tens of thousands of people taking in the races out front, there's kind of a solitude and quiet back in the paddock once the horses leave and go to the track, even though there are probably still a thousand people scattered around back here.

Looking up at the odds board one last time, and figuring I should just head out, I have a strange thought. At 13/1, betting the three thousand I've got left in my pocket on Mondatta to win would yield me about forty-two thousand if she gets home first. It would put me up for the trip and get me out of town on an amazing winning note. Maybe this was all meant to be. This is my horse. This has been my horse all summer, and my friend Mahoney has all the confidence in the world in her.

Renewed, I head to one of the betting windows back in the paddock area before I can talk myself out of it and put down my remaining thirty one-hundred dollar bills on Mondatta to win. I feel a sudden sense of relief once the bet is placed, and for some reason, my mood turns around. Just that possibility, that feeling of still having a fighting chance, brightens up the melancholy that I was experiencing for the last half hour.

I stroll over to a bank of television sets and stand next to a forty-something guy who's watching the horses load into the gate for the richest race in America.

"Who you got in here?" I ask the stranger.

"I'm on the favorite, Rturntoserve. He's my favorite horse," the man replies.

"Good luck, pal," I say back to him.

"*And awayyyy they go in the five-million-dollar Breeders' Cup Classic. Rturntoserve and Alexie Mattosie head out to the front early on, and no surprises here, Mondatta the filly is dead last early on.*"

Mondatta is probably fourteen or fifteen lengths behind the frontrunners early on, and even though I know she's a closer, I feel a little worried about how far back she is and how many good horses she's going to have to pass.

"*They turn onto the backstretch, and Alexie*

Mattosie and Rturntoserve continue to do battle on the front end. They got the opening half mile in a razor sharp forty-six-and-two-fifths seconds."

Rturntoserve is doing exactly what I had hoped he'd do. His jockey, Bernie Dalindo, took the bait, again, from Alexie Mattosie and is going way too fast early on. Mondatta is still far back, just a length or two behind Choctaw Nation who is also at the back of the pack.

"The field heads to the far turn and Rturntoserve takes over from Alexie Mattosie, who's now ridden along and not keeping pace. Windsong Destroyer moves into contention with Homer J starting a rally in third. It's two and a half more lengths back to Slew's Sargeant. Choctaw Nation is starting to kick it in, and Mondatta is starting her run from the back. She's passed three of her rivals and Juarez has her cranking up on the far outside."

The minute Juarez starts to push Mondatta and ask her to go, she immediately responds and takes off. She's finding gear after gear on the far turn, and as the field comes for home, she goes very wide, but has great momentum.

"C'mon Mondatta, c'mon girl, c'mon girl, for

all things holy keep going," I plead.

"*They come to the final furlong and Rturntoserve is all in, Choctaw Nation comes up to his outside, and Mondatta continues on the far outside, it's down to these three.*"

"C'mon Mondatta," I scream so loudly my voice cracks. Everything rides on these final hundred yards.

"*Choctaw Nation and Mondatta come up along with Rturntoserve, these three in a line with fifty yards to go. Choctaw Nation puts a nose in front, Mondatta trying to push on by in the final strides, but it's going to be Choctaw Nation to pull off a huge upset. He beat Mondatta by a neck with Rturntoserve back in third.*"

A neck.

A neck away from victory.

A neck away from security.

A neck short.

I can hear the hysteria going on out in front of the grandstand. The fact that it was Choctaw Nation who beat me doesn't help the situation. He was Maria's top pick, and I had chased him in every one of his races this summer, except the one that mattered most. Usually in these moments I'm flooded with thoughts of "why did this happen to me" or "I can't believe what bad luck I have." But this doesn't even feel like bad luck. This doesn't feel like anything I've known. It almost doesn't even feel.

I head toward the exits. As I walk through the turnstile, I look back at the Great Race Place. I see Maria walking from the television truck where she watched the race towards the winner's circle to do the interview with the winning connections. I can tell she has a skip in her step, as giving out a winner like that is something a public handicapper and paddock host like Maria can brag about for years to come.

The parking lot looks never-ending. As I start the walk back to the Motel 6, I'm hit with a strange calm that I've known before. There's a great calm in being busted, because I know that there's no more losing and no more of the pain that comes with it. The further I get from the track, and the closer I get to the motel, all I can think of is mom. Even looking at my phone, I scan through the contacts section to find her name. I haven't deleted her number. I don't think I ever will. That would make it permanent. Then she's really gone. She's been there to bail me out in these situations before. Thinking that no matter how bad I fucked up, and how much I blew, she was always there for me to get me back on my feet. Moms. They have such a way of appearing and being there for you even when they aren't even around. At least mine does. When I'd first left Mohawk Downs after having trouble keeping my panic attacks in check, she was on the first flight out. She drove me back home across country. Never asked a question. Just was there for her child. I just keep thinking that I wasn't thankful enough for her while she was here. For what she did when times were good and when they were bad. My relationship with her was the only time I knew I was the center of someone else's universe. My heart aches. The other thing I keep remembering is I don't even have enough money to pay my motel bill now, let alone for gas to get home.

I can call my Aunt. She'll gladly transfer me

the cash to at least get me home and back on my feet. Borrowing from family, though, has become a tired act that I've abused repeatedly.

Walking up the cement stairs at the Motel 6, I'm holding onto the railing for any support it can lend. My legs feel heavy as I lift each foot up another stair. Arriving at my room, I immediately shut the door and sit down on the bed. I take a deep breath and my eyes begin filling up with tears. Every impulse in my body is to reach for the television remote and at least fill some of the air with noise, because right now the silence feels like pain. The silence is reality. The silence is now.

Planting my face in my hands, the sobbing becomes uncontrollable. I lie down on my back and wail, as the tears fog my vision. Eventually, I curl up in a fetal position, and I feel that knot in my stomach every gambler, depressed person, or human being for that matter, feels when they reach rock bottom. My guttural howl bounces off the walls and windows, and straight back to me.

Where to go?

What to do?

Who to call?

As my eyes begin to dry, heavy and bloated, I turn over to look out the window. A three-inch gap in the blinds lets in not only sunlight, but also a small corner of Santa Anita that's still within view. I just want the blinds to shut, so I can disappear into the black. Sometimes you just don't want to be seen. Sometimes there's not a thing in this world to do, except be alone in it.

My phone vibrates in my pocket. It's my sister. I was hoping it was Maria. I was really hoping it was my mom. I hit the ignore button and open the Internet browser on the phone. After a quick check online, and finding the information I need, I pull myself up off the bed. It's amazing how light you feel after crying.

I head down those same stairs and into my car. The GPS on my phone tells me every turn to make. Ten minutes on the 210, off at Monrovia, a couple of right turns, and I park in front of an old green building. It looks completely out of place next to a brand new Chipotle and across from a shopping center. There's a tiny sign that says RC Services above the door. The paint is chipped. The sign has a hole in it, and it looks as if rocks were thrown through it. I head through the door, peak around, and find room three to my right. There are five people in the room. They look exactly like everyone else I've seen at these things. I reach out and open the door. All faces turn towards me.

"Hi. I'm Ryan. And I'm a compulsive gambler."

Acknowledgements

This book, and pretty much everything I've done with my life, would not have been possible without the love, help, and friendship of so many people. Please bear with me as I thank them here.

Most sincere thanks to all members of the Beem, Bender, Burr, Carr, and Wood families for always being the centerpieces of my life. I have so much love for all of you.

Thank you to all the members of the Beautiful Cohort for always being beautiful and for teaching me more than I ever thought I'd learn. You guys are going to change the world. Hell, you already have.

Thank you to Zara Kramer and everyone at Pandamoon Publishing.

Thank you and many hugs to Amanda Graff-Baker for sharing her heart, friendship, and love of hiking with me; to Tasney McNew for still making me laugh every time she speaks; to Sarah Jenkins for being a friend when I needed one most; to Jenn Hauth for introducing me to *The Office*, and watching *Indiana Jones* with me while I was blind; and to Sarah Lubak for her principles and goofiness.

I have some amazing friends and wish I could name you all here. I love you all. But special thanks to Chris Carpinito and family, Flynn Cochran, Ryan Callaghan, George Gagliardi, Ryan Reed, Ryan Armstrong, Tony Large, Paul Pipper, Team Phief, Bull Hurley, Chris Walbridge, Chad Bollacker, Members of Alpha Tau Omega, Chad Doing, Troy Rothermel, Kelly Morgan, Kearsten Holmdale, and Jared "Hairball" Werner.

I love horse racing and I've worked with some great people. I want to thank them for their friendship and for just being amazing. The General Jerry Kohls is still one of my favorite people on the planet and always will be. Vince Cyster is one of the sweetest people I've ever known. Gary Norton, who has to spend hours at a time with me in a tiny room and still always keeps things interesting. Steve and Debbie Peery, I love you both. Jessica Paquette, still the best friend I've never met. Thanks to Travis Stone. Thanks to Peter Aiello, Arnie, Jeff, Catfish, and everyone at River Downs. Thanks to Ben Root, Darrin Paul, and my friend and mentor Mr. Dave Martin (RIP). Thanks to Vestal, Mark, Lucas, Ben Edward Sabadoo, Bobby Baldwin, Mike, Keith, Sharon, and Kevin, Lori x 2, Patrick Kerrison, Brian, and to everyone at Portland Meadows. Thank you to Anne Sanguinetti and Mark Anderson. Thank you to everyone at Emerald Downs, especially to the great Robert Geller. Racing knows no classier gentleman and talent than you.

Thank you to Gavin Flynn, and everyone at Tigard Tuesdays and Fridays.

Thank you to Willy Vlautin, Lidia Yuknavitch, Vanessa Veselka, Pauls Toutonghi, and the late John O'Brien. Who knew words could change lives. Your guy's words have changed mine.

Thank you to Dwayne Yuzik for being a friend and ally at all times. Thank you to Vic Stauffer for being a friend, mentor, and for that Cesario call. Thank you to all the horse racing announcers. You guys inspire me on a daily basis.

Thank you to the horses, trainers, owners, grooms, jockeys, and gamblers who all make the great game go round.

Thank you to William Alempijevic. One of the great joys and learning experiences of my life has been getting to work with you. You've taught me so much, and more importantly, your loyalty and dedication to all of us is inspiring. Other people may doubt their boss's loyalty, but I've never doubted yours. It was I, however, who came up with "Wintertime Winner."

Thank you to devora moon holland and Andrew Price.

Special thanks to my aunt Brenda. You're the glue of our family, and we all love and appreciate you more than I think you know.

Lots of love to my sister Jacki. I'm so proud of you. Your sense of humor is one of the things I treasure most in life.

To my dad, Mark Beem. So much of my life involved you, both before and after your death. I miss you. Rarely a day goes by that I don't think of you and wish I could talk to you. Our relationship has been the most complicated I've ever known. I'll struggle with you as long as I live. But through that struggle, I'll play harder, longer.

And to my mother. You are all things. All things good. All things love. All things courage. All things beauty. All things grace. I've never known a greater blessing than you. You were the only sure thing in a life filled with long shots. This book and this life are written more for you than anyone. You are my hero.

CPSIA information can be obtained at www.ICGtesting.com
Printed in the USA
LVOW01s2317020414

380121LV00013B/327/P